Minorities in West Asia and North Africa

Series editors
Kamran Matin
University of Sussex
Department of International Relations
Brighton, United Kingdom

Paolo Maggiolini
Istituto per gli Studi di Politica Inter
Italian Institute for International Poli
Milano, Italy

This series seeks to provide a unique and dedicated outlet for the publication of theoretically informed, historically grounded and empirically governed research on minorities and 'minoritization' processes in the regions of West Asia and North Africa (WANA). In WANA, from Morocco to Afghanistan and from Turkey to the Sudan almost every country has substantial religious, ethnic or linguistic minorities. Their changing character and dynamic evolution notwithstanding, minorities have played key roles in social, economic, political and cultural life of WANA societies from the antiquity and been at the center of the modern history of the region. WANA's experience of modernity, processes of state formation and economic development, the problems of domestic and interstate conflict and security, and instances of state failure, civil war, and secession are all closely intertwined with the history and politics of minorities, and with how different socio-political categories related to the idea of minority have informed or underpinned historical processes unfolding in the region. WANA minorities have also played a decisive role in the rapid and crisis-ridden transformation of the geopolitics of WANA in the aftermath of the Cold War and the commencement of globalization. Past and contemporary histories, and the future shape and trajectory of WANA countries are therefore intrinsically tied to the dynamics of minorities. Intellectual, political, and practical significance of minorities in WANA therefore cannot be overstated. The overarching rationale for this series is the absence of specialized series devoted to minorities in WANA. Books on this topic are often included in area, country or theme-specific series that are not amenable to theoretically more rigorous and empirically wider and multi-dimensional approaches and therefore impose certain intellectual constraints on the books especially in terms of geographical scope, theoretical depth, and disciplinary orientation. This series addresses this problem by providing a dedicated space for books on minorities in WANA. It encourages inter- and multi-disciplinary approaches to minorities in WANA with a view to promote the combination of analytical rigor with empirical richness. As such the series is intended to bridge a significant gap on the subject in the academic books market, increase the visibility of research on minorities in WANA, and meets the demand of academics, students, and policy makers working on, or interested in, the region alike. The editorial team of the series will adopt a proactive and supportive approach through soliciting original and innovative works, closer engagement with the authors, providing feedback on draft monographs prior to publication, and ensuring the high quality of the output.

More information about this series at
http://www.palgrave.com/gp/series/15127

Kail C. Ellis
Editor

Secular Nationalism and Citizenship in Muslim Countries

Arab Christians in the Levant

Editor
Kail C. Ellis
Villanova University
Villanova, Pennsylvania, USA

Minorities in West Asia and North Africa
ISBN 978-3-319-89051-7   ISBN 978-3-319-71204-8   (eBook)
https://doi.org/10.1007/978-3-319-71204-8

This Palgrave Macmillan imprint is published by Springer Nature
The registered company is Springer International Publishing AG
The registered company address is: Gewerbestrasse 11, 6330 Cham, Switzerland

To all Christians in the Middle East, to all who labor for justice and equality in the region, and in appreciation for the work of the Sacred Congregation for the Oriental Churches and the Pontifical Oriental Institute.

PREFACE

This volume was inspired by the current plight of Christians and other vulnerable communities in the Middle East. In the aftermath of the disappointments of the Arab Spring of 2011, Islamist religious radicalism gained strength, particularly in the formation of militant groups such as al-Qaeda, the Islamic State of Iraq and the Levant (ISIS), and its offshoot, the Islamic Caliphate. In January 2014, ISIS fighters spread throughout western Iraq, adding new territory to their impressive territorial conquests in neighboring Syria. Their conquests in Iraq included the historically Christian villages and towns in the Nineveh Plains near Mosul, Iraq's second largest city and one of the historic centers for the Assyrian Church of the East, the Chaldean Catholic Church, and the Syriac Orthodox Church. ISIS's advances were extensively reported by numerous international news agencies with headlines such as *End of Christianity in Iraq?*; *Christianity Is Being Driven Out of the Middle East*; *Is This the End of Christianity in the Middle East?*; *Christians in Iraq: Should They Stay or Should They Go?* Extensive analyses of this situation appeared in newspapers, opinion pieces, academic journals, and think tank publications. Accounts also appeared about the persecution of other religious and ethnic groups such as Turkmen, Yazidis, Shabaks, and Shia Muslims, who were expelled or killed by ISIS. Human Rights Watch reported that the Islamic State seemed intent on wiping out all traces of minority groups from the area it controlled in Iraq.

Although religious persecution has been perpetrated by a variety of regimes and more recently by independent Islamist actors, notably in Iraq, Syria, and Egypt, it was ISIS's sudden capture of Mosul on 4–10 June 2014 that stunned the world. Mosul had a population of 1.5 million. Although much of this population had already fled, there were still an estimated 65,000 Christians (whose presence in Mosul dates to the second century) in the city when ISIS seized control. One of ISIS's first acts was to execute an estimated 4000 Iraqi Security Force prisoners. Then, after consolidating its hold over dozens of cities and towns in western and northern Iraq, the group formally declared itself the "Islamic Caliphate," dropping all mention of Iraq and Syria, and turned its attention to the destruction and defacement of Christian churches and monasteries. Christian properties were daubed with the Arabic letter for "N" (ن *nūn*, the first letter for the Arabic word, *Nasarrah*, "Christian") to indicate that they now belonged to the Islamic state. Christians were given the choice to either convert to Islam, pay a *jizya* (a tax levied on non-believers), or to leave. The Islamic Caliphate robbed at gunpoint some of those who fled via the road leaving the city. The ultimatum was widely reported and triggered an international wave of criticism; among the critics were Muslim scholars.

The brutal tragedy of the fall of Mosul and its surrounding areas, along with the difficult situation of Christians in Syria and in the region in general, spurred Villanova University and its Center for Arab and Islamic Studies to sponsor an academic examination of the historic presence of Christians in the Middle East. Included in this examination would be the Christian contributions to Islamic society as well as an examination of possible strategies that might improve their current situation as well as that of other vulnerable communities in the region. The initial title for this study, "Religious Minorities and the Struggle for Secular Nationalism and Citizenship in the Middle East," envisioned a comprehensive approach designed to acquaint the participants and the general public with the full range of the 2000-year presence of Christians in the Middle East. An international team of academics, diplomats, journalists, and members of the military—resident in the Middle East, Europe, and the United States—was consulted and asked to comment on the initial outline for the conference. Over 50 individuals were contacted, many of whom were gracious in their comments and suggestions. Fourteen of these individuals were selected to present talks. As a result of this consultation, the conference evolved to reflect current scholarship and to refine the topics under discussion. The term *minorities* was discarded in favor of "Christian communities in the Middle East and the Struggle for Secular Nationalism and Citizenship," and then, to better describe the subject matter, "The Struggle for Secular Nationalism and Citizenship in Muslim Countries:

Arab Christians in the Levant." The conference was held on 5–6 December 2016 at Villanova University with over 150 people in attendance.

The authors of the chapters in this volume use the current status of Christians as a lens to focus their analyses on three broad topics. The first, "Christian Cultural and Intellectual Life in the Islamic Middle East: A Shared History," deals with Christianity's historic roots in the Middle East and the modern history of Christianity in the wider Levant. Christian contributions to art, culture, and literature in the Arab world are given extensive coverage, as are the contributions of Christians to Arab politics. Finally yet importantly, this topic covers the essential role of education in the Arab world and Christian involvement in establishing schools, universities, hospitals, and other social services.

The second topic, "Human Rights, Combating Persecution and the Responsibility to Protect," focuses on the predicament of Arab Christians who supported authoritarian regimes in the belief that these regimes would better safeguard their rights, a view with which the author of one chapter disagrees. This shortsighted disregard of democratic principles, elections, parliamentary law, and constitutions had severe consequences. The other authors who address this topic advocate human rights as the best approach to protect Christians and other citizens. The last chapter in this section discusses strategies to protect Christians and other vulnerable groups from persecution. The discussion of the limits of current proposals to intervene militarily on the behalf of these groups or to establish safe areas for them is timely. According to reports at the time, aid groups were very concerned about the transfer of Syrian militants, their relatives, and other refugees from Lebanon into Syria bound for Idlib province in northern Syria, an area largely controlled by jihadists. The transfer involved more than 100 buses and was the largest formal repatriation of refugees to Syria since the war began in 2011. However, the lack of oversight by international aid groups raised concern about the refugees' welfare.

The third topic addresses "The Arab Spring, the Shia/Sunni Divide, and Their Impact on Regional and Geopolitical Tensions." The authors exploring this topic stress the importance of not oversimplifying the Shia/Sunni divide, as these groups are not monolithic. Rather, the emphasis should be on the rule of law and on economic development as the most effective measures to safeguard Christians and other vulnerable communities. The authors also stress the need for a strategic assessment of the security and political issues reshaping the Middle East today, and their impact on the Christian communities across the region. Particularly useful is the analysis of the impact of U.S. foreign policy on the political dynamics in the region under the Obama administration, as well as a preliminary analysis of President Trump's impact on regional security.

In my view as the editor of this volume, the topics and discussions of the conference presented provide three important insights. First is that despite widespread perception, persecution is not a major source for the numeric decline of Christians in the Middle East. Although persecution of Christians and other religious and ethnic communities who have suffered for their beliefs, been forced to flee their homes, and now are refugees must in no way be minimized, emigration and the higher birth rate of Muslims, not persecution, is the major cause for the numeric decline of Christians in the Middle East. Despite the current dire situation, church leaders such as the Chaldean Patriarch Louis Sako I are encouraging Christians to stay in their homelands. Pope Francis, speaking of Iraq and Syria, said, "We cannot resign ourselves to thinking about the Middle East without Christians, who for 2000 years have confessed the name of Jesus [there]."

It is critical to understand the dynamics of Christian emigration from the Middle East, the first phase of which began in the later part of the nineteenth century and continued until World War I. During that time, thousands of indigenous Christians left the Ottoman Empire in search of economic opportunities. After World War II, socio-economic factors continued to influence the emigration of Christians and to a lesser extent, of non-Christians. In the post-independence period, from the late 1940s to the present time, Christian emigration continued to rise, primarily due to economic insecurity but also due to political instability and military conflicts: the 1948 Palestinian–Israeli conflict, the Lebanese Civil War (1975–1990), and the series of wars in the Persian Gulf—the Iran–Iraq War (1980–1989), the First Gulf War (1990–1991), and the American invasion of Iraq, which began in 2003. Therefore, to focus on emigration and persecution in isolation from the demographic and socioeconomic factors, regional conflicts, the lack of human rights, and the rule of law is to risk viewing Christians solely as victims of persecution and mere relics of a fading past. Such a narrow focus robs Christians of agency as significant actors in their own societies.

Second, the reference to Christians as *minorities*, which aside from a numeric description, categorizes them as marginal and second class, is equally problematic. Arab Christians do not consider themselves minorities; they regard themselves as members of a pluralist society, albeit one in which they have suffered discrimination. Recent scholarship is changing the view that Arab Christians constituted segregated and victimized com-

munities in the nineteenth and twentieth centuries, and rightfully positions Christians and Jewish communities as integral parts of the larger
societies to which they belong—culturally, politically, and demographically. This emphasis was addressed powerfully by Cardinal Leonardo
Sandri in his letter greeting the participants in the Villanova conference of
5–6 December 2016 that is cited in this volume.

Third, there are longstanding developmental issues at the heart of the
instability in the Middle East: stagnant economic development, lack of
education, authoritarianism, and state repression. As several authors
emphasize, the most fundamental concepts that define states and the lives
of their citizens must be defined and validated, including the core issues of
statehood, nationhood, sovereignty, religiosity and secularism, communal
and national identity, and citizenship.

The recommendations represented by the authors and their topics are
essential in clarifying the causes of the current malaise in the region and in
securing equality, human rights, citizen participation, and the security of
all Middle Eastern communities. My hope is that this book will contribute
to a better understanding of Christians in the Middle East, as well as of the
fundamental principles that will help to improve the life of all citizens in
the region. Only by illuminating the historical context of the Arab Christians'
predicament, the many ways in which their environment changed, and by
developing strategies to address their situation in the future will there be
hope for all the vulnerable communities in the Middle East.

This volume is dedicated to the Vatican's Congregation for the Oriental
Church and the Pontifical Oriental Institute, which for the last hundred
years (1917–2017) have endured great changes in the Christian East. As
noted by contributor Anthony O'Mahony, these changes have included
the collapse of Ottoman Empire, the genocide and massacre of Armenian
and Syriac Christians, the Bolshevik Revolution, the destruction of the
Russian Orthodox Church, efforts to rebuild the churches in the interwar
period, World War II, the imposition of Communist rule in the Eastern
European states, the Cold War, the Second Vatican Council, and renewed
conflict in the Middle East. From the Arab–Israeli conflict to the current
conflict in Syria, the effects of war have challenged Christianity in the
Middle East to the point that many are concerned for its survival.
Throughout a century of turbulent events, the two institutions mentioned
above have protected the rights of the Christian churches of the East,
maintaining the liturgical, disciplinary, and spiritual patrimony of their
heritage, and making known to the Latin West their rich history of cultural, social, and political contributions to the region.

I would like to thank the many people who helped to make this volume possible. In particular, I would like to thank Father Peter M. Donohue, O.S.A., president of Villanova University, for his support of the conference and of the Center for Arab and Islamic Studies. My appreciation also goes to Mr. Antoine Frem and Mr. Masoud Altirs, who provided generous financial support, and to Most Reverend Paul Nabil Sayah, former Archbishop of Haifa and the Holy Land of the Maronite Church and Curial Bishop of the Maronite Catholic Patriarchate of Antioch, who reviewed the draft program and provided valuable advice. I am also indebted to Father Richard G. Cannuli, O.S.A., who created the beautiful icon, "Mary Queen of Peace," specifically for the conference. I would be remiss not to thank Ms. Lorraine McCorkel, the graphic designer of the attractive conference brochure, as well as all the staff in University Communications for their excellent assistance.

I would also like to express appreciation to the following people at Villanova University who have given their enthusiastic response to this conference: Dr. Patrick Maggitti, provost; Dr. Adele Lindenmeyr, dean of the College of Liberal Arts and Sciences; and my colleague Dr. Hafeez Malik, as well as to Dr. Helen Lafferty and the late Dr. M. Louise Fitzpatrick, dean of the College of Nursing at Villanova University, who provided invaluable moral support. Dean Fitzpatrick's death has left a deep void at the University as well as in the nursing profession where she was a respected leader. She will be missed by her many colleagues and friends.

As it was important to have the support of universities in the Middle East for this conference, I would like to thank Dr. Nabeel Haidar, provost of the American University of Science and Technology in Beirut, Lebanon, and Brother Peter Bray, FSC, vice chancellor of Bethlehem University, Bethlehem, Palestinian Authority, for co-sponsoring the conference on behalf of their respective universities.

Special thanks are due Nadia Barsoum, my administrative assistant, who gave tremendous assistance in handling the travel and accommodation arrangements, proofreading the manuscripts, collating the conference and book materials, and much more that made this endeavor a success, and to Angele Ellis, who provided indispensable editing support. To these individuals and many more too numerous to name, I offer my sincere thanks and appreciation.

Villanova, PA   Kail C. Ellis

CONTENTS

NOTES ON CONTRIBUTORS

Fateh Azzam is a senior fellow at the Carr Center for Human Rights Policy and an affiliate at the Middle East Initiative at Harvard Kennedy School. He was the former director of the Asfari Institute for Civil Society and Citizenship and senior policy fellow at the Issam Fares Institute for Public Policy and International Relations, both at the American University in Beirut. He previously served as the Middle East Regional Representative of the UN High Commissioner for Human Rights, director of Forced Migration and Refugee Studies at the American University in Cairo, Human Rights Program Officer at the Ford Foundation in Lagos and Cairo, and director of the Palestinian organization Al-Haq. He led the process of establishing the Arab Human Rights Fund. Azzam holds an LLM in International Human Rights Law from the University of Essex.

Alon Ben-Meir is a professor and senior fellow at New York University's Center for Global Affairs and senior fellow at the World Policy Institute. He received an M.A. in philosophy and a Ph.D. in international relations from Oxford University. He is the author of seven books related to the Middle East and his current manuscript is about violent extremism and deradicalization. He has been directly involved in negotiations between Israel and neighboring countries, and also with Turkey. He appears regularly on television, including ABC, NBC, CNN, Al Jazeera, Al Arabiya, Al-Hurra, and Russia Today.

Elie Chalala is associate adjunct professor of political science at Santa Monica College and the founding publisher and editor of *Al Jadid Magazine, A Review & Record of Arab Culture and Arts*. He taught political science as a teaching fellow at UCLA, from which he graduated, and has been teaching at Santa Monica since 1988. His research and publications focus on inter-Arab relations (Syria, Lebanon, and Iraq) and contemporary Arab political thought.

Kail C. Ellis is Assistant to the President, dean emeritus of the College of Liberal Arts and Sciences, former Vice President for Academic Affairs, and associate professor of political science at Villanova University. The founder-director of Villanova's Center for Arab and Islamic Studies, his Ph.D. is from The Catholic University of America. Currently he coedits the Journal of South Asian and Middle Easter Studies and was the editor of two books: *The Vatican, Islam and the Middle East*, (1987) and *Lebanon's Second Republic, Prospects for the Twenty-First Century*, (2002). He has also presented papers, published articles, and contributed book chapters related to the Middle East.

Sidney H. Griffith is Ordinary Professor Emeritus in the Department of Semitic and Egyptian Languages and Literatures in the School of Arts and Sciences at the Catholic University of America, where he earned the Ph.D. in 1977 with a thesis entitled, "The Controversial Theology of Theodore Abū Qurrah (c.750–c.820 AD): A Methodological, Comparative Study in Christian Arabic Literature." His areas of interest and academic responsibility are Syriac Patristics, Christian Arabic Literature, and the history of Christian/Muslim relations, especially within the World of Islam and in the Early Islamic period.

Brian Katulis is a senior fellow at the Center for American Progress. He focuses on U.S. national security strategy and counterterrorism policy. He has advised senior U.S. policy-makers and has provided expert testimony to U.S. Senate Committees. He received a B.A. in history and Arab and Islamic Studies from Villanova University, an M.A. from Princeton's Woodrow Wilson School, and was a Fulbright scholar in Jordan. He provides commentary for the "PBS News Hour," *The New York Times, The Washington Post*, and *The Wall Street Journal.* He is co-author with Nancy Soderberg of *The Prosperity Agenda*, on U.S. national security (2008).

Rami G. Khouri is an internationally syndicated political columnist, author, and journalist in residence and professor of journalism at the American University of Beirut. A senior fellow and former director at the Issam Fares Institute for Public Policy and International Affairs at AUB, his B.A. in political science and M.Sc. degree in mass communications are from Syracuse University. A nonresident senior fellow at the Kennedy

School of Harvard and visiting fellow at Georgetown University in Qatar, he also lectures annually at Northeastern University, and has been a visiting scholar at several universities including Harvard, Princeton, Villanova, Tufts, and Stanford.

Tarek Mitri is a director of the Issam Fares Institute for Public Policy and International Affairs at the American University of Beirut. A graduate of AUB with a doctorate from the Université de Nanterre Paris X, Mitri has written on religion and politics and interreligious and intercultural dialogue. He served in successive governments in Lebanon as Minister of Environment, Minister of Administrative Reform, Minister of Culture, Minister of Information, and Acting Minister of Foreign Affairs. He was also the special representative of the UN Secretary General and head of the UN Support Mission in Libya from 2012 to 2014.

Anthony O'Mahony is Reader in the History of Christianity and Director of Centre for Eastern Christianity, Heythrop College, University of London. He has published and lectured extensively on Christianity in the Middle East, Christian–Muslim relations and relations between Eastern and Western Christianity, with contributions to *The Cambridge History of Christianity: Eastern Christianity, Journal of Eastern Christian Studies; The International Journal for the Study of the Christian Church;* several volumes (as co-editor) in *Eastern Christianity in the Modern Middle East; The Catholic Church in the Contemporary Middle East; Christianity and Jerusalem: Studies in Theology and Politics in the Modern Holy Land; Christian Responses to Islam: A Global Account of Muslim-Christian Relations.*

Bernard Sabella is an elected Member of the Palestinian Legislative Council representing Jerusalem and Executive Secretary, Department of Service to Palestinian Refugees. He received his B.A. from Franklin and Marshall University, and his M.A. and Ph.D. degrees in sociology from the University of Virginia, Charlottesville. He is a former professor of sociology at Bethlehem University. From 2011 to 2015, he was chairperson of the Palestinian delegation to the Parliamentary Assembly of the Council of Europe in Strasbourg and served as executive secretary of the Department of Services to Palestinian Refugees in the Middle East Council of Churches.

Sami El-Yousef is the first lay Chief Executive of the Office of the Latin Patriarch in Jerusalem and former Regional Director of the Jerusalem field office of the Catholic Near East Welfare Association—Pontifical Mission for Palestine, an agency of the Holy See established in 1949 to aid

Palestinian refugees. He received a B.S. in chemical engineering from the University of Massachusetts-Amherst and an M.S. in industrial engineering from the University of Pittsburgh. He is a native of the Old City of Jerusalem, and belongs to one of that city's oldest Christian families. He spent 24 years of his academic career in a number of teaching and administrative positions at Bethlehem University.

General Anthony C. Zinni is a retired Marine Corps four-star general. He was commander of the joint task force and unified command (U.S. Central Command) from 1997 to 2000 and participated in presidential diplomatic and state department missions during the Israeli–Palestinian conflict and conflicts in Indonesia and the Philippines. In 1991, he was chief of staff and deputy commanding general of *Operation Provide Comfort* for Iraqi Kurds and director of operations for the Unified Task Force in Somalia from 1992 to1993. He has held academic positions at Duke University, Cornell University, the Virginia Military Institute, and the University of California, Berkeley.

CHAPTER 1

Introduction

Kail C. Ellis

The chapters in this volume are by an international team of academics, diplomats, journalists, policy institute scholars, NGO members, and the military from the Middle East, Europe, and the United States. The authors examine the importance of Christian history and presence in the Mashreq counties of the Middle East (Iraq, Syria, Lebanon, Palestine, and Egypt), from the rise of Islam to their contributions to Arab politics. Using the current status of Christians to focus their scholarship, the authors analyze the origins of the crises facing not only Christians and other vulnerable groups, but of all the peoples in the region, regardless of religion or belief. They also propose recommendations and strategies to foster religious freedom, human rights, and an inclusive political system that ensures equality of citizenship for all communities to participate fully in their societies.

The struggle for secular nationalism in the title stands in contrast to religious nationalism, which is the relationship of nationalism to a particular religious belief, dogma, or affiliation that can lead to the politicization of religion. Secular nationalism asserts the right of citizens to be free from religious rule and of governments that impose religion or religious practices upon their people. The Arab Christians of the subtitle are the volume's focus and reflects the volume's emphasis on full citizenship as a

K. C. Ellis (✉)
Arab & Islamic Studies, Villanova University, Villanova, PA, USA

© The Author(s) 2018
K. C. Ellis (ed.), *Secular Nationalism and Citizenship in
Muslim Countries*, Minorities in West Asia and North Africa,
https://doi.org/10.1007/978-3-319-71204-8_1

1

remedy for the problems facing Christians and other communities in the Middle East.

Christians have been an integral part of the Middle East for over two millennia. Eastern Christians made formative contributions to the theological development and richness of early Christianity. With the arrival of Islam they came under Muslim rule, but demographically they were the majority in many places until well into the eleventh century.[1] They contributed to the development of the arts, sciences, philosophy, and literature of what has come to be known as the Islamic Golden Age of the mid-seventh to mid-thirteenth centuries. They share the same history and a large part of the cultural heritage of the Muslim majority population. The only important difference, which has had numerous social and cultural consequences, is their adherence to the Christian religion. As Christians gradually diminished in number, Christian history, presence, and witness, as if frozen in time, was largely forgotten or neglected, both in the cultures they had a large part in shaping and in the West. Numerical decline is only a partial reason for the disappearance of Christians from serious scholarship on the Middle East. According to Paul S. Rowe, "Christians have long been viewed as the object of other actors. For some, they were products of Muslim societies that imposed upon them the debatably restricted or protected status of *ahl al-dhimmah*. For others, they were the appendages of external forces determined to use them as devices of their interests. The concerns of such external forces only contributed to Christians' portrayal as vehicles of imperialism."[2]

In an insightful article, "Recent Perspectives on Christians in the Modern Arab World," L.C. Robson cites several reasons why scholars of the modern Arab world largely avoided the topic of Christians. Among these reasons is that Islam was traditionally viewed as central to the definition of the region; therefore, secular scholars in the West and Arab historians in the Middle East were reluctant to engage in research on Arab Christian communities out of concern that the topic would inevitably raise questions about sectarianism and communal politics that they wished to avoid. Consequently, most scholars presented Arab Christians "as essentially marginal, appearing either as hapless victims of Muslim domination or as agents of the Western powers with which they had religious and political connections."[3] Robson cites Ussama Makdisi's conclusion that the reluctance of scholars to research the religiously sensitive topic of Christians, "perhaps in the interests of putative national unity, has allow[ed] the void to be filled with scholarship obsessed with the idea of perpetual hostility between Christians and Jewish minorities and an oppressive monolithic Muslim majority."[4] Only in the last several years have scholars sought to rectify this scholarly gap by exploring the ways in which Middle Eastern Christians function in their societies.[5] Anthony O'Mahony, a well-known scholar of Christianity in the Middle East, objects to the conventional characterization of the Middle East as "the Muslim World." Using this concept and phrase, he contends, automatically renders the ancient Christian community as "alien."[6]

Referring to Christians and other vulnerable communities as "minorities" poses another challenge. In common usage, the term "minority" is associated with inferiority, weakness, and subordination. The term serves to emphasize the marginal status of these communities, despite numerous instances of dominant and powerful minorities ruling over nations, such as Saddam Hussein's Iraq and the Assads of Baathist Syria.[7]

Nevertheless, the term "minority" can have multiple meanings. Besides its reference to a group's relative size, in the context of the Arab Middle East it also connotes an identity that is "ascribed" (i.e., assigned by others). When it refers to a group's religious identity, ipso facto it establishes the group's relationship to the state through confessional criteria, and reinforces sectarian behavior and interactions that can lead to political expectations and demands for privileges or, alternatively, to frustration or alienation.[8] The anthropologist Seteney Shami maintains that "minority," with its connotations of inferiority and exclusion from the body politic, leads to constructing a "majority" that is alleged to represent the nation. He cautions, "Even if the debate focuses on positive aspects such as minority rights, tolerance or diversity, or the privileging of a certain social group, the minority-majority pairing is a dichotomy that asserts the (often unwelcome) interruption of the allegedly homogenous or harmonious national community by a group that it is 'out of place.'"[9]

Another example of the use of the term "minority" to dominate a population is given by Benjamin T. White in his study *The Emergence of Minorities in the Middle East: The Politics of Community in French Mandate Syria*. During the French Mandate, "minority" was used to solidify French control of Syria, by "reinforcing religious divisions by distributing seats to representative bodies on religious communal grounds; by extending legal autonomy in matters of personal status to communities which had not previously been autonomous; and by granting territorial autonomy to certain religiously defined groups." According to White, "This policy adhered to the colonial theories of Marshal [Hubert] Lyautey, whose principle of *association* as opposed to assimilation had been developed in Morocco. Personal status law was crucial to French efforts to divide Syria's communities religiously."[10]

White argues that the contemporary use of the term is not useful in describing the place of "minorities" in relation to the wider society. He claims, "there was no articulated concept of 'minority' prior to the modern period because minorities did not exist." Rather, Islamic law placed all non-Muslims in a subordinate place, not because they were *minorities* but because they were non-Muslims, with no reference to number or ethnic identity. Since the term carries too much ideological baggage, White says it should be discarded as an analytical category.[11]

DEVELOPING THE CONCEPT OF "MINORITY" AND OTTOMAN REFORMS

The concept of "minority" developed from the *ahl al-dhimmah* status or "protected" status of the Christian and Jewish communities in the Ottoman Empire. It had its origin in the Islamic tenet that the prophetic tradition culminated from Judaism and Christianity and that the adherents of those religions, people with revealed books (*ahl al-kitāb*), had their place in Islamic society as "protected" communities (*ahl al-dhimmah*). In return—and as a mark of their submission—these communities were expected to pay the *jizya* (the root meaning of which is compensation, whereby they ratify the compact that assures them protection). It was a per capita yearly tax on able-bodied males of military age as a substitute for military service. However, *dhimmis* who chose to join military service were exempted from payment, as were those who could not afford to pay. Gradually, *dhimmi* protection was extended to other select religious communities.

After the conquest of Constantinople in 1453, the Ottomans developed the *millet* system to deal with their newly acquired sizable Christian communities that allowed them to choose their religious leaders, collect taxes, use their language, and have their personal laws and own courts. Although the system was built upon the foundation of the *ahl al-dhimmah*, by creating a structure of limited autonomous communities under their own religious leaders as a way to deal with religious diversity and coexistence, the *millet* system de facto separated these communities from their societies, paved the way for the introduction of the political ideology of European nationalism into the empire, and designated them as "minorities." As noted by White, the personal status laws of the Ottoman *millet* system were ready-made for adoption by the French Mandate to differentiate Syria's religious and ethnic communities, and were critical to maintaining French control of that country.

Although the *millet* system granted limited autonomy to non-Muslim communities, its primary function was to enable the Ottomans to rule a diverse population. The empire remained intensely Muslim. According to Ussama Makdisi, the "*millet* system reinforced the emphasis on religion in a profoundly unequal political and social order. At the top of this 'empire of difference' sat the 'shadow of God on earth,' the Sultan, whose rule was legitimated by his supposed upholding of Islam, his defense of the realm against infidels, and his stamping out of heresy within it."[12] Although Ottoman Muslim supremacy was deeply imbued within the ideological, political, and legal terrain of the empire, for Makdisi, the issue "is not that it [the empire] was 'tolerant' or 'intolerant'... Rather, the point that needs to be made is that the empire witnessed centuries of coexistence in which different Muslim and Christian and Jewish communities, and the ecclesiastical leaderships of different communities, accepted the fact that they were bound to live side by side—to literally coexist—for the foreseeable future."[13]

The French Revolution and the Napoleonic wars that spread the revolutionary principles of liberty, equality, and fraternity were the first powerful manifestations of European nationalism, which found its expression in the rational faith in a common humanity and liberal progress. As an ideology based on the premise that the individual's loyalty and devotion to the nation-state surpasses individual or group interests, European nationalism implicitly identified the state or nation with the people. Whereas previously for the different nationalities of Christendom as well as for those of Islam there was but one civilization—Christian or Muslim, and one language of culture, Latin (or Greek) or Arabic (or Persian), the principles of European nationalism were that each nationality should form an autonomous state.[14]

When European nationalism was introduced into the Ottoman Empire in the mid-to-late nineteenth century, it met a diverse population that had no previous experience of the separation of politics from religion. Although nationalism was a new concept, Albert Hourani has noted that "Christians could support such ideas without the hesitation of Muslims, whether Arab or Turkish, because they did not possess that deep and final loyalty to the empire, as the shield of Sunni Islam, which almost all Muslims had, and which was indeed the cause of their hesitations."[15] Thus the concept of nationalism was readily received in the religiously heterogeneous *millet* communities and provided the basis for numerous and competing nationalist movements. Nationalism also enabled the European powers to position themselves as protectors of the interests of the *millet* communities, giving them an inroad to interfere in the Ottoman Empire along religious lines. By the turn of the twentieth century, as noted by Benjamin White, nationalist movements within the empire had all but destroyed the previous notion of religious coexistence.[16] Reinforcing the emphasis on religion in a profoundly unequal political and social order, the *millet* system provided fertile ground for the political ideology of European nationalism. The growing national consciousness, coupled with a rising sense of ethnic nationalism, made nationalistic thought one of the most significant Western ideas imported to the Ottoman Empire.

Beginning from the late eighteenth century to the mid-to-late nineteenth century, the Ottoman Empire faced the challenges of defending itself against foreign invasion and occupation. European encroachments resulted in the loss of territory to Russia and its Balkan provinces to independence movements. Stunned by these losses and recognizing that it was perceived as "the sick man of Europe," the empire sought to redefine itself as a modern, bureaucratic, and tolerant state that was co-equal with the West but culturally distinct and independent of it.[17] The period called the *Tanzimat* (1839–1876) had as its centerpiece the Gülhane decree of 1839 whereby, for the first time, the Ottomans accepted the principle of legal and social equality of Muslim and non-Muslims Ottoman citizens and abolished the *millet* system. The *Hatt-I Hümayun* of 1856 promised full legal equality for all citizens of all religions. The principle of legal equality was formally incorporated in the Ottoman law of nationality of 1869 that gave juridical status to Ottoman citizens without an implied or overt reference to religion.

Muslim elites, according to Erik Freas, "worried that the reforms would undermine the traditional Islamic hierarchy, one rooted in the educational and legal structures that until then had constituted the basis of their rank and status."[18] Although the reforms encountered considerable Muslim resistance, Christians benefited from them materially, especially as they minimized the role of religion in government. Despite this, the reforms proved controversial for Christians who viewed traditional ecclesiastical establishments as the best way to secure their interests. Christians in the Balkans, for example, refused to support the reforms because they wanted an autonomy that would be more difficult to achieve under centralized power. In particular, Christians were leery of their new "equality" as it also entailed military service, an onus from which they were previously exempt. Nevertheless, it was acceptance of non-Muslims as equals that ultimately proved problematic, as many Muslims found it difficult to adjust to the idea of Christians being in positions of authority.[19] According to Hourani, the Ottoman Muslims' viewed the reforms as heralding the revival of the empire's strength, whereas Christians viewed them as a statement of rights. The fundamental basis of the Ottoman Empire remained intact; it was still a Muslim empire. Therefore, as Hourani concludes, "For the reforms to succeed, the empire would have to become a secular state on the European model."[20]

While the reforms allowed the Ottoman parliament to draw Christian members from various provinces of the empire, the emancipation of non-Muslims was greeted generally with dismay and, in some instances, with violence against Christians. One example was the 1860 civil war between Maronites and Druzes in Mount Lebanon, whose settlement resulted in a reversion to sectarianism in which the Ottoman and European powers hammered out a series of institutionalized sectarian political structures. According to Ussama Makdisi, this settlement "entrenched and reified the communal and naturalized the idea that sectarian representation was the only viable key to resolving the problem of religious pluralism."[21] Confessionalism subsequently became embedded in the 1861 "Règlement Organique" that ended that civil war in Mount Lebanon, as one of its provisions specified that a non-Lebanese Catholic Christian *mutasarrif* (governor), appointed by the Ottoman sultan, would hold the position. This arrangement lasted from 1861 until 1915, during which time seven Ottoman Christians from the Armenian, Melkite, and Roman Catholic communities were appointed to the position.[22] It was abolished at the outbreak of World War I.

SITUATION OF "MINORITIES" TODAY

Despite the argument of contemporary scholars that the term "minority" carries too much ideological baggage and is not useful, the use of the term persists today. Recognizing the limitations of the term, several Christian and Muslim leaders have advocated an alternative approach that would depict religious identity in terms of "presence." Cardinal Leonardo Sandri, a high-ranking Vatican official and Prefect of the Congregation for the Eastern Church, used the designation of presence in his greeting to the conference on Christians in the Middle East held at Villanova University in December 2016. Citing the tragedies in Syria and Iraq that have brought the dramatic condition of Christians of the Middle East to the attention of the world, Cardinal Sandri stated—

Many commentators have analyzed the situation, and not infrequently, with a typically Western eye, they tend to characterize these communities as 'minorities'. While applying a criterion of a numeric type is understandable enough, it risks obscuring the history of the cultures in question. It is important, therefore, also at the level of method and terminology, to abandon the term 'minorities' and train ourselves to think in terms of 'presence:' this expresses awareness of the fact—of which the Patriarchs, Bishops, and even the simple faithful often remind us—that, namely, Christians are original inhabitants of this region… Moreover, faith generates culture. Therefore it should be stressed that the Christian presence in the Middle East has contributed to the history of these peoples and nations, both in the past as in the present, through literary figures, philosophers, artists and thinkers, also in the social and political fields.[23]

"Freedom, Citizenship, Diversity and Integration," a conference held at the Islamic al-Azhar University in Cairo in 2017, also referred to non-Muslims as "citizens" rather than as "minorities." Conference attendees included Sunni Muslims, Shiite Muslims, Yazidis, Protestants, Orthodox Christians, and Catholics. At its conclusion, the participants signed a common declaration that called for a renewed alliance between all Arab citizens, regardless of their religion. The declaration called for the reinforcement of the National Constitutional state that is founded on the principles of citizenship, equality and the rule of positive law (laws enacted by governmental authority). It affirmed that the "exclusion of the concept of citizenship as a contract stipulated between citizens, society and the state, leads to the failure of the state." It also reinforced the idea that it is a misunderstanding of the concept of citizenship to talk about "minorities" and their rights:

> With this as a starting point, the declaration wishes that all men of culture and intellectuals be cautious regarding the risks implied in the use of the term 'minorities.' In fact, while it claims to affirm certain rights, it veils a sense of discrimination and separation. In the last couple of years, we have witnessed the re-appearance of the term 'minorities,' which we thought we had overcome with the end of colonialism. But it has recently come back into use to create differences between Muslims and Christians, but also between Muslims themselves, considering that it leads to dispersion of allegiance and favors foreign interests.[24]

While the al-Azhar declaration called on intellectuals to exercise caution in the use of the term "minority," it did not specify another term to take its place. Likewise, Cardinal Sandri's recommendation that scholars should train themselves to think in terms of "presence" (as an affirmation that Christians are original inhabitants of this region) is not always possible given the context of usage and the numeric connotation of the "minority-majority" designation. Nevertheless, this editor accepts the limitations of the word; and, wherever possible, this volume will avoid the use of "minority," except in cases where it is used by scholars in specific contexts, as the following discussions demonstrate.

Elizabeth Picard's study of the role of the authoritarian regimes in promoting discriminatory legislation in the post-independence period of the 1950s and 1960s is a case in point. Picard states that the "minority/majority" dichotomy was a means used by authoritarian regimes to solidify their new and often fragile powers by appealing to the Islamic religious identities of the majority population. Legislation, such as blasphemy laws, has had a chilling effect on basic religious freedoms in the Christian community, especially for those who might be engaged in proselytizing. In addition, atheists and secular Muslims have also been threatened with prosecution and imprisonment for perceived negative comments against Islam.

Picard notes that authoritarian leaders amended the constitutions of their nationalist states to stress the Islamic nature of their regimes, especially in the areas of personal and family law. This enabled authoritarian regimes to make social identities "confessional," and validate their claims to protect non-Muslims communities by means of social contracts or pacts (under which individuals surrendered some or all their personal liberties for that protection). Consequently, Christians and other groups were reduced de facto to secondary citizenship. Picard concludes that "we cannot but acknowledge that several religious and confessional minorities do not enjoy freedom in their homeland where they may be symbolically excluded from the public sphere and political life and more than often oppressed and even condemned to exile."[25] Picard's analysis of the second-class status that Arab Christians (and per force, other communities) face today is a core subject of this volume.

Despite widespread concerns, the greatest threat to the Christian presence in the Middle East today is not persecution but emigration and the related socioeconomic and political distress fostered by disparity and the lack of rights. From the later part of the nineteenth century to the First World War, thousands of indigenous Christians left the Ottoman Empire in search of economic opportunities. Emigration continued from the late 1940s to the present time, primarily due to political instability, economic factors, civil war and military conflicts.

More recently, the Arab Spring of 2011, which began as a revolutionary wave of demonstrations and protests instigated by dissatisfaction with the rule of despotic regimes, led to the rise of religious radicalism and militant groups. The rise of these groups and their maltreatment of Christians and other non-Muslims created new pressures that contributed to the exodus of Christians from the Middle East. The brutal persecution of Christians, Yazidis, and other marginalized communities by ISIS and other radical Islamist groups was condemned in a joint statement by the United Nations Human Rights Council in Geneva in 2015.[26] Significantly, the importance of Christian presence in the region has also been affirmed by Muslim religious and political leaders,[27] notably King Abdullah II of Jordan. In a speech given to the United Nations in September 2014, the king proclaimed, "Islam prohibits violence against Christians and other communities that make up each country. Let me say once again: Arab Christians are an integral part of my region's past, present, and future."[28]

The papers in this volume do not pass over the longstanding political, socio-economic, and demographic issues (such as the higher birth rate of Muslims) that have contributed to the relative decline of the Christian presence in the Middle East over the last century. Nor do they assert that Christians are the only community under threat. However, Christians, as the largest non-Muslim sect in the region, are given special attention. Not only are their presence, history, and culture intertwined with Muslim cultural heritage, but their status provides a gauge for the possibility of peaceful coexistence for all vulnerable ethnic and religious communities in the Middle East.

This volume examines three broad areas: (1) Christian Cultural, Intellectual Life, and Shared History in the Islamic Middle East; (2) Human Rights, Combating Persecution, and the Responsibility to Protect; and (3) The Arab Spring, the Shia/Sunni Divide, and their Impact on Regional and Geopolitical Tensions. The authors represent a variety of views based on their professional and varied backgrounds and places of residence. While their perspectives do not always agree, the multiple dimensions of their assessments, particularly their analyses of sectarianism, authoritarian regimes, the role of Islamic law, the persecution of religious and ethnic communities, and the "duty to protect," provide valuable insights into crucial issues. Most importantly, underlying many of these issues is the neglect of authoritarian regimes to promote socio-economic development, which has resulted in a crisis of despair among under-educated and underemployed youth, and has fed the rise of radical groups and the resultant resentment and persecution of Christians and other communities. The analyses of these issues give this volume its unique perspective.

PART I: CHRISTIAN CULTURAL AND INTELLECTUAL LIFE IN THE ISLAMIC MIDDLE EAST—A SHARED HISTORY

This section examines the historic roots of Christianity in the Middle East; Christian contributions to art, culture, and literature in the Arab-Islamic world; Christian contributions education and social advancement in the region; and the Christian contributions to Arab politics and religious freedom.

Sidney Griffith's chapter, "Christianity's Historic Roots in the Middle East: Christians at Home in the World of Islam," deals with the Arabic sources of the Christian heritage in Middle East. Despite the impression many Christians have from the Book of Acts in the New Testament, the missionary journeys of the apostles were not only westward through Greece and the Mediterranean world and on to Rome.[29] Griffith reminds us that almost simultaneously, Aramaic-speaking disciples brought the Gospel eastward to the far-flung territories of the Persian Empire, across the Silk Roads into China, southward into Arabia, and ultimately to India. Along with Greek and Latin, Aramaic is the third patristic language and the Qu'ran itself is the most important evidence of the presence of Christians in Arabia, which flourished 600 years before the rise of Islam. Under the Abbasid caliphate in the tenth century, Christian scholars in Baghdad worked with Jews and Muslims to translate Greek philosophy into Arabic and Latin in a multicultural Islamic environment. Scholars in each community pursued knowledge and lived the ideal of philosophical life in a culture they could share, and expressing their differing confessional views by using philosophy to support and clarify their positions.

After the destruction of Baghdad in 1258, this vibrant intellectual activity shifted to Damascus and Cairo. Although Christians per se in this period were not normally subject to persecution in the world of Islam, the accumulated pressures of *dhimmitude* set in motion the demographic decline of the Christian communities. Christians went from a near majority in Abbasid times to demographic insignificance in most of the Middle East by the end of the twentieth century. Despite the diminished numbers of indigenous Christians, Griffith states that historians must take note of not only their extraordinary contributions (and that of the Jews) in the world of Islam but also the role they played in almost every realm of human endeavor, up to and including the present day. These contributions are treated in the following chapters in this section.

Anthony O'Mahony's chapter, "Christianity in the Wider Levant Region: Modern History and Contemporary Contexts," is an analysis of the status of Arab Christians in the contemporary Middle East. The emigration of the educated and dynamic Arab Christian middle classes, especially for economic reasons, has long been the trend in the Middle East. In Iraq, this was aggravated by the rapid spread of underlying sectarian conflicts, intensified by the United States–led invasion in 2003 and the subsequent breakdown of civil and political order. Likewise, the brutal conflict in Syria has resulted in the departure of approximately half of the Christian population or some 600,000 people, who have either left the country or been displaced.

While Egypt has not experienced war since the 1990–2000 period, relations between Egyptian Copts and Muslims have been increasingly marked by the growing communal identity in opposition to the other. This situation was further aggravated by the ascension of the Muslim Brotherhood during 2011–2013, a period in which Islam became the dominant political force and Shari'a law became a marker in Muslim identity; this had a profound impact upon Christians and other non-Muslims.

The potential transformation of political governance associated with the Arab Spring of 2011 has encouraged Christian leaders, such as the Maronite Patriarch, Cardinal Bechara al-Raï, to express the hope that the Arab regimes "are transformed into democratic regimes, should separate religion from the state, strengthening civil liberties and human rights, the right to respect difference, and embrace diversity in unity." Likewise, Christian theologians, such as the Egyptian Coptic Jesuit Fr. F. Sidarouss, have called for the local churches to take up the social teachings of the universal church to respond to the numerous religious, political and cultural questions currently engaging the region such as the exodus of Christians. Similarly, the former Melkite Archbishop of Beirut, Grégoire Haddad, argued for an open *laïcite* and a new "political-theology" which takes seriously the reordering of religious culture across the region.

Finally, O'Mahony asserts that Christian theologians in Middle East should focus on "liberation," rather than on "survival," as "survival" connotes a risky state of paralysis for Christian witness in the Arab world. Arab Christians need to re-center their witness on the demands of liberation, which modern Arabs desire, rather than on "survival," which resembles a spiritual death. As the Catholic ecumenist Jean Corbon writes, "The Christians of the Middle East appear as the microcosm of the universal ecumenism: there where the greatest diversity had abounded in division, the grace of Communion in unity has over abounded." Therefore, the meaning of the presence of indigenous Christians in the Middle East and whether they will remain an ongoing presence raises the question of the possibility of real citizenship (*muwatana*) based in a state under the rule of law and governance which seeks the common good, a theme that is expanded upon in other chapters of this volume.

Bernard Sabella's chapter, "Christian Contributions to Art, Culture, and Literature in the Arab-Islamic World," discusses the important role that Christian Arabs and Arab Jews played in the Arab "Cultural Awakening" (*Nahda*) of the late nineteenth and early twentieth centuries. Sabella's study belies the perception that Christians, in particular, were an extraneous import to the region when in fact, they were deeply rooted in their respective societies, particularly in Iraq and Egypt. Increased contact with Western culture was stimulated by the role of printing presses that facilitated the dissemination of theological, philosophical, literary, journalistic, and theatrical works. Lebanese literary figures were indisputably the pioneers in implanting the roots of literary renovation, reform, and renaissance in the Arab world. The Maronite Catholics of Mount Lebanon preserved the Arabic language and literature by publishing dictionaries and encyclopedias and opening newspapers and literary magazines. In the mid-nineteenth century, European and American missionaries established schools, universities, and social welfare institutions throughout the Middle East.

The resulting cultural ferment gave rise to illustrious literary figures who shaped the *Nahda* and argued for a society open to all. Today, Arab Christians and other like-minded Arabs still believe in a common future—as witnessed by the writings, artistic performances, political affiliations, and other personal and public manifestations that continue to attest to the possibility of a joint vision of living together. Nevertheless, they face the challenge of how to mold this communal vision, given the current destruction and violence that has plagued intercommunal and interreligious relations. Since their literary and cultural talents gave rise to the *Nahda*, Christians, in cooperation with other like-minded Arabs, should continue their advocacy to recapture that vision. Sabella also states that involvement in politics is a must for those [Arab Christians] who seek change, but this involvement needs to be in the context of political alliances with groups and parties that view the future as one that ensures intercommunal citizenship.

Tarek Mitri takes up this challenge in his chapter, "Christians in Arab Politics." Mitri notes that the enthusiasm that greeted the Arab Spring of 2011 was soon displaced by disillusionment and uncertainty. Yet no one should think that the yearning for dignity, freedom, and political participation that motivated the uprisings was ephemeral. Mitri asserts that the social demands for democracy that ethnic and religious communities, especially Christians, used to shake loose the "protected status" (*dhimmah*) of the Ottoman *millet* system, must continue in efforts to shape a new social and political order that would recognize Christians as equal citizens.

The path to equality of citizenship has not been without pain, as Mitri notes. Although the weakened Christian community was able in the nineteenth and early twentieth centuries to achieve self-affirmation, economic prosperity, and subtle forms of political power because the Western education of the missionary schools exposed them to a new type of culture, the majority of Muslims had limited access to such opportunities. This created unanticipated problems. While a large number of Christians used their new confidence to emphasize their common ethno-cultural identity with Muslims and form what came to be the "pact of citizenship" (which superseded the former *dhimmah* pact), Muslim self-awareness began to express itself in resentment because of the failures of these modern, more or less secular, independent, and authoritarian governments. This resentment was sometimes directed toward the Christian community. The leaders of authoritarian regimes and some Christian politicians used this resentment to overstate and exacerbate Muslim anger to gain support for their regimes. Conversely, some Christian politicians used Muslim antipathy to frighten and dominate their constituents, while pretending to protect them against Muslims. Subsequently, Mitri states, two negative approaches were developed by those seeking equality of citizenship: those who withdrew to an exclusively minority-centered militancy, and others who chose silence either out of fear or resignation.

A third, more positive (but as yet unrealized), approach tried to revitalize the "pact of citizenship" that would bind Christians and Muslims in a renewal of the role they played in the *Nahda*. The rationale for this approach was the shared humanity of both communities and the realization that the anxiety experienced by Christians was also lived and experienced by a considerable number of Muslims, reflecting common problems within society as a whole. The "pact of citizenship" approach affirmed the need for the mutual liberation of Christians and Muslims as a necessary condition for both communities. The basis of the bond between the two communities, however, was not Muslim domination over Christians, but rather the shared aspiration for justice, political participation, human rights, and national dignity. This approach holds great promise and, according to Mitri, the most hope for both communities to ensure equality of citizenship and human rights.

Sami El-Yousef examines the important role of social institutions in Arab society in his chapter, "Christian Contributions to Education and Social Advancement." A native of the Old City of Jerusalem, El-Yousef belongs to one of the oldest Christian families in Jerusalem who have had a continuous presence in the city for centuries. As the current Chief Exectutive Officer of the Latin Patriarchiate of Jerusalem and the former director of the Jerusalem office of the Catholic Near East Welfare Association/Pontifical Mission, El-Yousef is uniquely qualified to give a personal account of the social work that Christians oversee in the Holy Land and across the Middle East. Although this work continues to have great impact on the social development of the Middle East, it was not always regarded as entirely benevolent, as one objective of the missionaries—at least initially—was to bring enlightenment in the form of Christianity to the region. Even today, the well-known Islamic scholar Seyyed Hossein Nasr notes that some Muslims regard these activities with suspicion, and oppose what they call the continuation of aggressive missionary proselytization in several Islamic countries.[30] Despite opposition and misgivings, the work of non-governmental social agencies in the current tragic situation of civil unrest, wars, violence, administrative governmental corruption, and foreign occupation, is accepted as indispensable to the welfare of the civilian population.

El-Yousef reiterates that the Christian presence in Palestine and the Middle East covers a wide variety of churches. Jerusalem alone is the seat of 13 heads of churches, including the Orthodox, Catholic, and the Evangelical (from the Arabic *Injili* that is used to designate Protestant churches in the Middle East). There are over 125 Catholic religious congregations that function in the Holy Land (Israel and Palestine). Some are monastic in nature, while others are service ministries in the fields of education, health care, and social services, and provide quality services to all segments of society regardless of religious affiliation.

While the numerical presence of Christians in the Middle East has declined, El Yousef argues that the contributions of Christians to education, health care, and social advancement are huge—but face great challenges. For this important Christian witness that benefits Arab societies as a whole to continue, more funding and subsidies must be secured.

In certain geographic and political areas, for example, Christians have had to comply with imposed interpretations of Islamic customs and laws in the running of their institutions. This is especially true in schools in areas of conflict and violence such as Gaza, where single-sex education for students and teachers has been imposed, albeit temporarily. Other chal-

lenges mentioned by El-Yousef include the Israeli separation wall that iso-
lates youth on both sides who grow up without knowing the "other," the
ongoing 50-year Israeli occupation, and the unresolved conflict between
Israel and Palestine, which seems to have no end. This is the most difficult
challenge faced by all Palestinians, including Christians. Despite these
challenges, El-Yousef gives assurances that Christian institutions are committed to supporting the less advantaged regardless of religious affiliation. They have been first responders during wars and conflicts and
according to El-Yousef, "We never existed to support only Christians, and
we never will."[31]

Part II: Human Rights, Combating Persecution, and the Responsibility to Protect

The chapters in this section examine the existential issues facing Christians
and other vulnerable communities in the contemporary Middle East. The
first, Elie Chalala's "The Arab-Christian Predicament Before and After the
Rise of the Islamic State," probes the underlying causes and consequences
of the potential loss of cultural and religious diversity in the region, with a
specific focus on Iraq and Syria. According to Chalala, Lebanese-born editor of the California-based journal *Al Jadid: A Review & Record of Arab
Culture and Arts*, the threats to Christians and other groups of persecution and forceful expulsion from their ancestral lands predate the aftermath of the Arab Spring of 2011. He cites two important factors to
support his argument: the end of the Ottoman *millet* system after the First
World War that ended the state's protection of non-Muslim religious communities, and the interwar period in which many Christians in the Levant
became receptive to the appeal of totalitarian and extremist nationalist
parties, some of which were overtly sympathetic to Nazi Germany.

Faced with the choice between a liberal, democratic party and a nationalist, socialist-communist one that would guarantee equality regardless of
their sects, class, or numbers, many Christians of the intellectual elite
chose the totalitarian and extreme nationalist parties. As an explanation,
Chalala states that the sectarian underpinnings of the Ottoman *millet* system proved difficult to overcome. Many Christians were reluctant to give
up their "protected" community prerogatives even when this came at the
expense of equality of citizenship. Likewise, they feared the prospect of
elections that might lead to majority rule and the potential tyranny of the
Muslim majority. Therefore, they gravitated to regimes that were inspired

by nationalist, Baathist, and communist parties. In Iraq, for example, Christians sided with Saddam Hussein, at the cost of alienating the Shiite majority, which was persecuted by the Iraqi Baathist regime. The consequences of this decision are evident today. Chalala believes that the Arab Christians' fears of majority rule and their dismissal of Western democratic concepts such as constitutions, parliaments, elections, and the rule of law (regardless of how flawed these institutions might have been), has resulted in their current precarious position.

Chalala notes that as the Syrian conflict intensified, the Syrian regime coopted the Christians by using their neighborhoods to attack Sunni districts. When, as might have been expected, retaliation by the Sunnis ensued, the Christians were backed into de facto support of the regime. The neutrality that some Christians had worked so hard to cultivate during the conflict was compromised; it was destroyed further when the Church's hierarchical leadership led the Christian community into siding with the Assad regime, to the detriment of their own congregations.

Even in the midst of the Syrian conflict, many Christians remained hostile toward political systems that are based on freedom, economic liberalism, and democratic pluralism. Chalala argues that unless this approach changes and the decades-old lens through which some Arab Christians view questions of nationalism and despotism is altered, Christians will remain imperiled. He urges Arab Christians to reflect on the effects of their formerly expedient alliances, and to adjust their positions to embrace the concepts embodied in constitutions, parliaments, elections, and the rule of law, regardless of the perceived flaws of these institutions.

Fateh Azzam's chapter, "A Human Rights Perspective on the Protection of Christians and Other Minorities in the Middle East and North Africa," posits that human rights can provide a set of standards to monitor, inform, and offer the needed protection for vulnerable groups of the Middle East and North Africa. He focuses on the Maghreb countries of North Africa in his chapter, but the principles he espouses are applicable to all states. Quoting the first article of the Universal Declaration of Human Rights of 1948 (UDHR), "All human beings are born free and equal in dignity and rights. They are endowed with reason and conscience and should act towards one another in a spirit of brotherhood,"[32] Azzam cautions that human rights do not implement themselves. Rather, they exist within the broader political and institutional context of the region as well as the global frameworks for the protection of rights. The realization of these principles will require mobilization and advocacy on the part of an informed public. In addition, a holistic approach to these principles must include an understanding of the political economy of repression and brutality, a long view of history, and a clear vision of a future where all can be equal and equally protected.

When it comes to the multiplicity of minority communities in the richly diverse Middle East, Azzam joins other authors in this volume to argue that the region currently is experiencing a serious failure of legal and moral responsibility. A low-intensity level of discrimination exists in a number of countries, although few have experienced the dire consequences of the genocidal acts perpetrated by ISIS in Iraq and Syria.

Sectarianism is a powerful tool of autocratic leadership to maintain control, power, and wealth. Azzam points to the retention by Arab states of the *millet* system of the Ottoman Empire that created the schism between penal law and civil laws. On one hand, "minority" differences and the exercise of community prerogatives were protected; on the other, the legal status of individual members of those communities was differentiated at the expense of equality of citizenship. Further complicating this situation, the Arab Spring of early 2011 opened a Pandora's box of authoritarianism and sectarianism by both governments and armed groups in Syria, Iraq, Libya, Yemen, and elsewhere, resulting in the chaos of today. As tempting as it may be to come to the rescue of Christians, Azzam cautions against privileging one group over another, as it would further sectarian divisions. Everyone needs protection, and every community that is persecuted needs to be protected or saved equally. Finally, Azzam argues that human rights principles and their treaties and conventions offer an approach that can provide protection to religious and other groups, as they are based on the inherent dignity of all humanity.

General Anthony Zinni's chapter, "The 'Responsibility to Protect' and the Dangers of Military Intervention in Fragile States," discusses what Pentagon strategists today describe as "volatile, complex, uncertain, and ambiguous" situations in the world. General Zinni's analysis is informed by his former position as commander of the United States Central Command with responsibility for all military functions and operations in the Middle East. He was also the Bush Administration's envoy to the Middle East Peace Process in 2002, where he engaged with Israeli and Palestinian leaders and would often meet with the leaders of the 13 Christian denominations in the region. In 2015, he was part of a delegation from the Middle East Institute examining the U.S.–Egyptian relationship, and had discussions with the Coptic Pope and Muslim religious leaders in Cairo regarding anti-Christian events in Egypt during the reign of the Muslim Brotherhood.

General Zinni evokes the end of the Cold War in 1989–1990, and the resulting relief and euphoria that led to heady talk of a new world order and of a peace dividend. In the two decades that followed, the United States felt a compassionate and honor-bound need to intervene militarily in a number of conflicts that were "values-based" as opposed to "interests-based." For the most part, military interventions to protect at-risk groups from potential religious cleansing and genocide have not succeeded. The reason, General Zinni, argues, is that U.S. interventions, even going back to Vietnam, were marked by a lack of strategic or long-term view of what the end state should or could look like. "We get in but can't get out."

The same situation has prevailed with peace agreements. While in principle an agreement can be signed by all parties, its implementation often is not achieved. Besides, the use of the military to protect or ensure peace is expensive and costly and tends to last indefinitely. General Zinni cites the Carter Administration's commitment to station U.S. forces in the Sinai as an assurance that came with the Egyptian–Israeli Peace Treaty of 1979. Those forces are still in place. He points out that the United States still has troops in Europe and Japan long after the end of World War II in 1945, as well as in in South Korea since 1950. The deployments of U.S. troops in Iraq and Afghanistan are well into their second decade. He argues that military intervention is not the solution to such conflicts, as it can freeze a situation or relieve the symptoms only temporarily.

In General Zinni's view, in war zones and in failed and fragile states that threaten entire ethnic, religious, or tribal groups, it is unlikely that "boots on the ground" will stop the catastrophic bleeding and suffering. He agrees with strategists who have stressed the need for carefully defining the national security interests of those involved before undertaking such initiatives. Clear objectives, engaging in a thorough assessment of the risks and costs, setting an exit strategy, and analyzing the potential consequences of any U.S. action should be necessary before any such undertaking. The key to success is in securing both the continuing support of the American people and broad international support before undertaking any intervention.

The military has plenty of robust and dynamic war plans that are continually updated, exercised, and adjusted, if it wishes to engage in a "responsibility to protect" intervention. Nevertheless, despite the moral commitments and the good intentions of leaders to alleviate suffering and genocide, General Zinni points out that such intervention is doomed to failure if there is no consideration of a "responsibility to rebuild" plan by other government agencies that exist to deal with post-conflict societies. In part, this is due to the lack of resources provided to the State Department, USAID, and other government agencies that should have been responsible for such planning. But it is also due to the absence of a "planning culture" in these agencies. Few experts truly exist or are developed within these agencies, as compared to the military. Coordinating and addressing these governmental deficiencies, Zinni argues, is necessary for U.S. policy to be effective.

Alon Ben-Meir expands upon General Zinni's concerns and adds another responsibility, namely, the "responsibility to prevent" as a way to deal with these crises, in his chapter, "The Persecution of Minorities in the Middle East." Ben-Meir lists several countermeasures that can be taken to stem the rising tide of religious discrimination as well as other human rights violations in the Middle East. Among these are (1) efforts to end raging regional conflicts; (2) employing preventive diplomacy and timely intervention at any sign that acts of persecution or human rights violations might take place; (3) monitoring and exposing infractions committed against religious and other vulnerable groups throughout the world; (4) providing incentives, such as significant funding for educational programming, so that citizens of a given country can develop legal practices and cultural tools which offer training and instruction in religious and human rights tolerance; (5) using coercive diplomacy, such as leveraging international trade or other political deals with a demand of ending violations against vulnerable religious communities; (6) promoting education to foster religious tolerance and inter-religious dialogue; and (7) use of quiet diplomacy to make objections clear to allied nations, to compel them to correct their records on religious freedom and human rights violations.

Ben-Meir points out that the root causes of the threats to vulnerable communities emanating today from groups such as ISIS, al-Qaeda, and other Takfiri groups (those willing to break the law of the Qu'ran by declaring other Muslims to be apostates and killing them), are religious teachings, albeit distorted, under the guise of defending purist Sunni Islam (or Shia Islam, in the case of Iran). The ultimate aim of these groups is to infect (and recruit) susceptible Muslim youths for whom religion provides an escape and a sense of belonging. By waging a war on Western cultural and religious precepts, violent extremists attempt to fuse their brutal acts into the identity of their own jihadist community, thereby gaining recognition as the representative of the larger Muslim community, especially by the media. Christians, given the ties between the Western world and mainstream Christianity, have become a "natural" target for groups that seek to frame their conflict as one of epic religious proportions.

Although Ben-Meir offers a strategy to combat persecution, his analysis recognizes the difficulties that impede progress toward mitigating it. As persecution of vulnerable groups can be allayed only partially, this phenomenon will remain for the foreseeable future. As a result, Christians and other groups may not be able to restore the status quo and live in harmony with their largely Muslim neighbors in the near term.

Finally, Ben-Meir warns that the plight of Christians and other communities in the Middle East has ramifications on the West. The rise of populism and tribalism has become a visible global phenomenon. The world is witnessing the growth of nationalism not only in the Middle East but also in Western Europe and the United States. This phenomenon brings with it a desire for social homogeneity and a tendency to blame others for one's plight. Ben-Meir argues that this global phenomenon cannot be ignored, but must be countered by providing countries with significant funding to develop legal practices and cultural tools that offer training and instruction in religious tolerance and human rights, promoting education to foster religious tolerance and inter-religious dialogue, and monitoring and exposing infractions committed against religious groups throughout the world.

Part III: The Arab Spring, the Shia/Sunni Divide, and Their Impact on Regional and Geopolitical Tensions

In his chapter, "The Answer to the Vulnerability of Arab Christians and other Minorities Is Citizenship Rights Under the Rule of Law," Rami Khouri contends that to use the narrow and somewhat exaggerated Shiite/Sunni divide to assess vulnerable group realities and threats in the Middle East is deceptive. This divide was mentioned only rarely until about 2003, when the Anglo-American war eliminated Iraq's state structure. Essentially, Khouri argues, sectarian identity is strengthened by internal stresses within states as well as by regional conflicts among states and non-state actors. But Christians and other communities across the Arab region are more affected by the lack of definition and validation of the most fundamental concepts that define states and the lives of their citizens. These include core, critical ideas such as statehood, nationhood, sovereignty, religiosity and secularism, communal and national identity, and citizenship. Lack of genuine state-hood is reflected in the slow degradation in the fundamental quality of life for a large number of the region's people and has created mass discontent. These ills include poverty, socio-economic disparities, quality of education, labor informality, and other obstacles to living a decent life.

Sectarian tensions between Sunnis and Shiites represent only the most recent serious threat that impacts the lives of millions of people, whether characterized as "majorities" or as "minorities." Khouri decries the fact that Arab citizens have never had the opportunity—have never even been asked—to define the critical elements that create security in their lives, at the individual, family, community, or national levels. In desperate times, people will naturally turn to their religion, or to their tribal and ethnic identity, to find protection if the state leaves them living in wretched con-ditions. This has been the case for many Arabs in the past half century.

Khouri lists ten key trends that have shaped the current conditions and trajectories in the Arab region, and that demonstrate the deep structural malignancies that go beyond facile explanations of the Arab uprisings, ter-rorism, political violence and the Shia-Sunni rivalry. The answer promised in the title of his chapter is genuine citizenship, based on a clear under-standing of the need for citizens to define and validate their own govern-ment systems, state borders, power structures, and national values.

Brian Katulis explores the theme of broader regional struggles in "The Impact of the Shia-Sunni Political Struggle and Future Strategies for Christian and other Vulnerable Communities in the Middle East." Katulis confirms that Christians are but one community that has been rendered defenseless and exposed by the internal and regional Shia-Sunni sectarian struggles, and not only in Iraq and Syria. The rise and fall of political Islamist forces in countries such as Egypt has also placed Christians and other vulnerable groups in the crosshairs of a dangerous battle.

Geographically, the Middle East is at the epicenter of a broader "arc of crisis" that has a significant impact on security beyond the region, of which the current refugee crisis in Europe is a prime example. Geo-strategically, the region has long served as a vital land and sea transit route for global trade and commerce whose continued security is vital to Europe and the global economy. With this as the background, Katulis provides a strategic assessment of the security and political dynamics reshaping the Middle East. He describes how these overarching security dynamics impact

Christian communities across the Middle East, highlighting the diversity of circumstances facing the region's Christians. He then argues that the continued presence of Christians and other vulnerable groups in the region will require a shift in policy planning on the part of the United States, Europe, and Russia that involves working with regional partners to develop a positive agenda that supports religious freedom, equality, and basic rights for all its people. Finally, Katulis analyzes the impact of U.S. foreign policy on these dynamics during the latter part of the Obama administration, concluding with some preliminary analysis on the impact of President Donald Trump and his new administration on these dynamics.

CONCLUSION

The chapters that form the basis of this volume were initially inspired by the necessity to address the contemporary persecution of religious communities in the Middle East and, in particular, the threat to the continued existence of Christians in the region. The authors who have contributed to this study have moved beyond that immediate tragedy and have highlighted the importance of the struggle for secular nationalism and citizenship for imperiled communities. In shifting the analysis to the root causes of inequality, they have reframed the discussion on the plight of vulnerable communities, and enabled the reader to explore policy implications that will foster reconciliation, equality, human rights and citizenship. It is their contention that only by examining these fundamental issues will the politics and daily life of the Middle East be transformed to ensure equality and the human rights of all.

NOTES

1. Griffith, Sidney H. "'People of the Gospel; People of the Book'": Christians and Christianity in the World of Islam," *The Church in the Shadow of the Mosque: Christians and Muslims in the World of Islam* (Princeton University Press, 2008), 11.
2. Paul S. Rowe, "The Middle Eastern Christian as Agent," *International Journal of Middle East Studies*, Vol. 42, No. 3 (August 2010), 472–474.
3. L.C. Robson, "Recent Perspectives on Christians in the Modern Arab World," *History Compass*, 9/4, 2011, 312–325.
4. Ussama Makdisi, *The Artillery of Heaven: American Missionaries and the Failed Conversion of the Middle East* (Ithaca and London: Cornell University Press, 2008), 8.

5. Rowe, op. cit.
6. Anthony O'Mahony, "The Contributions of Ancient Christian Communities to the Contemporary Middle East," Conference on *Christianity and Freedom: Historical and Contemporary Perspectives*, Rome, Italy, December 13–14, 2013.
7. See: Anh Nga Longva, Anne Sofie Roald (eds.), *Religious minorities in the Middle East: Domination, Self-empowerment, Accommodation* (Leiden, Boston: Brill, 2012), 5. Seteney Shami, "'Aqualliyya'/Minority in Modern Egyptian Discourse," Carol Gluck and Anna L. Sing (eds.), *Words in Motion* (Durham, NC: Duke University Press, 2009), 151–173. Also, Eliz Sanasarian, *Religious Minorities in Iran* (Cambridge: Cambridge University Press, 2000), 66.
8. Anh Nga Longva, Anne Sofie Roald (eds.), op. cit., 5.
9. Seteney Shami, op. cit., 151–173. Also, Eliz Sanasarian, *Religious Minorities in Iran* (Cambridge: Cambridge University Press, 2000), 66, who states that during the discussions on the formulation of the constitution of the Islamic Republic of Iran in 1979, the Armenian deputy requested that Christians be referred to as a "community" rather than a "minority." The author states, "there was a possibility that the forum was being used to convey a message to those who had equated Western imperialism with Christian minorities in Iran."
10. Benjamin Thomas White, *The Emergence of Minorities in the Middle East: The Politics of Community in French Mandate Syria* (Edinburgh: Edinburgh University Press, 2011), 26–31.
11. Ibid.
12. Ussama Makdisi, "The Problem of Sectarianism in the Middle East in an Age of Western Hegemony," in Nader Hashemi and Danny Postel (eds.), *Sectarianization: Mapping the New Politics of the Middle East* (Oxford, NY: Oxford University Press, 2017), 26.
13. Ibid.
14. Hans Kohn, "Nationalism," *Encyclopaedia Britannica*, Encyclopedia Britannica, Inc., 2017, Web. 19 July 2017. https://www.britannica.com/print/article/405644
15. Albert Hourani, *Arabic Thought in the Liberal Age: 1798–1939* (Cambridge: Cambridge University Press, 1983), 95.
16. Benjamin Thomas White, op. cit., 26–31.
17. Ussama Makdisi, "Ottoman Orientalism," *American Historical Review*, Vol. 107, No. 3 (June 2002), 770.
18. Erik Freas, *Muslim-Christian Relations in Late Ottoman Palestine: Where Nationalism and Religion Intersect* (New York: Palgrave Macmillan, 2016), 157–158.
19. Ibid.
20. Hourani, *Arabic Thought in the Liberal Age*: op. cit.

21. Ussama Makdisi, "The Problem of Sectarianism in the Middle East in an Age of Western Hegemony," in Nader Hashemi and Danny Postel (eds.), *Sectarianism: Mapping the New Politics of the Middle East* (Oxford, NY: Oxford University Press, 2017), 27.

22. Engin Deniz Akarli, *The Long Peace: Ottoman Lebanon, 1861–1920* (Berkeley: University of California Press, 1993), 31–33.

23. Letter of greeting to participants in the Villanova conference on Christians in the Middle East, December 6, 2016. Cardinal Sandri hold the third most important position within the Vatican (after the Cardinal Secretary of State and the Pope himself), serving essentially as the chief of staff of the Secretariat of State. As Prefect of the Congregation for the Oriental Churches, he heads the curial congregation that handles matters regarding the Eastern Catholic Churches and is the ex officio Grand Chancellor of the Pontifical Oriental Institute that deals with Islam.

24. "There Are No Minorities, only Citizens: The al-Azhar declaration calls for a renewed alliance between all Arab citizens: Muslims, Christians and those of other religions," *Oasis: Christians and Muslims in the Global World*, April 13, 2017. http://www.oasiscenter.eu/articles/religions-and-the-public-sphere/2017/04/13/there-are-no-minorities-only-citizens

25. Elizabeth Picard. *Conclusion: Nation-Building and Minority Rights in the Middle East*, "Religious Minorities in the Middle East: Domination, Self-empowerment, Accommodation," Brill, 230–255, 2012. https://halshs.archives-ouvertes.fr/halshs-00715384/document

26. Holy See Press Office, *Joint Statement on "Supporting the Human Rights of Christians and Other Communities, particularly in the Middle East" at the 28th Session of the Human Rights Council (Geneva, 13 March 2015)*, 13.03.2015. https://press.vatican.va/content/salastampa/en/bollettino/pubblico/2015/03/13/0186/00415.html

27. *Muslim leaders in Lebanon condemn persecution of Christians in the Middle East.* "In the name of religious, humanitarian and national principles, the summit condemns religiously motivated attacks against Eastern Christians, including attacks against their homes, villages, property and places of worship, when in fact the Prophet had recommended that they be respected, protected and defended." http://www.catholicnewsagency.com/news/muslim-leaders-in-lebanon-condemn-persecution-of-christians-in-the-middle-east-56617/

28. Remarks of His Majesty King Abdullah II, Plenary Session of the 69th General Assembly the United Nations, New York, 24 September 2014. http://www.un.org/en/ga/69/meetings/gadebate/pdf/JO_en.pdf

29. Philip Jenkins, *The Lost History of Christianity: The Thousand-year Golden Age of the Church in the Middle East, Africa and Asia,—and how it died* (New York: Harperone, 2008), 5–12.

30. Seyyed Hossein Nasr, "Muslim Dialogue with the Church after Nostra Aetate," *Nostra Aetate*, Pim Valkenberg, Anthony Cirelli (eds.), (Washington, DC: The Catholic University of America Press, 2016), 110. http://www.jstor.org/stable/j.cttlg69zbs.15, Downloaded Wed, 15 March 2017.
31. Sami El-Yousef, "Jerusalem Situation Update," October 15, 2015, The Catholic Near East Welfare Association, *Pontifical Mission: the papal agency for Middle East relief and development.*
32. Universal Declaration of Human Rights, adopted by the U.N. General Assembly on 10 December 1948.

Christian Cultural and Intellectual Life in the Islamic Middle East: A Shared History

Christianity's Historic Roots in the Middle East: Christians at Home in the 'World of Islam'

Sidney Griffith

PROLEGOMENA

The canonical scriptures of the New Testament originally composed in Greek, particularly the Acts of the Apostles and the Epistles ascribed to St. Paul, record Christianity's spread from its homeland northward and westward into the Greek- and Latin-speaking realm of the Roman Empire. For this reason and to this day, albeit that Jesus the Messiah, his apostles, and disciples were speakers of Aramaic whose scriptures were written in Hebrew and Aramaic and whose historic roots were deeply planted in the East, most people in the West still think of Christianity's early history as almost exclusively a Greek and Latin phenomenon. But the fact is that just about simultaneously with the spread of Christianity from the Holy Land westward, Aramaic-speaking disciples were already bringing the Gospel eastward, beyond the borders of the Roman Empire into the far-flung territories of the Persian Empire and beyond, eventually across the Silk Roads into China, southward into Arabia, and ultimately to India. Their stories

S. Griffith (✉)
Department of Semitics and Egyptian Languages and Literatures, The Catholic University of America, Washington, DC, USA

© The Author(s) 2018
K. C. Ellis (ed.), *Secular Nationalism and Citizenship in Muslim Countries*, Minorities in West Asia and North Africa,
https://doi.org/10.1007/978-3-319-71204-8_2

29

are recorded in the Christian church's third patristic language, the widely spoken dialect of Aramaic called Syriac. As fate would have it, even the earliest Syriac Christian texts of the Middle East came too late to be included among the canonical scriptures. But they nevertheless clearly attest to Christianity's flourishing in the Middle East and beyond for 600 years and more before the rise of Islam in the seventh century A.D. Moreover, the Syriac-speaking Christians brought Christianity from the peripheries of Arabia into the heartlands of the Arabic-speaking communities to whom Muhammad would bring the Qur'ān in the first third of the seventh century A.D.

CHRISTIANS IN PRE-ISLAMIC ARABIA

There is a wealth of information scattered in mainly Greek, Syriac, and Arabic texts about the Christian communities that found their way in the fifth, sixth, and seventh centuries into the Arabic-speaking heartland. In recent years, scholars have indefatigably gathered every shred of available information they have been able to glean from all of these sources and more, thereby providing sufficient material for the composition of a more or less continuous narrative of Christian presence in Arabia and its environs from the fourth century to the time of Muhammad.[1] And it seems clear from these sources that the major Christian communities who made headway among the Arabs in the several centuries just prior to the rise of Islam were associated with the communities or denominations that later Muslim writers would customarily identify as the 'Melkites,' 'Jacobites,' and 'Nestorians.'[2] Their principal ecclesiastical language was Syriac, or Christian Palestinian Aramaic among the 'Melkites,' albeit that their ecclesial identities were largely determined by the positions their communities adopted in the Christological controversies of the fifth and sixth centuries. These controversies in turn were largely concerned with texts translated from Greek into Syriac from the fifth century onward.[3] In South Arabia, there was also a significant Ethiopian presence, and while their Christological sympathies were with the 'Jacobites' and the Copts of Egypt, their ecclesiastical language was Ge'ez.[4] The historical record preserves no memory of any other significant Christian presence thriving among the Arabs or in their environs in the crucial period from the fifth century to the first third of the seventh century. In particular, as we shall discuss below, there is no indisputable, documentary evidence for the presence of any notable 'Jewish Christian' group thriving as such in Arabia in this period. Modern scholars who have postulated their presence have done so, as we shall argue, on the basis of extrapolations from their theological interpretations of certain passages in the Arabic Qur'ān. But it nevertheless seems also to have been the case that the 'main-line' Christian communities (i.e., the 'Melkites,' Jacobites,' and 'Nestorians'), whose bishops, priests, and monks represented established Christianity in the Syriac and Arabic-speaking communities by the seventh century, also still carried with them much of the lore and literature of earlier Christian groups. These included the Aramaic-speaking Ebionites, Elchasaites, and Nazarenes, along with the memory of the more or less contemporary 'Marcionites' (Marcion d.c. 160) and the followers of Bardaysān of Edessa (154–222), to name only the most prominent of earlier Christian groups. But there was one important community from Christian antiquity that still flourished in the seventh century, even among the Arabs, and contemporary with the 'Melkites,' 'Jacobites,' and 'Nestorians,' namely, the followers of the Aramaic-speaking, third-century teacher and self-styled apostle and prophet, Mani (c. 216–276), whose disciples also carried with them the memories and traditions of the earlier groups.[5] Indeed, the recollection of Marcion, Bar Daysān, and Mani still appears prominently centuries later in early Islamic heresiography.

Given the evidentiary presumption then that Christianity came among the Arabic-speaking peoples by way of their contacts with Aramaic, Syriac, or Ge'ez-speaking Christians on the periphery of Arabia proper, a question arises about the language of Christianity among the Arabs. It seems unlikely a priori that indigenous, Arabic-speaking Christians in the Arabian heartland, who would have learned their Christianity from the communities on the Arabian periphery, would have adopted the Aramaic, Syriac, or Ge'ez languages along with their Christian faith. Rather, the historian's presumption must be that the Arabs on the periphery translated Christianity at least orally into their own Arabic language. This would not have been a surprising development because of the likely bilingualism of the Arabs living on the periphery of Arabia proper, especially in Syria and Mesopotamia. In northern Mesopotamia there was an entire region between the city of Nisibis and the Tigris river called in Syriac, Bēt 'Arbāyê, or 'the homeland of the Arabs.'[6] Here in the sixth century, the Syrian Orthodox holy man and bishop Mār Ahūdemeh (d. 575), had considerable success in evangelizing the Arab tribes, who would in due course come to have their own 'Bishop of the Arabs.'[7] Some of their number would become known in early Islamic times precisely for their bilingualism, speaking both Syriac and Arabic.[8] The situation must have been similar already in the fifth century in Palestine, where the monastic founder St. Euthymius (d. 473) evangelized Arab tribesmen and established an episcopal hierarchy among them.[9] In the areas controlled by the 'Jacobite' Ghassanids and the 'Nestorian' Lakhmids in the sixth century, Arabic may already have been the dominant language,[10] but their ties with the Syriac-speaking 'Jacobite' and 'Nestorian' churches were continuous. Presumably, the same may be said even of the Christian communities in southern Arabia, and particularly in Najrān, where ties with the Syriac-speaking mother-churches seem to have been continuous up to the rise of Islam.[11] In the fifth and sixth centuries, the south Arabian tribal group called Kinda gained ascendancy among the Arab tribes even of central and northern Arabia, and there were notable Christian and Jewish converts among them. And while it may well have been the case that the Christians among them played a major role in the spread of the knowledge of Christianity among the Arabic-speaking peoples; their major exploits all seem to have been mostly political in nature and to have transpired normally on the Arabian periphery, among the Romans in Palestine or the Persians in Mesopotamia.[12]

It is scant, but there is some explicit evidence in the Greek, Syriac, and even Arabic historical sources for a presence of Christians among the Arabic-speaking peoples of central Arabia and the Hijāz in the sixth and seventh centuries,[13] where presumably only Arabic was commonly spoken. And the contents of the Arabic Qur'ān that has its origins in just this Arabic-speaking milieu testifies to the fact that by the first third of the seventh century knowledge of Christianity, of its scriptures, its lore, its doctrines, and practices must have been widespread in the Arabic-speaking heartland. For as we shall see, the Qur'ān presumes a detailed knowledge of these matters on the part of its audience. So the question is, how did they acquire it? The answer seems to be that by the time of the Qur'ān, detailed knowledge of the Christian Bible, the creed, and liturgy had already spread orally among the Arabs, presumably transmitted originally from those Arameans and Arabs living on the Arabian periphery. They were in more immediate contact, both with the Syriac-speaking Christians whose faith and practice the Qur'ān largely echoes, and the Ge'ez-speaking Christians of Ethiopia and South Arabia, who were themselves influenced by Syriac Christianity.[14] While very few traces of Christian texts in Arabic prior to the rise of Islam have so far come to light, the Arabic Qur'ān itself, given the high quotient of its Christian awareness, emerges as the most important document in evidence of the presence of Christians in its Arabian milieu.

Arabic-speaking Christians were in the audience to whom much of the Qur'ān was addressed, especially in the Medinan phase of Muhammad's career when he came into direct controversy with Christians. At the time, the Qur'ān called the Christians whom it addressed 'Nazarenes' (*an-Nasārā*), a name for them that would persist wherever Arabic was spoken thereafter, including among Christians themselves, who within a century after the Islamic conquest of the Middle East had themselves adopted Arabic as their daily language.

CHRISTIAN ARABIC

The study of the Christian heritage in Arabic has never been more important than it is today, when in many places in the Near and Middle East Arabic-speaking Christians are becoming fewer and fewer in the populations of their homelands. Many communities, especially among those whose patristic and liturgical patrimony is Syriac, are in danger of disappearing altogether from now predominantly Muslim Palestine, Syria, and Iraq, where their forebears made substantial intellectual and religious contributions to what has been called 'Islamicate' culture. It is an awkward term that is meant by those who use it to refer to the multicultural and multi-religious factors inherent in the formation of what we customarily think of as the classical culture of the World of Islam.[15] Typically scholars have used it in reference to such historical phenomena as the role Christians played in the so-called Graeco-Arabic Translation Movement of early Abbasid times, the Christian and Jewish contributions to the history of philosophy in Arabic,[16] or the influence wielded by wealthy Christians or Christian physicians over the Muslim elite in the milieus of Baghdad or Cairo in their heydays.[17] Scholars have also highlighted in this connection what they have perceived to be the indebtedness of the evolving Islamic religious and political doctrine and practice in its formative period to concurrent Jewish and Christian thought and life.[18] All of this refers to Christian contributions to Islam consequent upon the adoption of the Arabic language by the originally Greek and Syriac-speaking Christian communities who after the mid-seventh century came under Arab Muslim rule, and who by the mid-to-late eighth century had adopted the Arabic language as their own.

After the Arab conquest and occupation of almost all of the territories of the Oriental Patriarchates of the Christians (Alexandria, Antioch, Jerusalem) in the course of the seventh Christian century, large communities of hitherto Greek, Syriac, Coptic, and Armenian-speaking Christians joined the already Arabic-speaking Christians of the original milieu of Muhammad and the Qur'ān as 'People of the Book,' living in the midst of the Muslim 'Community of Believers,' with a guaranteed legal status of their own, albeit one that required them to pay a special poll tax and to adopt a low social profile as subaltern citizens in the World of Islam.[19] For in due course, and within about two centuries after the death of Muhammad, the territories under Arab rule had grown into what a modern scholar has called the Islamic Commonwealth,[20] which nevertheless thought of itself as the World of Islam (*dār al-Islām*). As Albert Hourani memorably wrote—

> By the third and fourth Islamic centuries (the ninth or tenth century AD) something which was recognizably an "Islamic World" had emerged.... Men and women in the Near East and the Maghrib lived in a universe which was defined in terms of Islam. ... Time was marked by the five daily prayers, the weekly sermon in the Mosque, the annual fast in the month of Ramadan and the pilgrimage to Mecca and the Muslim calendar.[21]

The process of integrating the several communities of Christians into this new social reality, among many other adjustments on their part, most notably involved the adoption of the Arabic language, not only as the idiom of public life in the caliphate, but as an ecclesiastical, even liturgical, theological, and everyday language. It began as a project to translate the scriptures and many other Christian texts originally written in Greek and Syriac into Arabic,[22] an ecclesiastical translation movement that pre-dates and in some ways may even be said to have eventually encompassed the more well-known Abbasid project to translate Greek scientific, logical, and philosophical texts into Arabic. Simultaneously, and as an integral part of the process of social integration, Christians also began to write original theological and apologetic texts in the Arabic idiom of the contemporary Islamic religious discourse.[23]

The adoption of Arabic on the part of the hitherto Greek, Coptic, and Syriac-speaking Christian communities indigenous to the Levant culminated eventually in a large Christian presence in the intellectual and cultural life of the formative period of the history of the Islamicate world, extending from ninth-century Iraq well into the thirteenth and fourteenth centuries in Egypt.[24] During this half-millennium and more of Jewish, Christian, and Muslim *convivencia* in the heartlands of the Arabic-speaking peoples after the Islamic conquest,[25] relations between Muslims and Christians were constant, often intellectually and culturally complimentary, mutually comprehensible, but both confrontational and cooperative at the same time. In the end, from the thirteenth century onward, due to numerous disabling factors,[26] including developments in Islamic religious thinking,[27] the numbers of Christians living in the Islamic world gradually declined to demographic insignificance in some areas, reaching crisis proportions in certain places by the dawn of the twenty-first century.[28]

Over the course of the long, early history of Arab Christian relations with Islam, extending roughly from the mid-ninth century to the mid-thirteenth century, in the environs first of Baghdad and then of Cairo, several areas of Christian intellectual and cultural accomplishment stand out. These areas of Arab Christian accomplishment may the most usefully be identified under three headings: translation and cultural assimilation, inter-religious colloquy, and the Islamochristian cultivation of philosophy, especially in Baghdad and its environs from the ninth to the eleventh centuries.

BAGHDAD IN ABBASID TIMES

Baghdad in the tenth century, like Paris in the thirteenth century, was a city alive with an intellectual enthusiasm generated in no small part by a movement to translate Greek logical and philosophical texts into the local scholarly languages, Arabic and Latin, respectively.[29] In both instances, the heydays of the translation movements were in the preceding centuries: the ninth century in Baghdad and the twelfth century in Europe.[30] In ninth-century Baghdad, perhaps the now most famous of the translators was the Christian Hunayn ibn Ishāq (808–875), whose enterprise involved a whole circle of other translators, working both from earlier Syriac versions of Greek texts and from Greek originals as well.[31] And already in the ninth century in Baghdad, thinkers such as Abū Yūsuf Ya'qūb ibn Ishāq al-Kindī (d. 866/870), and Abū Bakr Muhammad ibn Zakariyā ar-Rāzī (850–925) were doing philosophy in dialogue with the translated texts of Aristotle, Plato, and Galen, to name only the most prominent thinkers. They were followed in the tenth century by masters such as the Christian Abū Bishr Mattā ibn Yūnus (d. 940); the Jewish thinker, Sa'adyah ha-Ga'ōn ibn

Yūsuf al-Fayyūmī (882–942); the Muslim, Abū Naṣr al-Fārābī (d. 950)—
'the second master' after Aristotle, as he was called; and the Christian,
Yaḥyā ibn 'Adī (893–974)—the leader of the Aristotelians in Baghdad in
the third quarter of the tenth century—and his circle of disciples, both
Christian and Muslim.[32]

In addition to medicine, logic, and other philosophical topics, and
along with the defense of the religious claims of their own religious communities, particularly the central doctrine of monotheism (*at-tawḥīd*), all
the Baghdad thinkers of the period, Jews, Christians, and Muslims, were
interested in ethical, moral, and political issues, both private and public.
These included concerns about how best to dispel sorrows and achieve
happiness, how to instill virtues and extirpate vices, how to envision 'the
perfect man' (*al-insān al-kāmil*) and lead the philosophical life, and, not
least, how society should best be structured and under which legal system
(*sharī'ah*) it should be governed. Interestingly, it is in this latter context
that one often finds references to inter-religious concerns and to the
imperative for the cultivation of 'humane values' (*al-insāniyyah*) in the
relationships between communities, almost as if for these thinkers philosophy itself and the philosophical way of life could provide the only reason-
able approach to inter-communal dialogue and social harmony.[33] Finally,
there was also the question of right religion. The scholars of the period—
Jews, Christians, and Muslims—were eager to make use of their Late
Antique philosophical heritage to commend the veracity of their own religious traditions.

The Christian translator and philosopher Ḥunayn ibn Isḥāq seems to
have envisioned this inter-communal role for philosophy already in the
ninth century, according to a passage in the *Kitāb ādāb al-falāsifah*, a text
often attributed to him. The bulk of the work is a collection of sayings of
Greek and Persian sages and philosophers, transmitted from both ancient
and seemingly contemporary, gnomological sources.[34] But the opening
narrative is an interesting, if idiosyncratic, sketch of the history of philosophy, which assimilates even religious thinking and ritual behavior to the
philosophical way of life. The remarks attributed to Ḥunayn about Jews,
Christians, and Muslims highlight their joint participation in philosophy.[35]
He brings them up in the context of his discussion of the Stoics, a group
of philosophers who conducted their discussions in a specific place, i.e., in
the porches or porticoes of the cities where they lived, as their name
implies, and the usual appointments of which he describes in some detail.[36]

It seems that this mention of a special place for doing philosophy is what brings the Jews, Christians, and Muslims to mind.

Hunayn says that the Jewish philosophers imitated the Stoics. They too, he says, occupied a porch made of trees and vine cuttings, where their sages used to gather every year, as on a feast, during a week appointed for consultations and disputations. Hunayn says that they used to decorate the place with various kinds of fruit; and there, he says, their scholars would confer about knowledge (*ʿilm*) and study the prescribed books of their ancestors.[37] According to Hunayn, the meaning of the hanging fruit in the porches/booths was that "these [fruits] were the original maxims/wise sayings, for which the fruit stood, and with which souls are pleased and which hearts love."[38] Hunayn then goes on to speak of how the Stoics used to confer with one another about knowledge and studied their philosophy in their porticoes, all the while going in and out, so as to bestir their minds and their ardor by the bodily movement. Similarly, he now says—

> Jews and Christians occupied porticoes in gathering places (*al-kanāʾis*); they would gather in them to study the books they had, and to teach the young how to intone the chants and recite them; they would be moving around, both standing and sitting, to enkindle their ardor. The Jews do this to the present day.[39]

Hunayn then says that "the source of the chants of the Jews and the Christians is 'Music,' from which they took the chants."[40] He mentions David and the Psalms and says that to this day the Christians intone the Psalms in the chants of David. Both the Jews and the Christians, he says, build sanctuaries and put pillars in front of them, and so it is that "the Muslims too install pillars and porticos in their mosques, where the teachers teach the Qurʾān to the youngsters. They recite it in a sing-song way and in chants." "All this," Hunayn says, "was taken from Music."[41]

Finally, Hunayn offers a description of a church almost as if it were a philosophical academy and its priests and ministers were philosophers and their disciples and their liturgies were conferences of sages. He says—

> The Christians arrange the seats of the sanctuary one rank above another. The seat of the major, spiritual master, the teacher, is in the center of the sanctuary, while the philosophers are in the highest rank, the lowest of them being the disciples, whose station in rank is according to their level in science and philosophy.[42]

Hunayn's undertaking here to make a place for the Jews, Christians, and Muslims in his account of the history of philosophy echoes the earlier efforts of some Jewish and Christian intellectuals in Late Antique times, from Philo Judaeus and Origen of Alexandria onwards, to fold Jewish and Christian religious thinking into the wider discursive fabric of the Hellenistic philosophical schools. In the Islamic milieu of Baghdad, Hunayn's imaginative transformation of Jewish, Christian, and Muslim synagogues, churches, and mosques, with their liturgical rites, into philosophical schools, with their customary academic usages and procedures, seems to have been an effort on his part to promote the primacy of philosophy in public discourse in the Arabic-speaking, religiously plural polity in which he and his colleagues lived. To this end, Hunayn said of philosophy in his time that "God, mighty and exalted be He, conferred a blessing on us and taught us Arabic, so that we might bring it out of Greek, Hebrew, Syriac, and Greek into the clear, Arabic language."[43] It is against the background of this way of thinking that one approaches the study of the careers and works of several Christian intellectuals of Baghdad as they conversed with Jewish and Muslim contemporaries.

Yahyā ibn ʿAdī

Unlike the more-well-known Muslim thinkers of the period, men such as Abū Bakr ar-Rāzī, al-Kindī and al-Fārābī, and the Jewish philosopher/theologian Saʾadya Gaʾon, the Christian philosophers of tenth-century Baghdad are seldom studied in modern Western scholarship. In Baghdad, in the tenth century, the pursuit of knowledge and the ideal of the philosophical life offered Jews, Christians, and Muslims alike a culture they could share and an idiom in which they could talk with one another, even about their differing confessional views, which scholars in each community called upon philosophy to support and clarify. We find this colloquy underway in the works of Yahyā ibn ʿAdī and his circle of colleagues and students.[44]

Yahyā ibn ʿAdī at-Takrītī was born in Takrīt, Iraq, in 893. Takrīt had been, since the 640s, the seat of the Syrian Orthodox, or 'Jacobite,' metropolitan bishop, called the *Maphriān*. His mission was to serve the Syriac-speaking 'Jacobite' Christians living in Persian territories prior to the Islamic conquest; the see retained its special significance in Islamic times.[45] The city became a center for 'Jacobite' scholarship; and in the generation prior to that of Yahyā two Christian scholars in particular from Takrīt were well known in the 'Jacobite' community. They were Habīb ibn Khidma Abū Rā'itah (d. before 850), and his nephew, Nonnus of Nisibis (d.c. 862), both of whom were fluent in Syriac and Arabic, and both of whom wrote apologetic tracts in defense of the truth-claims of the 'Jacobite' Christians vis-à-vis the challenges of both Muslims and other Christian creedal communities.[46] Given the fact that in later years, Yahyā ibn ʿAdī would emerge as a formidable 'Jacobite' theologian in his own right, it is likely that his theological education began already in his youth in Takrīt. But it was philosophy and Aristotelian logic that called him to Baghdad.

Sometime in the first quarter of the tenth century, Yahyā came to Baghdad to study. In his *Kitāb at-tanbīh wa l-ishrāf*, the Baghdadī historian, al-Masʿūdī (d. 956), says of Yahyā that while he, Yahyā, was the sole person he knew in Baghdad who could trace his scholarly lineage back to Abū Naṣr Muhammad al-Fārābī (d. 950), Yahyā's "beginnings, his views and his practice were in the study of the practice of Muhammad ibn Zakariyyāʾ ar-Rāzī (d. 925), and it was the view of the Pythagoreans in 'first philosophy.'"[47] While some have been skeptical about this report that Yahyā ibn ʿAdī began his studies with ar-Rāzī, al-Masʿūdī was certainly in a good position to know about it. And it was certainly the case that Yahyā's most important teachers were the well-known 'Nestorian' logician of the time, Abū Bishr Mattā ibn Yūnus[48] and the aforementioned 'second master' after Aristotle, al-Fārābī.

After the death of Abū Bishr, and al-Fārābī's departure from Baghdad in the year 942, Yahyā ibn ʿAdī emerged in the city as the master of a circle of students of Aristotelian philosophy and logic, both Muslim and Christian. But he made his living as a bookman and a copyist. According to Muhammad ibn Ishāq an-Nadīm, Yahyā at one time boasted to him that he had already twice copied the *Tafsīr* of at-Tabarī and so many works of the *mutakallimūn* that they were beyond counting. What is more, Yahyā claimed that he normally copied a hundred leaves at a time, working day and night.[49] Another source reports that in his work as a copyist, Yahyā "used to write in a clear, sedate hand."[50] Yahyā also worked as a translator, translating mostly philosophical and logical texts from Syriac into Arabic, or correcting and revising earlier translations. An-Nadīm cites a number of translations, or revisions of earlier translations, for which Yahyā was responsible. But not everyone was pleased with the quality of his translation work. For example, his disciple, Abū Hayyān at-Tawhīdī, makes the remark that his master was "ill-suited for translation and bad at interpretation."[51]

Personally, according to Abū Hayyān, Yahyā ibn 'Adī was a man of tender character, even somewhat timid in disposition, yet very talented in bringing out in conversation the different shades of opinion on any given subject. These qualities allowed Yahyā to excel in the *majlis*. Nevertheless, again according to Abū Hayyān, Yahyā had a distaste for metaphysical subtleties and he would readily lose his way when they were brought up in the course of the conversations in the *majlis*. His forte, as his *laqab*, i.e., *al-mantiqī*, suggests, was logic.

In addition to the buying and selling of books, his work as a copyist, and his participation in the scholarly *majālis* of the socially elite in Baghdad, Yahyā ibn 'Adī was also the author of a large number of works on a wide variety of learned topics. The medieval historian of scholarship, al-Qiftī, lists almost 50 different titles attributed to Yahyā, while his modern bibliographer, Gerhard Endress, lists more than double that number of texts, including translations, that are attributed to Yahyā ibn 'Adī in the surviving manuscripts.[52] One can trace the wide range of Yahyā's interests in the subject headings of Endress' bibliography, which systematically and analytically present the many texts attributed to our author: translations, commentaries on the works of Aristotle and Alexander of Aphrodisias, propaedeutics and logic, physics and mathematics, metaphysics, ethics, philosophical questions, Christian theology, medicine, and even a bit of poetry.[53] An interesting feature of a number of the texts is the insight they afford the reader into the course of the philosophical and theological colloquies in which Yahyā took part with his Jewish, Christian, and Muslim interlocutors. Their names are sometimes mentioned in the texts, but their now missing works, or personal messages to Yahyā, are currently available, at least in part, only in Yahyā's quotations from them.

It is difficult to determine from the tenor of his surviving works if Yahyā ibn 'Adī was more a philosopher or a theologian. He certainly had a large interest in both areas of inquiry. In philosophy, his main preoccupation seems to have been with the proper understanding of the Aristotelian corpus, particularly the works on logic, the *Organon*, and Porphyry's *Eisagoge*, along with the *Topics* and the *Physics*, the two works that have been identified as being of particular interest for inter-faith discourse in the era of the translation movement in Baghdad.[54] In theology he defended the rationality of the Christian doctrines of the Trinity and the Incarnation against Muslim objections, and in Christian theology as such he was concerned principally with the defense of the Christological formulae of his own 'Jacobite' community against the rival doctrinal formulations of the

'Nestorians' and the 'Melkites.' In all, Yaḥyā seemed to think that proper logical definitions and care for the validity of Aristotelian syllogisms would settle most controversial questions in both philosophy and theology. As befits a student of the 'second master' after Aristotle, the Muslim philosopher, al-Fārābī, Yaḥyā was also concerned with matters pertaining to the virtuous life and the requisite dispositions for life in a reasonably well ordered society.

Yaḥyā ibn 'Adī died on 13 August 974. He was buried in the church of St. Thomas in the Daqīq quarter of Baghdad. The inscription on his tomb survives, preserved by Ibn Abī Usaybi'ah. It was inscribed on Yaḥyā's commission by one of his students, his fellow 'Jacobite,' Abū 'Alī 'Īsā ibn Zur'a (943–1008), a famous scholar in his own right, of whom we shall speak below. The text highlights Yaḥyā's devotion to knowledge; it gives the following advice—

> Many a dead man lives on through knowledge,
>> while one left behind is dead of ignorance and fecklessness.
> Acquire knowledge to attain immortality;
>> do not reckon life in ignorance to be worth living.[55]

Many of Yaḥyā ibn 'Adī's works provide information about the scholarly networks of his time and due to his habit of quoting large sections of text from the works of those with whom he takes issue on one point or another, his own compositions more than once have preserved significant portions of the texts of the works of his adversaries which are themselves otherwise lost. For example, it is due to Yaḥyā's essay in refutation of an otherwise unknown, anti-Trinitarian tract by the Muslim philosopher Abū Yūsuf Ya'qūb ibn Isḥāq al-Kindī (d. 870) that major portions of the work have survived in Yaḥyā's quotations from it,[56] enabling the modern editors of the philosophical and scientific works of al-Kindī to include this otherwise lost text in their edition of the philosopher's philosophical and scientific works.[57]

Even more importantly, it is due to Yaḥyā ibn 'Adī's habit of quoting large portions of the texts of those with whose ideas he disagrees in his refutations of them that a significant portion of the lost work of an important comparative religionist in the early Islamic period, Abū 'Īsā al-Warrāq (d.c. 862), has survived, allowing a modern editor to bring out an edition of what he considers to be the major part of Abū 'Īsā's anti-Christian work.[58] Abū 'Īsā's ideas are otherwise known only by the largely hostile references to them found in the works of other early scholars; he was considered by the establishment of his time to have been a freethinker and a crypto-Manichaean. However, this may be, one can see in the quotations from his work preserved by Yaḥyā that Abū 'Īsā was a careful scholar, taking care accurately to describe the views of those whose systems of thought he would then submit to scrutiny and criticism.

Similarly, from another one of Yaḥyā ibn 'Adī's works one gains some idea of how discussions were conducted in his philosophical circle in Baghdad. The text is a minor one among Yaḥyā's works; it discusses the relative importance of sexual abstinence as a spiritual exercise in the philosophical life.[59] But it affords the reader a rare insight into the processes of the intellectual colloquy between Yaḥyā and his interlocutors when he put one of his treatises into circulation. In the form in which we have it, this particular work is an unfinished composite text, consisting of three parts: an original essay (*maqālah*) that Yaḥyā composed on the Christian ideal of lifelong celibacy; a selection of comments on the essay by several readers, from which Yaḥyā quotes extensively from a note or 'communication' (*mukhātabah*) sent to him by one reader, before replying to the comments and then putting forward three important questions of his own for his commentator; and finally a transcript or 'copy' (*nuskhah*) of his interlocutor's answers to Yaḥyā's questions, along with Yaḥyā's response to them. It is interesting to note the detail that at the beginning of this last piece of the exchange, Yaḥyā's interlocutor asked that the master send him a response on the reverse side of his own document. In the end, Yaḥyā refers his colleague back to his initial essay, which he says his interlocutors should now be able to read with a full understanding. This somewhat involved account of a composite work affords one an insight into how Yaḥyā's text was read by several of his colleagues, whose remarks were sent to him in writing, to which he then replied in detail, quoting liberally from their remarks, and sending his replies back to them, presumably at least once on the back of the same sheets on which the comments were communicated to him. This was in all likelihood the process by which many issues were discussed in the Aristotelian circle of Yaḥyā ibn 'Adī in Baghdad in the tenth century and perhaps it was a common process employed by other contemporary intellectuals as well.

Yaḥyā ibn 'Adī was networked with many other scholars of his time, Jewish, Christian, and Muslim, a number of whose names he mentions in his works as he responds to their queries or to positions he knows that they have maintained. With some of them he was in correspondence. An interesting example of the latter is furnished by Yaḥyā's response to 14 queries posed for him by the Jewish scholar of Mosul in Iraq, Ibn Abī Sa'īd 'Uthmān al-Yahūdī, who sent his questions by the hand of one Bishr ibn Simsān ibn 'Urs ibn 'Uthmān al-Yahūdī on the 24th of Dhū l-Hijjah, 340 AH or 23 May 952. Yaḥyā replied promptly on the 29th. The questions and answers concerned topics in logic, physics, metaphysics, and medicine, such as queries about Anaxagoras' and Aristotle's views of space, time, and the forces of the heavenly sphere, various issues in logic such as the categories, judgments, definitions of technical terms, and God's providence, with two final questions on medicine.[60] Clearly, in tenth-century Baghdad there was an active measure of scholarly *convivencia* between Jews, Christians, and Muslims, and on that account as well as in view of several other features of their scholarly and literary interests, a number of modern scholars have not hesitated to speak of the currency in those days of a certain philosophical, literary, and even political humanism in the Islamic world.[61]

From Baghdad to Cairo

After the destruction of Baghdad and the Abbasid caliphate in the year 1258 A.D., Christian and Muslim intellectual life in Arabic shifted from Baghdad westward to Damascus and Cairo. Already in the late twelfth century, perhaps even prior to Salāh ad-Dīn Yūsuf ibn Ayyūb's (1138–1193) dramatic defeat of the western Crusader armies at the battle of the 'Horns of Hattīn' in the year 1187, the 'Melkite' scholar and bishop of Sidon in today's Lebanon, Paul of Antioch (*fl.* late twelfth, early thirteenth centuries), composed a clever apologetic tract in Arabic entitled, *Letter to a Muslim Friend*. In it Paul argued, on the basis of selected, idiosyncratically interpreted passages from the Qur'ān, that Muhammad was not sent to the Christians, nor is the Qur'ān itself addressed to them, nor is Islam meant to be the religion of Christians. What is more, he says, Christians are neither polytheists nor infidels, and that in fact, when read carefully, the Qur'ān can be seen to affirm Christian beliefs and practices. In the *Letter* Paul wraps these arguments in a frame story in which he tells of his recent visit "to the homelands of the Romans, Constantinople, the country of Amalfi, some Frankish provinces, and Rome," where he says he came into conversation with "the most important people ... their most eminent and learned men." Paul says that his Muslim friend wanted to know what these learned Romans thought of Muhammad and in the rest of the *Letter* he proceeds to recount what they reportedly had to say about the Muslim prophet, the Qur'ān, and Islam, along with what Paul presents as their defense of basic Christian teachings by way of a Christian interpretation of selected passages from the Qur'ān. Paul concludes the *Letter* by expressing his wish that if the report pleases his Muslim friend, God be praised "since He will have made quarreling cease between His servants the Christians and the Muslims." Otherwise, says Paul, he would be willing as a mediator to convey his Muslim friend's objections to the learned Romans in expectation of a suitable reply.

It was not long before Paul's *Letter* came to the attention of some scholarly Muslim jurists in Cairo in the first third of the thirteenth century, and it could already have been known to Abū l-Baqā' Taqī ad-Dīn Sālih ibn al-Husayn al-Ja^{c}farī (1185–1270), although he does not mention it. Al-Ja^{c}farī wrote an influential polemical tract against the local Christians under the title: *Takhjīl man harrafa l-Tawrāh wa-l-Injīl*, in which he counters positions typically defended by earlier Christian apologists. What is more, it is clear that in this work, al-Ja^{c}farī relied heavily on the earlier work of the aforementioned Rabban at-Tabarī, his *ar-Radd ^{c}alā n-nasārā*, which seems to have gained a renewed currency in Ayyubid Cairo. The Coptic scholar, as-Safī Abū l-Fadā'il Mājid ibn al-^{c}Assāl (c.1205–c.1265) had already taken the trouble to compose a virtually line by line refutation of at-Tabarī's *Radd* in a text he called, *as-Sahā'ih fī jawāb an-Nasā'ih*, in which he made a passing reference to Paul of Antioch's *Letter to a Muslim Friend*, and not long thereafter, unwillingly and at the prodding of his patriarch, as-Safī also produced a refutation of al-Ja^{c}farī's *Takhjīl* under the title, *Nahj as-sabī l fī jawāb Takhjīl al-Injīl*. In the meantime, the Muslim jurist, Shihāb ad-Dīn Ahmad ibn Idrīs al-Qarāfī (1238–1285), drawing heavily on al-Ja^{c}farī's *Takhjīl* among other polemical texts,[62] composed his own anti-Christian text entitled, *al-Ajwibah l-fākhirah ^{c}an al-as'ilah l-fājirah fī radd ^{c}alā l-millah l-kāfirah*, in which, without naming Paul of Antioch or his *Letter to a Muslim Friend*, he nevertheless prominently included in his work a point by point refutation of Paul's arguments. But the saga of Paul's *Letter* did not end here.

In the early years of the fourteenth century, well into Mamlūk times, an enthusiastic, Cypriot reader of Paul's *Letter*, in all probability a 'Nestorian' Christian, revised and expanded the *Letter* and promptly sent copies to two prominent Muslim scholars of the day, one to Ibn Abī Tālib ad-Dimashqī (d. 1327) and one to none other than the redoubtable, Abū l-^{c}Abbās Taqī d-Dīn Ahmad ibn ^{c}Abd al-Hākim ibn Taymiyyah

(1263–1328), both of whom wrote responses to it.[63] Ibn Taymiyyah prominently mentioned the letter as an occasion for writing his book, which would become a monument in Muslim anti-Christian polemic thereafter, *Al-Jawāb as-Sahīh liman Baddala Dīn al-Masīh*.[64] Energized by Ibn Taymiyyah's approach, subsequent Muslim scholars, like Ibn Taymiyyah's younger contemporary, Ibn Qayyim al-Jawziyyah (1292–1350) in his *Hidāyat al-Hayārā ᶜalā l-Yahūd wan-Nasārā*, carried on in the same heightened vein of aggressive polemics, complete with a high quotient of ridicule and demeaning vocabulary reminiscent of the manner of speaking employed in the earlier polemical works of al-Jaᶜfarī and al-Qarāfī.

Another notable feature of the anti-Christian texts composed by mostly Muslim jurists from Ayyubid times onward, in addition to the heightened aggressiveness of the discourse, is the close attention paid to the exegesis of proof-texts drawn from the Bible. While already from the eleventh and twelfth centuries, major Muslim scholars such as Ibn Hazm (994–1064) and al-Ghazālī (1058–1111) were concerned to refute the scriptural reasoning of Christians by demonstrating in great detail the unreliability of their scriptures, beginning in Ayyubid times something different was beginning to happen. Christian and Muslim scholars began arguing with one another about the details of biblical passages as the Christians actually had them and weaving their polemical exegeses of them into the fabric of their apologies for their respective doctrinal positions. Whereas in the past, Christian and Muslim controversialists each deployed their own list of proof-texts within their own interpretive frameworks, without much interaction with one another about the interpretive details, in Cairo in the thirteenth century they began arguing with one another in earnest about the proper quotation and interpretation of individual proof-texts. Muslim polemicists began to take a keener interest in the texts of the Bible as the Christians actually had them. For example, as Diego Sarrio Cucarella has recently shown, in al-Jaᶜfarī's *Takhjīl* and al-Qarāfī's *al-Ajwibah al-Fākhirah* there are 51 biblical proof-texts, quoted fairly accurately and cited in support of just the one claim that the coming of Muhammad as a prophet was foretold in the Bible! At other points in their works they similarly adduce accurately quoted, biblical proof-texts in support of the Qur'ān's and Islamic theology's positions regarding other matters as well and particularly concerning the truth about Jesus of Nazareth from an Islamic perspective, in response to what they regarded as Christian exaggerations. On the Christian side of the conversation, the posture became generally one of reaction. For example, apologists such as the aforementioned as-Safī ibn al-ᶜAssāl now offered detailed critiques of the interpretations of particular, biblical proof-texts employed by the Muslim writers and attempted to show that they could not rightfully be used to contravene Christian teaching.

There are many factors that lie in the background of the turn to heightened polemics in Christian/Muslim exchanges in the thirteenth century and the novel, close textual attention now paid to accurately quoted, scriptural proof-texts, beyond just the provocative role played by Paul of Antioch's *Letter to a Muslim Friend*. As a matter of fact, albeit that Paul's *Letter* and its Cypriot, expanded revision caused a considerable stir among Muslim jurists at the turn of the thirteenth and fourteenth centuries, due perhaps in large part to its Qur'ānic, scriptural reasoning, Paul's *Letter* was not actually the precipitating factor in the surge in Christian/Muslim altercations in thirteenth-century Cairo. Already prior to al-Qarāfī's refutation of the *Letter* in his *Al-ajwibah al-fākhirah*, local Christian and Muslim intellectuals in controversy with one another had already begun a new phase in their exegesis of one another's scriptures in their efforts more effectively to argue in behalf of the truth claims of their opposing doctrines. One supposes that political and social changes were among the precipitating factors for this new phase in Christian/Muslim interactions, factors such as the victories over the Crusaders from the late twelfth century onward, the change from Fatimid (909–1161) to Ayyubid (1169–1260) rule in Cairo and Damascus, and from the mid-thirteenth century onward, the intellectual and cultural shift from Baghdad to Cairo and the subsequent change from Ayyubid to Mamlūk (1250–1517) rule, not to mention the increasing social tensions at the time between Muslims and Copts in Egyptian civic life.

In addition to the change in tone and method of Christian/Muslim exchanges that came to the fore in Ayyubid times, another notable mutation in interreligious discourse that begins to become evident thereafter, and especially in the Mamlūk era, is a shift in the intellectual horizon against the background of which Arabophone Christian scholars thought and wrote. Twentieth-century historians of Christian Arabic literature have been in the habit of describing the thirteenth century in Egypt as a golden age of Arabophone literary production. While this is certainly true in terms of the abundance and quality of the work of such scholars as Būlus al-Būshī (c.1170–c.1250), the *Awlād al-ᶜAssāl (fl.* mid-thirteenth century), and Shams ar-Ri'āsah Abū 1-Barakāt (d. 1321), also known as Ibn Kabar, the fact is that a striking feature of their compositions is both their summary, even ecumenical character, and their retrospective horizon. Abū 1-Barakāt's *A Lamp in the Darkness*, for example, is virtually an encyclopedia of Christian theology in Arabic, into which he subsumed texts of many earlier writers from the several Arabophone Christian communities, to the extent that his work is almost a reference book for Christian theology and ecclesiastical practice in Arabic, from its beginnings to the his own time.[65] And much the same could be said of al-Mu'taman ibn al-ᶜAssāl's *Majmūᶜ usūl ad-dīn wa-masmūᶜ mahsūl al-yaqīn*, not to mention his Coptic-Arabic lexicon, *as-Sullam al-muqaffā wal-dhahab al-musaffā*. Thereafter the intellectual horizon begins to shift. Whereas from the late eighth century to the thirteenth century, Arabophone Christian theologians wrote in tandem with the intellectual developments in Muslim thought and expression, from the fourteenth century onward, concurrent with major changes in the demography of the *dhimmī* communities, their attention turns more and more beyond the World of Islam, to Constantinople, Rome, and Paris. But that is a topic for another time. Suffice it to say now that from its beginnings in the eighth century to its apogee in thirteenth-century Cairo, Christian philosophy and theology in Arabic were very much attuned to their Muslim counterparts, and even expressed in an Arabic idiom inspired by developments in Islamic philosophical and religious thought. What is more, Christian philosophers such as Yahyā ibn ᶜAdī (d. 974) portrayed their world as virtually an Islamo-Christian polity,[66] and historians, such as Saᶜīd ibn Batrīq/ Eutychios of Alexandria (877–940) and his continuators, folded ecclesiastical history into the framework of the history of the Abbasid caliphs.[67] But Christian life in the World of Islam was nevertheless never free from the constant call to Islam, nor from the numerous religious and civil disabilities imposed upon Christians as so-called 'People of the Book' or 'Scripture People' (*ahl al-kitāb*), whose subaltern position in Islamic society was theoretically governed by restrictive legal stipulations rooted in interpretations of selected passages in the Qur'ān. As their numbers grew ever smaller from Mamlūk times onward, with a slight upward trend in the Ottoman period, Christians at home among Middle Eastern Muslims gradually lost demographic significance, a factor in their eventual loss of political power and upward social mobility at home that made emigration an ever more attractive option.

DHIMMITUDE

Hovering over the life of Christians at home in the World of Islam from the time of the Arab conquest even until now has been the special status stipulated for them in Islamic legal theory, a status which has recently been designated by the neologism, *Dhimmitude*,[68] a term which echoes the Arabic word '*adh-dimmah*', literally 'protection' with a note of disapproval, which designates the legal standing of 'Scripture People,' mostly Jews and Christians in Islamic society, who are consequently often referred to by the adjective, '*dhimmī*'.[69] A key provision of *Dhimmitude* is the payment of a special poll-tax (*al-jizyah*), which according to the Qur'ān is to be demanded of the 'Scripture People' living among the Muslims; the passage specifies that the tax is to be paid with an air of submission (IX *at-Tawbah* 29). Historically, after the conquest and the consolidation of Islamic rule in the conquered territories, and over a period of time, a legal instrument known as the *Covenant of 'Umar* gradually came into being to govern this submissive, low social profile expected of the Christians, Jews, and others who paid the tax. The stipulations came originally from the treaties concluded between the Muslims and the cities and garrisons the Arab armies conquered in the seventh century in the time of the second caliph, 'Umar I (634–644), hence the name of the compilation of these and later stipulations, the *Covenant of 'Umar*.[70] Over time, other considerations dictated a more ideal approach to the matter and by the middle of the ninth century, when the *Covenant* seems to have reached its classical form, legal scholars had elaborated several theoretical schemes for the governance of non-Muslims in Islamic society, some of which included a whole series of stipulated civic, religious, and personal disabilities thought to be appropriate to the status of those who by then were being called the *dhimmī* populations.[71]

Classically, the tax (*al-jizyah*) came to be considered the price to be paid by the 'People of the Book' for the special 'protection' or 'covenant of protection' (*adh-dhimmah*) which the Islamic government would then assume for them. It was thought of as a kind of answerability, even responsibility on the government's part for dependent persons, not without a note of dispraise in the verbal root of the Arabic word, which basically means 'to affix blame' or 'to find fault.' Persons in this situation are then described, as mentioned above, by the Arabic adjective *dhimmī*, meaning someone under the protection and responsibility of the Islamic government. In present-day discussions of the situation, the neologism

Dhimmitude has come to express this theoretical, social condition of Jews, Christians and others living under Muslim rule.[72] In classical Islamic times, the *dhimmī* populations were to be governed through the offices of their own leaders, who were then held responsible for both the taxes and the good behavior of those under their care. In later Ottoman times, this arrangement came to be called the *millet* system, a term frequently used for it by modern scholars.[73]

There is no doubt then that in view of the stipulations of the *Covenant of 'Umar* the *dhimmī* populations of Christians in the Islamic world were what we would now call 'second class citizens,' subaltern populations. The legal disabilities, which governed their lives, required subservience, often accompanied by prescriptions to wear distinctive clothing and to cease from the public display of their religion, and, of course, to refrain from inviting converts from among the Muslims. Christian wealth, buildings, institutions and properties were often subject to seizure. As a consequence, over the course of time, the number of bishoprics, churches, monasteries and schools gradually decreased, having fallen victim to the very conditions of the official establishment of Islam. These circumstances of a necessity put *dhimmī* groups such as the Christian communities at risk; in spite of their numbers, they became sociological minorities, subaltern populations subject to discrimination, disability and at times even persecution.[74] In response, their disadvantaged situation in life under Muslim rule inevitably elicited from the subject Christians both a discourse of accommodation and a discourse of resistance.

There was no general, government mandated persecution of Christians for religious reasons in the Islamic world until our own day. On the contrary, there were even some legal protections for them as 'People of the Book,' as we have seen, albeit that amid the sorrows of *Dhimmitude*, at various times and places in particular circumstances Christians and Jews were in fact victims of violence and massacre. On these occasions, it was often the case that the causes of violence were an amalgam of social, political, economic and even ethnic hostilities affecting the pursuit of power, and not religion as such, although religion may often have been an aggravating factor. Sometimes in these circumstances, because of their perceived implication in these hostilities, local Christians and other 'People of the Book,' not to mention Muslims themselves, were deemed by some Muslim authorities to have forfeited the statutory protection (*dhimmah*) otherwise normally guaranteed to them in virtue of their payment of the special poll tax (*al-jizyah*) and general maintenance of a low social profile as the

Qur'ān demands of them (IX *at-Tawbah* 29). So, while Christians were certainly sometimes the victims of atrocities at the hands of Muslims, which are a matter of historical record in the chronicles written by Christians and others in Syriac and Arabic from the early Islamic period onward, Christians were not normally subject to outright persecution in the World of Islam simply for being Christian. Nevertheless, the accumulated pressures of *Dhimmitude* over time, not to mention the vicissitudes of history in the Middle East from the thirteenth and fourteenth centuries onward, gradually brought about the long, demographic decline of the Christian communities in their homelands from a near majority in Abbasid times, in the heyday of Baghdad's cultural sway, to virtual demographic insignificance in most of the Middle East, with some notable exceptions such as Egypt and Lebanon, by the end of the twentieth century. Looking back from the middle of the first third of the twenty-first century, historians must notice not only the extraordinary contributions of the indigenous Jews and Christians in the world of Islam to the formation of the classical culture of that world in its early days, but also their continued role in almost every realm of humane endeavor up to the present day.

NOTES

1. See J. Spencer Trimingham, *Christianity among the Arabs in Pre-Islamic Times* (London & New York: Longman, 1979); Theresia Hainthaler, *Christliche Araber vor dem Islam* (Eastern Christian Studies; Leuven: Peeters, 2007) with its rich and comprehensive bibliography. See also the monumental work of Irfan Shahid, *Rome and the Arabs: A Proloegoenon to the Study of Byzantium and the Arabs* (Washington, DC: Dumbarton Oaks, 1984); *Byzantium and the Arabs in the Fourth Century* (Washington, DC: Dumbarton Oaks, 1984); *Byzantium and the Arabs in the Fifth Century* (Washington, DC: Dumbarton Oaks, 1989); *Byzantium and the Arabs in the Sixth Century* (vol. I, parts 1–2; Washington, DC: Dumbarton Oaks, 1995); *Byzantium and the Arabs in the Sixth Century* (vol. II, part 1; Washington, DC: Dumbarton Oaks, 2002); *Byzantium and the Arabs in the Sixth Century: Economic, Social, and Cultural History* (vol. II, part 2; Washington, DC: Dumbarton Oaks, 2009). The series is projected to conclude with volumes on the seventh century. See too Fergus Millar, "Christian Monasticism in Roman Arabia at the Birth of Mahomet," and Robert Hoyland, "Late Roman Provincia Arabia, Monophysite Monks and Arab Tribes: A Problem of Centre and Periphery," in *Semitica et Classica* 2 (2009), pp. 97–115 & 117–139.

2. One uses the names 'Melkite', 'Jacobite' and 'Nestorian' with some reluctance, realizing that they are anachronistic and polemical in origin, coined by the adversaries of the communities to which they are applied, viz. the Eastern/Greek Orthodox Church, the Syrian/Oriental Orthodox Churches, and the Assyrian Church of the East respectively. The problematic names were used for centuries by both Muslim and Christian writers and have become commonplace. See Sebastian Brock, "The 'Nestorian' Church: A Lamentable Misnomer," *Bulletin of the John Rylands University Library of Manchester* 78 (1996), pp. 23–35.

3. See D.S. Wallace Hadrill, *Christian Antioch: A Study of Early Christian Thought in the East* (Cambridge: Cambridge University Press, 1982); Jaroslav Pelikan, *The Spirit of Eastern Christendom (600–1700)* (The Christian Tradition, vol. 2; Chicago: University of Chicago Press, 1974); Adam H. Becker, *Fear of God and the Beginning of Wisdom: The School of Nisibis and Christian Scholastic Culture in Late Antique Mesopotamia* (Philadelphia, PA: University of Pennsylvania Press, 2006); Stephen J. Davis, *Coptic Christology in Practice: Incarnation and Divine Participation in Late Antique and Medieval Egypt* (Oxford Early Christian Studies; Oxford: Oxford University Press, 2008); Volker L. Menze, *Justinian and the Making of the Syrian Orthodox Church* (Oxford Early Christian Studies; Oxford: University Press, 2008).

4. For a brief historical sketch and bibliography, see Wolfgang Hage, *Das orientalische Christentum* (Die Religionen der Menschheit, vol. 29.2; Stuttgart: Verlag W. Kohlhammer, 2007), pp. 202–206.

5. See in particular Moshe Gil, "The Creed of Abū 'Āmir," *Israel Oriental Studies* 12 (1992), pp. 9–47; Róbert Simon, "Mānī and Muḥammad," *Jerusalem Studies in Arabic and Islam* 21 (1997), pp. 118–141; François de Blois, "Elchasai—Manes—Muḥammad: Manichäismus und Islam in religionshistorischen Vergleich," *Der Islam* 81 (2004), pp. 31–48.

6. See R. Payne Smith, *Thesaurus Syriacus* (2 vols.; Oxford: Clarendon Press, 1879–1901: reprint; Hildesheim & New York: Georg Olms, 1981), vol. II, col. 2983.

7. See Hainthaler, *Christliche Araber vor dem Islam*, pp. 106–110. See too Jack Tannous, "Between Christology and Kalām? The Life and Letters of George, Bishop of the Arab Tribes," in George A. Kiraz (ed.), *Malphono w-Rabo d-Malphone: Studies in Honor of Sebastian P. Brock* (Piscataway, NJ: Gorgians Press, 2008), pp. 671–716.

8. See the report of Michael the Syrian in J.-B. Chabot (ed. & trans.), *Chronique de Michel le Syrien, patriarche jacobite d'Antioche, 1166–1199* (4 vols.; Paris: Leroux, 1899–1924), vol. II, p. 422 (Syriac) & vol. IV, p. 432.

9. See Hainthaler, *Christliche Araber vor dem Islam*, pp. 41–42.

10. See the discussion of Louis Cheikho's claims for pre-Islamic, Arabic literature in Camille Hechaïmé, *Louis Cheikho et son livre: Le Christianisme et la littérature chrétienne en Arabie avant l'islam; etude critique* (Beyrouth: Dar el-Machreq, 1967). See now Irfan Shahid, *The Arabs in Late Antiquity: Their Role, Achievement, and Legacy* (The Margaret Weyerhaeuser Jewett Chair of Arabic, Occasional Papers; Beirut: The American University of Beirut, 2008); Shahid, *Byzantium and the Arabs in the Sixth Century*, vol. II, part 2, pp. 297–302; 321–337. See also Elizabeth Key Fowden, *The Barbarian Plain: Saint Sergius between Rome and Iran* (Berkeley, CA: University of California Press, 1999).

11. See René Tardy, *Najrán: Chrétiens d'Arabie avant l'Islam* (Recherches, 8; Beirut: Dar el-Machreq, 1999).

12. See Irfan Shahid, "Kinda," in *EI*, rev. ed., vol. V, pp. 118–120; Gunnar Olinder, *The Kings of Kinda of the Family of Ākil al-Murār* (Lund: H. Ohlsson, 1927). See also Irfan Shahid, "Byzantium and Kinda," *Byzantinische Zeitschrift* 53 (1960), pp. 57–73; *idem*, "Procopius and Kinda," *Byzantinische Zeitschrift* 53 (1960), pp. 74–78.

13. See Hainthaler, *Christiliche Araber vor dem Islam*, pp. 137–142; Ghada Osman, "Pre-Islamic Arab Converts to Christianity in Meca and Medina: An Investigation into the Arabic Sources," *The Muslim World* 95 (2005), pp. 67–80.

14. See A.M. Butts, "Ethiopic Christianity, Syriac Contacts with," in S.P. Brock et al. (eds.), *Gorgias Encyclopedic Dictionary of the Syriac Heritage* (Piscataway, NJ: Gorgias Press, 2011), pp. 148–153; Christian Julien Robin, "Ethiopia and Arabia," in Scott Fitzgerald Johnson (ed.), *The Oxford Handbook of Late Antiquity* (Oxford: Oxford University Press, 2012).

15. The adjective 'Islamicate' was invented by Marshal Hodgson, who said that it "would refer not directly to the religion, Islam, itself, but to the social and cultural complex historically associated with Islam and the Muslims, both among Muslims themselves and even when found among non-Muslims." Marshall G. S. Hodgson, *The Venture of Islam: Conscience and History in a World Civilization* (3 vols.; Chicago: University of Chicago Press, 1974), vol. I, p. 59.

16. Dimitri Gutas, *Greek Thought, Arabic Culture: The Graeco-Arabic Translation Movement in Baghdad and Early ʿAbbāsid Society (2nd–4th/8th–10th Centuries)* (London & New York: Routledge, 1998).

17. See, e.g., Raymond Le Coz, *Les médecins nestoriens au moyen âge: Les maîtres des Arabes* (Paris: L'Harmattan, 2004); Kurt J. Werthmuller, *Coptic Identity and Ayyubid Politics in Egypt 1218–1250* (Cairo & New York: The American University in Cairo Press, 2010).

18. See, e.g., John Wansbrough, *The Sectarian Milieu: Content and Composition of Islamic Salvation History* (Oxford: Oxford University Press, 1978); Patricia Crone, *God's Rule: Government and Islam; Six Centuries of Medieval Islamic Political Thought* (New York: Columbia University Press, 2004).

19. See Youssef Courbage & Philippe Fargues, *Christians and Jews under Islam* (trans. Judy Mabro; London & New York: I.B. Tauris, 1997); Yohanan Friedman, *Tolerance and Coercion is Islam: Interfaith Relations in Muslim Tradition* (Cambridge: Cambridge University Press, 2003); Milka Levy-Rubin, *Non-Muslims in the Early Islamic Empire: From Surrender to Coexistence* (Cambridge, UK: Cambridge University Press, 2011).

20. See Garth Fowden, *Empire to Commonwealth: Consequences of Monotheism in Late Antiquity* (Princeton, NJ: Princeton University Press, 1993).

21. Albert Hourani, *A History of the Arab People* (New York: Warner Books, 1992), pp. 54–57.

22. In this connection, see Alexander Treiger, "Syro-Arabic Translations in Abbasid Palestine: The Case of John of Apamea's 'Letter on Stillness' (Sinai ar. 549)," *Parole de l'Orient* 39 (2014), pp. 79–131; *idem*, "The Fathers in Arabic," in Ken Parry (ed.), *The Wiley Blackwell Companion to Patristics* (Chichester, West Sussex, UK: Wiley Blackwell, 2015), pp. 442–455; *idem*, "Christian Graeco-Arabica: Arabic Translations of the Greek Church Fathers," *Intellectual History of the Islamicate World* 3 (2015), pp. 188–227; *idem*, "Unpublished Texts from the Arab Orthodox Tradition (1): 'On the Origins of the Term 'Melkite' and 'On the Destruction of the Maryamiyya Cathedral in Damascus,'\'," *Chronos: Revue d' Histoire de l'Université de Balamand* 29 (2014), pp. 7–37; *idem*, "Unpublished Texts from the Arab Orthodox Tradition (2): Miracles of St. Eustratius of Mar Saba (Written ca. 860)," *Chronos: Revue d'Histoire de l'Université de Balamand* 33 (2016), pp. 7–20.

23. See Sidney H. Griffith, "The Monks of Palestine and the Growth of Christian Literature in Arabic," *The Muslim World* 78 (1988), pp. 1–28; "From Aramaic to Arabic: The Languages of the Monasteries of Palestine in the Byzantine and Early Islamic Periods," *Dumbarton Oaks Papers* 51 (1997), pp. 11–31.

24. See Samir Khalil Samir, *Foi et culture en Irak au XIe siècle: Élie de Nisibe et l'Islam* (Collected Studies Series, 544; Aldershot, UK: Variorum/Ashgate, 1966); Sidney H. Griffith, *The Church in the Shadow of the Mosque: Christians and Muslims in the World of Islam* (Princeton, NJ: Princeton University Press, 2008); *idem*, "Syrian Christian Intellectuals in the World of Islam: Faith, the Philosophical Life, and the Quest for an Interreligious Convivencia in Abbasid Times," *Journal of the Canadian Society for Syriac*

Studies 7 (2007), pp. 55–73; Samuel Noble & Alexander Treiger (eds.), *The Orthodox Church in the Arab World 700–1700: An Anthology of Sources* (Dekalb, IL: Northern Illinois University Press, 2014); Diego R. Sarrió Cucarella, *Muslim-Christian Polemics across the Mediterranean: The Splendid Replies of Shihāb al-Dīn al-Qarāfī (d. 684/1285)* (History of Christian-Muslim Relations, vol. 23; Leiden: Brill, 2015).

25. The Spanish term *'convivencia'* is normally used to describe the living situation of Jews, Christians and Muslims in al-Andalus in the medieval period. Some writers view the period somewhat romantically, envisioning a time of tolerance and enlightenment. See, e.g., María Menocal, *The Ornament of the World: How Muslims, Jews, and Christians Created a Culture of Tolerance in Medieval Spain* (Boston: Little, Brown, 2002). The present writer views this account of affairs in Spain to be more legendary than real; see Griffith, *The Church in the Shadow of the Mosque*, pp. 154–155. Nevertheless, *convivencia* is an apt term to suggest the modes of mutual accommodation of Jews, Christians, and Muslims in the wider World of Islam and particularly in reference to Baghdad and its environs from the ninth to the twelfth centuries. See Griffith, "Syrian Christian Intellectuals," cited in the previous note.

26. See the accounts of difficulties, disabilities, and persecutions in Bat Ye'or, *The Decline of Eastern Christianity under Islam: From Jihad to Dhimmitude; Seventh-Twentieth Century* (Madison, NJ: Fairleigh Dickinson University Press, 1996). One must be aware of the extreme anti-Islamic prejudice of this and other recent publications by Bat Ye'or. Nevertheless, it is to this author's credit to have highlighted the need for systematic study of the cumulative effects over time of the Islamic legislation regarding the People of the Book on the factual diminution of Jewish and Christian communities in the world of Islam.

27. These developments are discussed with characteristic insight in Fazlur Rahman, *Revival and Reform in Islam: A Study of Islamic Fundamentalism* (ed. Ebrahim Moosa; Oxford: One World, 2000/2003).

28. See Jean-Pierre Valognes, *Vie et mort des chrétiens d'Orient: Des origines à nos jours* (Paris: Fayard, 1994); Andrea Pacini (ed.), *Christian Communities in the Arab Middle East: The Challenge of the Future* (New York: Oxford University Press, 1998).

29. On the translation phenomenon as an important stimulus in the development of philosophy in the Islamic world and Western Europe, see the collection of studies in Jacqueline Hamesse & Marta Fattori (eds.), *Rencontres de cultures dans la philosophie médiévale: Traductions et traducteurs de l'antiquité tardive au XIVe siècle* (Actes du Colloque International de Cassino, 15–17 juin 1989; Louvain–La-Neuve & Cassino: Université Catholique de Louvain & Università degli Studi di Cassino, 1990). On the

intellectual importance of Baghdad see Javier Teixidor, *Hommage à Bagdad: Traducteurs et letters de l'époque ɔabbasside* (Paris: CNRS Éditions, 2007); Jens Scheiner & Damien Janos (eds.), *The Place to Go: Contexts of Learning in Baghdād, 750–1000 C.E.* (Princeton, NJ: The Darwin Press, 2014); Damien Janos (ed.), *Ideas in Motion in Baghdad and Beyond: Philosophical and Theological Exchanges between Christians and Muslims in the Third/Ninth and Fourth/Tenth Centuries* (Leiden: Brill, 2016).

30. See respectively Dimitri Gutas, *Greek Thought, Arabic Culture: The Graeco-Arabic Translation Movement in Baghdad and Early 'Abbasid Society (2nd–4th/8th–10th Centuries)* (London & New York: Routledge, 1998) and H. Daiber, "Lateinische Übersetzungen arabischer Texte zur Philosophie und ihre Bedeutung für die Scholastik des Mittelalters. Stand und Aufgaben der Forschung," in J. Hamesse & J. Fattori (eds.), *Rencontres de cultures dans la philosophie médiévale* (Louvain-la Neuve & Cassino: Institut d'Études Médiévales de l'Université Catholique de Louvain & Università degli Studi di Cassino, 1990), pp. 203–250; Jean Jolivet *La théologie et les Arabes* (Paris: Les Éditions du Cerf, 2002); See also Richard E. Rubenstein, *Aristotle's Children: How Christians, Muslims, and Jews Rediscovered Ancient Wisdom and Illuminated the Middle Ages* (Orlando, FL: Harcourt, 2003).

31. See Myriam Salama-Carr, *La traduction à l'époque abbaside: L'école de Hunayn ibn Ishaq et son importance pour la traduction* (Paris: Didier, 1990); Barbara Roggema, "Hunayn ibn Ishāq," in David Thomas & Barbara Roggema (eds.), *Christian-Muslim Relations: A Bibliographical History* (vol. I (600–900); Leiden: Brill, 2009), vol. I, pp. 768–779.

32. See especially Joel L. Kraemer, *Humanism in the Renaissance of Islam: The Cultural Revival during the Buyid Age* (Leiden: Brill, 1986); idem, *Philosophy in the Renaissance of Islam: Abū Sulaymān al-Sijistānī and his Circle* (Leiden: E.J. Brill, 1986). See also the earlier essays by Marius Canard, "Baġdād au IVe siècle de l'hégire (Xe siècle de l'ère chrétienne)," *Arabica* 9 (1962), pp. 267–287.

33. In this connection, see John W. Watt, "The Strategy of the Baghdad Philosophers: The Aristotelian Tradition as a Common Motif in Christian and Islamic Thought," in J.J. van Ginkel et al. (eds.), *Redefining Christian Identity: Cultural Interaction in the Middle East since the Rise of Islam* (Orientalia Lovaniensia Analecta, 134; Louvain: Peeters, 2005), pp. 151–165; *idem*, "Christianity in the Renaissance of Islam: Abū Bishr Mattā, al-Fârâbî and Yahyâ in 'Adī," in Martin Tamcke (ed.), *Christians and Muslims in Dialogue in the Islamic Orient of the Middle Ages: Christlich-muslimische Gespräche im Mittelalter* (Beiruter Texte und Studien, 117; Beirut: Orient Institut & Würzburg: Ergon Verlag in Kommission, 2007), pp. 99–112. See also the earlier essays, Michel Allard, "Les chrétiens à Baġdād," *Arabica* 9

(1962), pp. 375–388; Georges Vajda, "Le milieu juif à Baġdād," *Arabica* 9 (1962), pp. 389–393; Steven M. Wasserstrom, *Between Muslim and Jew: The Problem of Symbiosos under Early Islam* (Princeton, NJ: Princeton University Press, 1995).

34. See Gutas, *Greek Wisdom Literature in Arabic Translation: A Study of the Graeco-Arabic Gnomologia* (American Oriental Series, vol. 60; New Haven: American Oriental Society, 1975) and Mohsen Zakeri, "Ādāb al-falāsifa: The Persian Content of an Arabic Collection of Aphorisms," in Emma Gannagé *et al.* (eds.), *The Greek Strand in Islamic Political Thought* (Mélanges de l'Université Saint-Joseph, vol. 57; Beirut: Université Saint-Joseph, 2004), pp. 173–190.

35. See the fuller discussion in Sidney H. Griffith, "Hunayn ibn Ishāq and the *Kitāb ādāb al-falāsifah*: The Pursuit of Wisdom and a Humane Polity in Early Abbasid Baghdad," in George A. Kiraz (ed.), *Malphono w-Rabo-Malphone: Studies in Honor of Sebastian P. Brock* (Piscataway, NJ: Gorgias Press, 2008), pp. 135–160.

36. See Abdurrahman Badawi (ed.), *Hunain ibn Ishâq, Âdâb al-falâsifah (Sentences des Philosophes)* (Safat, Koweit: Éditions de l'Institut des Manuscrits Arabes, 1985), pp. 40–43.

37. Hunayn seems to be alluding to some of the rites and practices of the Jewish feast of Succoth, a term which is usually translated into English as meaning booths or huts. See Jeffrey L. Rubenstein, *The History of Sukkot in the Second Temple and Rabbinic Periods* (Brown Judaic Series, 302; Atlanta: Scholars Press, 1995).

38. Badawi, *Hunain ibn Ishâq, Âdâb al-falâsifah*, p. 40.

39. Badawi, *Hunain ibn Ishâq, Âdâb al-falâsifah*, p. 40.

40. Badawi, *Hunain ibn Ishâq, Âdâb al-falâsifah*, p. 40. Perhaps Hunayn's ideas about 'Music' and its philosophical significance parallel those of his Muslim contemporary, and sometime patron, the philosopher al-Kindī. See Peter Adamson, *al-Kindī* (Great Medieval Thinkers; Oxford: Oxford University Press, 2007), pp. 172–180, 201.

41. Badawi, *Hunain ibn Ishâq, Âdâb al-falâsifah*, p. 41.

42. Badawi, *Hunain ibn Ishâq, Âdâb al-falâsifah*, p. 41.

43. Badawi, *Hunain ibn Ishâq, Âdâb al-falâsifah*, p. 43.

44. On Yahyā see Augustin Périer, *Yahyâ ben 'Adî: Un philosophe arabe chrétien du Xe siècle* (Paris: J. Gabalda, 1920); Kraemer, *Humanism in the Renaissance of Islam*, pp. 116–139; E. Platti, "Yahyā ibn 'Adī," in D. Thomas & A. Mallett (eds.), *Christian-Muslim Relations: A Bibliographical History* (vol. II (900–1050); Leiden: Brill, 2010), pp. 390–438.

45. See J.M. Fiey, "Tagrît: Esquisse d'histoire chrétienne," *L'Orient Syrien* 8 (1963), pp. 289–342; reprinted in J.M. Fiey, *Communautés syriaques en Iran et Irak dès origins à 1552* (Collected Studies Series, 106; London: Variorum Reprints, 1979).

46. See Sandra Toenis Keating, *Defending the 'People of Truth' in the Early Islamic Period: The Christian Apologies of Abū Rā'itah* (The History of Christian-Muslim Relations, vol. 4; Leiden: Brill, 2006); Sidney H. Griffith, "The Apologetic Treatise of Nonnus of Nisibis," *ARAM* 3 (1991), pp. 115–138.

47. Abū l-Hasan 'Alī ibn al-Husayn ibn 'Alī al-Mas 'ūdī, *Kitāb at-tanbīh wa l-Ishrāf* (ed. M.J. De Goeje, Bibliotheca Geographorum Arabicorum, part VIII; Lugduni-Batavorum: E.J. Brill, 1894), p. 122. See Sahban Khalifat, *Yahyā Ibn 'Adī: The Philosophical Treatises* (Amman: University of Jordan, 1988), pp. 13–14; Dominique Urvoy, "Abū Bakr al-Rāzī and Yahyā ibn 'Adī," in Peter Adamson, *In the Age of al-Fārābī: Arabic Philosophy in the Fourth/Tenth Century* (Warburg Institute Colloquia, 12; London-Turin: The Warburg Institute-Nino Aragno, 2008), pp. 63–70.

48. See Gerhard Endress, "Mattā b. Yūnus (Yūnān) al-Kunnā'ī," *EI*, 2nd rev. ed., vol. VI, pp. 844–846.

49. See Muhammad ibn Ishāq ibn an-Nadīm, *Kitāb al-Fihrist* (ed. Gustav Flügel, 2 vols. in 1; Beirut: Khayats, 1964), vol. I, p. 264. English trans. in Bayard Dodge (ed. & trans.), *The Fihrist of al-Nadīm: A Tenth-Century Survey of Muslim Culture* (2 vols.; New York: Columbia University Press, 1970), vol. II, p. 631. Both Ibn Abī Usaybi'ah and al-Qiftī repeat this information.

50. Jamāl ad-Dīn Abī l-Hasan Alī ibn Yūsuf al-Qiftī, *Ta'rīkh al-Hukamā'* (ed. Julius Lippert; Leipzig: Dieterich'sche Verlagsbuchhandlung, 1903), p. 341.

51. Abū Hayyān at-Tawhīdī, *Kitāb al-Imtā 'wa l-Mu'ānasah* (3 parts; Cairo: Lajnat al-Ta'līf, 1939–1944), part I, p. 37.

52. See Gerhard Endress, *The Works of Yahyā bin 'Adī: An Analytical Inventory* (Wiesbaden: Dr. Ludwig Reichert Verlag, 1977).

53. Publications of the works of Yahyā ibn 'Adī include the following: Augustin Périer, *Petits traits de Yahyâ ben 'Adî* (Paris: J. Gabalda & Paul Geuthner, 1920); Emilio Platti, *Abū 'Īsā al-Warrāq, Yahyā ibn 'Adī: De l'incarnation* (CSCO, 490 & 491; Louvain: Peeters, 1987); *idem*, "Un compilation théologique de Yahyā ibn 'Adī par al-Safi ibn al-'Assāl," *Mélanges de l'Institut Dominicain d'Études Orientales du Caire* 13 (1977), pp. 291–303; *idem*, "Deux manuscripts théologiques de Yahyā b. 'Adī," *Mélanges de l'Institut Domicain d'Études Orientales du Cairo* 12 (1974), pp. 217–229; *idem*, *La grande polémique antinestorienne (et la discussion avec Muhammad al-Misrī)* (CSCO, vols. 427 & 428; Louvain: Peeters, 1981); *idem, Yahyā b. 'Adī, théologien Chrétien et philosophe arabe; Sa théologie de l'Incarnation* (Orientalia Lovaniensia Analecta, 14; Leuven: Katholieke Universiteit Leuven, Departement Orientalistiek, 1983); Yahyā ibn 'Adī, *Traité sur la continence* (Vincent Mistrih, ed. & trans., Studia Orientalia Christiana Collectanea, 16; Cairo: Éditions du Centre Franciscain d'Études

Orientales Chrétiennes, 1981); Sahban Khalifat, *Yahyā Ibn ʿAdī: The Philosophical Treatises; a Critical Edition win and Introduction and a Study* (Amman, Jordan: Department of Philosophy, Faculty of Arts, University of Jordan, 1988); Yahyā ibn ʿAdī, *The Reformation of Morals: A Parallel Arabic-English Edition* (Samir Khalil Samir, ed., Sidney H. Griffith, trans.; Provo, UT: Brigham Young University Press, 2002).

54. See Dimitri Gutas, *Greek Thought, Arabic Culture: The Graeco-Arabic Translation Movement in Baghdad and Early ʿAbbasid Society (2nd–4th/8th–10th Centuries)* (London & New York: Routledge, 1998), pp. 61–74.

55. Ahmad ibn-al Qāsim ibn Abī Usaybiʿah, *Kitāb ʿuyūn al-anbaʾ fī tabaqāt at-Tibbāʾ* (ed. August Müllwr; 2 vols.; Cairo & Königsberg: n.p., 1882–1884), vol I, p. 235.

56. See Augustin Périer, "Un traité de Yahyâ ben ʿAdî: Defense du dogme de la trinité contre les objections d'al–Kindî," *Revue de l'Orient Chrétien* 3rd ser., 2 (1920–1921), pp. 3–21.

57. See Roshdi Rashed et Jean Jolivet (eds.), *Oeuvres philosophiques et scientifiques d'al-Kindī* (vol. 2, Métaphysique et Cosmologie; Leiden: Brill, 1998), pp. 119–128.

58. See David Thomas, *Anti-Christian Polemic in Early Islam: Abū ʿĪsā al-Warrāq's "Against the Trinity"* (University of Cambridge Oriental Publications, no. 45; Cambridge: Cambridge University Press, 1992); *idem, Early Muslim Polemic against Christianity: Abū ʿĪsā al-Warrāq's "Against the Incarnation"* (University of Cambridge Oriental Publications, no. 59; Cambridge: Cambridge University Press, 2002). See also David Thomas, "Abū ʿĪsā l-Warrāq," in Thomas & Roggema, *Christian-Muslim Relations: A Bibliographical History*, vol. I, pp. 695–701.

59. Yahyā ibn ʿAdī, *Traité sur la continence* (Studia Orientalia Christiana Collectanea, 16, ed. & trans. Vincent Mistrih; Cairo: Éditions du Centre Franciscain d'Études Orientales Chrétiennes, 1981). See the discussion of the somewhat complicated composition of this treatise in Sidney H. Griffith, "Yahyā ibn ʿAdī's Colloquy on Sexual Abstinence and the Philosophical Life," in James E. Montgomery (ed.), *Arabic Theology, Arabic Philosophy: From the Many to the One; Essays in Celebration of Richard M. Frank* (Orientalia Lovaniensia Analecta, 152; Leuven: Uitgeverij Peeters en Departement Oosterse Studies, 2006), pp. 299–333.

60. See the detailed analysis by Shlomo Pines, "A Tenth-Century Philosophical Correspondence," *Proceedings of the American Society for Jewish Research* 23 (1954), pp. 103–136. The text of the *risālah* is published in Dr. Sahban Khalifat, *Yahyā ibn ʿAdī: The Philosophical Treatises; a Critical Edition with an Introduction and a Study* (Amman: University of Jordan, Department of Philosophy, 1988), pp. 314–336.

61. See, e.g., Joel L. Kraemer, *Humanism in the Renaissance of Islam: The Cultural Revival during the Buyid Age* (Leiden: E.J. Brill, 1986); Lenn E. Goodman, *Islamic Humanism* (Oxford: Oxford University Press, 2003).
62. Diego Sarrio Cucarella has shown that al-Qarāfi was also indebted to the work of two Andalūsī, anti-Christian writers, Ahmad ibn ᶜAbd as-Samad ak-Khazrajī's (d. 1187), Maqāmiᶜ al-sulbān and Ahmad ibn ᶜUmar al-Qurtubī's (d. 1258), Al-Iᶜlām bimā *fi Di an-Nasārā min al-fasād wal-awhām*. See his important study: Diego Sarrio Cucarella, *Muslim-Christian Polemics across the Mediterranean: The Splendid Replies of Shihāb al-Din al-Qarāfi (d. 684/1285)* (Leiden: Brill, 2014).
63. See Rifaat Ebied & David Thomas, *Muslim-Christian Polemic during the Crusades: The Letter from the People of Cyprus and Ibn Abi Tāib al-Dimashqī's Response* (The History of Christian-Muslim Relations, vol. 2; Leiden: Brill, 2005).
64. Taqī d-Dīn Ahmad ibn-Taymiyyah, *Al-Jawāb as-Sahīh li-man Baddala Din al-Masīh* (4 vols. in a2; Jiddah: Maktabat al-Madanī, n.d.). Partial English translation in Thomas Michel, *A Muslim Theologian's Response to Christianity: Ibn Taymiyya's al-Jawāb al- Sahih* (Delmar, NY: Caravan Books, 1984).
65. See the text published in Samir Khalil Samir (ed.), *Misbāh az-Zulmah fi īdāh al-khidmah* (Cairo: Maktabat al-Kārūz, 1971).
66. See Sidney H. Griffith, "A Christian Philosopher in Abbasid Baghdad: Yahyā ibn ᶜAdī on Right Religion and the Cultivation of Virtue," in press. See Griffith's fuller discussion in George A. Kiraz (ed.), *Malphono w-Rabo-Malphone: Studies in Honor of Sebastian P. Brock* (Piscataway, NJ: Georgias Press, 2008), 135–160.
67. See Sidney H. Griffith, "Apologetics and Historiography in the Annals of Eutychios of Alexandria: Christian Self-Definition in the World of Islam," in R. Ebied & H. Teule (eds.), *Studies on the Christian Arabic Heritage* (Eastern Christian Studies, 5; Leuven: Peeters, 2004), pp. 65–89.
68. The term seems first to have been used by the Christian president of Lebanon, Bashir Gemayel, in a speech he delivered on 14 September 1982.
69. The popular writer Bat Ye'or popularized the neologism in her books, *The Decline of Eastern Christianity under Islam: From Jihad to Dhimmitude; Seventh-Twentieth Century* (Madison, NJ: Fairleigh Dickinson University Press, 1996); *eadem, Islam and Dhimmitude: Where Civilizations Collide* (Madison, NJ: Fairleigh Dickinson University Press, 2002).
70. See Yohanan Friedmann, *Tolerance and Coercion in Islam: Interfaith Relations in the Muslim Tradition* (Cambridge, UK: Cambridge University Press, 2003); Milka Levy-Rubin, *Non-Muslims in the Early Islamic Empire: From Surrender to Coexistence* (Cambridge, UK: Cambridge University Press, 2011).

71. See Milka Levy-Rubin, "*Shurūt ᶜUmar* and its Alternatives: The Legal Debate on the Status of the *Dhimmīs*," *Jerusalem Studies in Arabic and Islam* 30 (2005), pp. 170–206.

72. See note 69 above.

73. See M.O.H. Ursinus, "Millet," in *The Encyclopaedia of Islam: New Edition*, ed. C.E. Bosworth et al., vol. 7: pp. 61–64 (Leiden: Brill, 1993).

74. See Youssef Courbage & Philippe Fargues, *Christians and Jews under Islam* (trans. Judy Mabro; London & New York: I.B. Tauris, 1997).

CHAPTER 3

Christianity in the Wider Levant Region: Modern History and Contemporary Contexts

Anthony O'Mahony

In recent times, the trend toward the study of "world Christianity" with a focus on Asia, Africa, and Latin America, has emerged. However, little attention has been given to the Eastern Christian churches, despite the fact that Eastern Christians constitute one of largest Christian traditions in the world.[1] The Christian scholar Dyron B. Daughrity poses a prudent warning: "the 'North to South' metaphor has been helpful and challenging, but before we adopt it as rigid paradigm, we must face up to the absence of the East in that typology."[2] Eastern Christian churches are mainly concentrated in Russia, Eastern Europe, the Middle East, East Africa, and in a number of countries of diaspora in the West.[3] Eastern Christianity has somewhere between 250 to 300 million members worldwide (estimates vary), constituting approximately 12 percent of the global Christian population.[4]

Eastern Christianity in its various traditions is the dominant character of Christianity in the Middle East.[5] The churches of the Middle East can be grouped into five families. The Oriental Orthodox family includes

A. O'Mahony (✉)
Centre for Eastern Christianity, Heythrop College, University of London, London, UK

© The Author(s) 2018
K. C. Ellis (ed.), *Secular Nationalism and Citizenship in Muslim Countries*, Minorities in West Asia and North Africa, https://doi.org/10.1007/978-3-319-71204-8_3

Armenian, Coptic, and Syriac churches. The Eastern Catholic family includes Armenian, Chaldean, Coptic, Latin, Maronite, Melkite, and Syriac churches. The Eastern Orthodoxy comprises the patriarchates of Constantinople, Antioch, Alexandria, and Jerusalem. The final two families are the "Assyrian" Church of the East and the various Protestant dominations, which are grouped as one.[6]

The ecclesial context for Middle Eastern Christianity is complex. Its origins are as old as Christianity itself, encompassing deep cultural, linguistic, and theological diversity.[7] Middle Eastern Christianity, despite being a small part of global Christianity (certainly less than 1 percent), has great significance and importance in the wider Christian tradition. Sidney H. Griffith, a contributor to this volume, stresses the centrality of Christianity during the first five centuries of Islam:

> It is important to take cognizance of the seldom acknowledged fact that after the consolidation of the Islamic conquest and the consequent withdrawal of "Roman/Byzantine" forces from the Fertile Crescent in the first half of the seventh century perhaps 50 percent of the world's confessing Christians from the mid-seventh to the end of the eleventh centuries found themselves living under Muslim rule.[8]

The Oriental Orthodox family (including Coptic, Armenian, and Syriac churches) is dominant in the Middle East, with the Coptic Orthodox Church being the largest among these churches.[9] The doctrinal position of these churches is based on the teachings of the first three ecumenical councils: Nicaea (325), Constantinople (381), and Ephesus (431). They have traditionally rejected the Council of Chalcedon (451). The Oriental Orthodox family comprises the following ecclesial communities: Coptic Orthodox Patriarchate of Egypt; Syrian Orthodox Patriarchate of Antioch and All the East, Damascus; Armenian Apostolic Church: See of Etchmiadzin, Armenia and Catholicosate of Antelias, Lebanon; Orthodox Church of Ethiopia; Orthodox Church of Eritrea; and Syrian Orthodox Church of Malankar. In the Middle East, the Armenian Apostolic Church governs a community of some nearly eight million people scattered, like all the Armenians, across the globe. The Armenian Church is represented today by two Catholicosates: Etchmiadzin, which has primacy in the Caucasian and diaspora region; and Sis, which has authority over most of the Orthodox Armenians of the Middle East; and two Patriarchates: Jerusalem and Constantinople. The Syrian Orthodox Church, whose

Patriarch Ignatius Aphrem I is based in Damascus, is today connected to the many millions of Syriac Christians in India through the Malankara Orthodox Syrian Church. The Coptic Orthodox Church is mainly based in Egypt.

The Eastern Orthodox churches have often been depicted in Western and Byzantine church history as living in isolation from the rest of the Christian world, and as concerned with mere survival. This is true to a certain extent. A significant feature of Eastern Orthodoxy has been persecution and genocide suffered under Byzantine, Muslim, and Ottoman powers. On the whole, relations between the Eastern Orthodox churches and the Latin Crusader states tended towards openness, which at times encouraged important ecclesial and theological dialogue. In the modern period, the Eastern Orthodox Christian tradition has been marked by suffering, including martyrdom on a large scale, leaving deep wounds on its life, witness, theology, and spirituality.

The Eastern Orthodox Church in the Middle East comprises the four ancient patriarchates of Constantinople, Alexandria, Antioch, and Jerusalem. These are autocephalous churches, each independent and self-governing. The independence between the four churches is administrative. The preeminence granted to the ecumenical patriarch of Constantinople is one of honor and not authority. Each patriarch has his own metropolitans, bishops, and synod. The four patriarchates have a shared identity based upon doctrine, patristic theology, liturgy, ecclesiology, and canon law.

History has imposed common challenges on Eastern Orthodoxy in the Middle East: relations to Islam, relations to Russian Orthodoxy and the Russian State; relations to Rome and Eastern Catholicism; relations to Protestantism, first European then American; friction and conflict among the four sees; and relations between the Greek hierarchy and the Arab Orthodoxy. Eastern Christianity in the Middle East has faced these challenges within the context of Islamic conquest, conversion, and settlement. During the long centuries of Ottoman rule, the only difference that really mattered in religious terms was the difference between Muslims and other communities, and an emerging modern synthesis between Orthodoxy and nationality, which was a Christian "revivalist" response to political domination by Muslims in the late Ottoman period.

Structurally, Orthodoxy is divided between the four Patriarchates. The Patriarchate of Antioch, which has authority over the Orthodox communities in Syria and Lebanon (which are Arabic-speaking) as well as those of the Orthodox Syrian and Lebanese diaspora, represents the majority of its faithful in the Middle East. Its head, currently Patriarch John X, who resides in Damascus, is considered the leader of the Orthodox in the Arab Middle East. Eastern Orthodox Christians of the Syrian and Lebanese diaspora number at least 500,000 people, two-thirds of whom are in South America (primarily in Brazil and Argentina); the remainder are in North America. These expatriate communities are under the Patriarchate of Antioch. In the past century, Antioch has experienced a significant ecclesial and theological renewal. This renewal, however, is imperiled by the ongoing civil conflict in Syria, which threatens the long-term prospects for Christianity in that country.[10]

The Patriarchate of Jerusalem leads a community of about 70,000 Arabic speaking faithful, divided between Israel, Palestine, and Jordan. However, the senior clergy, including the Patriarch, are Greek; the Patriarchate's *raison d'être* is above all the exercise of Orthodox rights in the Holy Places.[11] The Orthodox Patriarchate of Jerusalem is also home to Arab Orthodox Palestinian Christians, who have developed a distinctive religious and political culture in the context of their roots in the Holy Land and the Palestinian-Israeli conflict.[12] This community has been supplemented by large numbers of Orthodox Christians now living in the State of Israel, either as migrant workers (including thousands of Romanians) or as part of the wave of Russian "Jewish" immigration to Israel in the last two decades of the twentieth century.[13]

The Eastern Catholic families of churches, like their Orthodox counterparts, have a complex ecclesiology, which broadly reflects that of their sister-churches of the same rite. There are six patriarchal churches in this family: Latin, Melkite, Syrian, Armenian, Coptic, and Chaldean.

The emergence of Hebrew Catholicism in the modern state of Israel might be interpreted as the most recent expression of Eastern Christianity in the Middle East. Another recent addition to Eastern Christianity are millions of Catholic Christians, especially Syriacs from India, who live and work in the Gulf states.[14]

The Maronite Church, which has its origins in the fourth or fifth century, has no Orthodox equivalent. It emerged gradually over many centuries in the province of the Patriarchate of Antioch, from a small rural Syrian community distinct from the rest of the Chalcedonian Church, which was then in decline. Maronite identity is complex: Maronites accept the Council of Chalcedon, are Syriac in rite but Catholic in faith and discipline, and exist in ultimate union with the See of Rome. The Maronite

Church has approximately 1 million members in Lebanon, but over 3.5 million faithful scattered throughout the world (700,000 in Argentina, 500,000 in Brazil, 150,000 in Mexico, 200,000 in North America, and 150,000 in Australia). The future of the Maronite Church, although it does not bring together all the Lebanese Christians, has been conflated with that of Lebanese Christianity, even that of Lebanon itself, because it incarnates the Lebanese spirit of survival through difficult times.

The other Eastern Catholic Churches are all branches of the Orthodox and pre-Chalcedonian Churches. The oldest is the Catholic Chaldean Church, formed in 1553. Today, with over 640,000 adherents, it is larger than its equivalent, the "Assyrian" Church of the East. Its main strength is in Iraq, with minorities in Iran and Lebanon.[15] The relatively small Syrian Catholic Church was formed following a schism in the Syrian Orthodox Church in 1663, but was not definitively established until the end of the eighteenth century. Mostly represented in Syria and Lebanon, it is led by a "Patriarch of Antioch and the East of the Syrians," and has 205,440 members.[16] Since the eighteenth century, the Armenians have had a Catholic branch, called the "Patriarchate of Cilicia of the Armenians," which brings together 736,134 faithful who live both in the Middle East and in other countries of the world.[17] In the late nineteenth century, the Coptic Catholic Church emerged; it is based in Egypt, has its own patriarch, and has nearly 175,000 members. The Greek Catholic "Melkite" Church was born in the eighteenth century following a schism in the Antiochian Patriarchate of the Greek Orthodox Church. It is as large as its Orthodox equivalent, but fewer than half its members (approximately 1.5 million) live in the Middle East, mainly in Syria and Lebanon. This church, Byzantine in rite and Arabic-speaking, only has one Patriarchate, of "Antioch, and all the East, Jerusalem and Alexandria."[18] The Latin Patriarchate of Jerusalem, re-established in 1847, has 27,500 members in Israel, including about 500 Hebrew-speaking Catholics. In addition, its members include 50,000 migrant workers, 20,000 members in the Palestinian territories, 50,000 members in Jordan, plus 35,000 workers from a number of countries and some Iraqi Catholic refugees.[19]

The Assyrian Church of the East[20] is one of the oldest Christian churches in existence, founded on the eastern marches of the Byzantine Empire and in Persia following the condemnation of Nestorianism (the doctrine that there were two separate persons, one human and one divine, in the incarnate Christ) by the Council of Ephesus. In 1964, it was split into two branches, one of which is the "Catholicosate of the East of the Assyrian

Church of the East." Its previous leader, Catholicos Mar Dinkha IV, lived in Detroit; however, the recently elected Mar Gewargis III (the 112th patriarch of the Church of the East) has now returned to reside in northern Iraq. The leader of the other branch, the "Catholicosate of the East of Old Catholic and Apostolic Church," is Mar Addai II, who lives in Baghdad. The Church of the East, after many centuries of isolation from the rest of the Christian world, renewed itself in the latter part of the twentieth century; ecumenical dialogue was an essential element of that revival. Mar Dinkha IV met Pope John Paul II in 1984, and signed a "Common Declaration of Faith" in 1994. An unprecedented Eucharistic-sharing agreement signed in 2001 in the Vatican between the Church of the East and the Chaldean Catholic Church crowned these achievements.[21]

Samir Khalil Samir of the Pontifical Oriental Institute asserts that Middle Eastern Christianity is significant due to its cultural richness, its pride in apostolic origins that go back to the beginning of Christianity, its rejection of the term "minority," and its understanding of its vocation as a unifying bridge between cultures, civilizations, and religions, both East and West.[22] The idea that the Christians in the Middle East are representatives of a minority is viewed as a mischaracterization of a region defined by its religious plurality, not merely by majority-minority markers. However, Todd M. Johnson has noted that one of the most profound changes in the global religious landscape has been "the unrelenting proportional decline of historic Christian communities in the Middle East."[23] Contemporary challenges to Christian presence in the region are underscored by a dearth in the imagination of global Christianity in understanding the implications of the decline of Middle Eastern Christians for all Christians—at a time when it is estimated that Christians account for over a third of humanity.[24] At no point in historical memory has one religious tradition been so vast and so geographically spread. Jewish sacred spaces in Jerusalem (one-third of all Jews live in Israel) and Islamic sacred spaces, both in Jerusalem and in the Arabian Peninsula (20 percent of Muslims live in the Middle East), are assured of a living and strong religious presence. The same cannot be said for Christian Holy Places and territory; as Christian communities decline in number, the fate of these places seems less secure.

In 1910, Christians composed 13.6 percent of the population in the region, but by 2010, they accounted for only 4.2 percent. Johnson believes that this proportion could decline to 3.6 percent by 2025, while noting that this figure could be even lower if the flight of Christians from Iraq and Syria continues. The Middle East is becoming more Muslim, with numbers increasing from 85 percent in 1910 to 92.3 percent in 2010. The increasing lack of religious plurality in the region is one of the principal forces for change and destabilization.[25] As Catherine Mayeur-Jaouen describes the situation today:

> The taking of Mosul by the Islamic State (Daesh) [otherwise referred to as ISIS or ISIL] led to a massive exodus of Christians from the plain of Nineveh to Iraqi Kurdistan. The payment of a tribute (*jizya*) imposed on the last Christians of Raqqa in Syria in February 2014 by a "pact", then the beheading of 21 Copts in Libya a year later, together with the ostentatious destruction of churches, indicate the Christianophobia at work in the ideology of Daesh ... And we can fear that enforced departure and massacres may end by emptying these countries of their Christians, already few in number. Confronted with a general wave of migration, which for Christians seems like a haemorrhaging, prophets of the 'death' of 'Eastern Christians'—a literary genre in a West which feels itself threatened—are not short of arguments for condemning the millions of Christians living in the Near East to imminent disappearance.[26]

Christianity in the Near and Middle East today is a minority religion in terms of numbers. In Egypt,[27] Lebanon,[28] and among Palestinian Christians,[29] the departure of the educated and dynamic middle classes has long been a trend.[30] We might add to these reasons the rapid spread of underlying sectarian conflicts, aggravated by the United States-led invasion of Iraq in 2003. The Christians of Iraq have been one of the main communal causalities of the breakdown in civil and political order in the country. Christians have found it difficult to hold a position as a minority community spread across the country after the carving-up of regions between various ethnic and religious groups, including Sunnis, Shiites, and Kurds. The church in Iraq, comprising the Assyrian Church of the East and the Chaldean Church, represented a historic Christian culture, which evolved beyond the confines of the Roman Empire in almost total isolation from the influences of Hellenistic culture. This distinctive rite is the product of a fusion between Judeo-Christianity and Assyro-Babylonian and Iranian cultures. It uses Syriac, a language close to Aramaic, the language used by Christ and the disciples, and was culturally embedded in the landscape of Mesopotamia.[31] The loss of Christians in Iraq profoundly alters not just the character of those lands, but also their future.[32]

The conflict in Syria has generated a justified concern that the fate of Christians in Iraq is one that might befall Syrian Christians, as a consequence of religious and ethnic confrontation. The Melkite Greek Catholic

Archbishop of Aleppo, Jeanbart, stated in January 2012: "We are very worried about the consequences of an overthrow of the regime which will drive many of our faithful to emigrate, just as in Iraq after the fall of Saddam Hussein. Christians have no confidence in an extremist Sunni power. We fear the domination of the dogmatic Muslim Brotherhood."[33] The Syrian crisis began in March 2011; since then, approximately half the Christian population—some 600,000 out of a total of 1.2 million—has left Syria or has been displaced within the country or to Lebanon. As in Iraq, significant damage has been done to the infrastructure of the Christian communities, including destruction of churches, schools, and communal property. This has led many Syrian Christians to decide that they have no future in their country.[34] In the zones held by the opposition or by radical Islamists groups, the Christian population has almost completely disappeared, relocating into the government-held areas.[35] In the Syrian Government zones, due to the movement of populations since 2011, there has been an increase in the percentage of minority communities: Alawites, Shiites, Druze, Christians, and others.

In previous crises, many Christians from across the region took refuge in Lebanon to settle and rebuild communal and religious life.[36] Today, however, many Christians who are leaving Iraq and Syria for Lebanon regard their stay there as a stepping-stone to exile, emigration, and diaspora.[37] Lebanese Christians are now concerned that they could be the next victims of the elimination of Christians from the Middle East, which began with the Armenian and Syriac Christian massacres of the end of the nineteenth century.

The challenge for Christians in the region has been how to position themselves in relation to a host of regional actors, in particular Saudi Arabia, Turkey, Iran, and Qatar, countries whose politics have developed around sectarian associations. In the current regional confrontation between Shi'a and Sunnis, which began in 2005, there is increasing concern for the future of a multi-confessional states such as Iraq, Lebanon, and Syria. In Egypt, the rise of a "Coptic question: and the exercise of power by the Muslim Brotherhood (2011–2013) have altered the traditional image of peaceful coexistence.[38] The "oasis" of Jordan seems fragile, due to ongoing tensions in society and government, along with a growing Islamist movement and larger numbers of Sunni Muslims displaced in the border areas with Syria.[39] Palestinian Christians have long suffered from political impasse, economic crisis, and from the violence in the occupied Palestinian territories.[40] The rise of political Islam and Jihadism means that

Christians can be threatened or killed in the Middle East just because they are Christians.[41] It is increasingly asserted that the recent upsurge in violence toward Middle Eastern Christians is the inescapable continuation of the 1915 genocide, proof of the deadly threat that "the crisis" in Islam and the temptation toward religious nationalism represents for Christians and other religions in the region.[42]

The Eastern Christian world of West Asia has from its beginning aligned itself with a variety of cultures and pluralities (Armenian, Coptic, Greek, or Syriac).[43] Paolo Dall'Oglio, an Italian Jesuit who founded the new monastic community of Deir Mar Musa al-Habashi in Syria, which is dedicated to ecumenism and relations between Christian and Muslims, considers this ecclesial plurality as an essential aspect of maintaining a religious and political plurality in the Middle East region today.[44]

Eastern Christianity was born in 395, with the division of the Roman Empire between the two sons of Theodosius. Although this did not immediately lead to the formation of two separate churches, it created conditions for a divergent development between the Christian communities of West and East. The destruction of political unity deepened the existing cultural divisions between the Greek and Latin territories of the Empire. Despite its political and social importance, this divide in Christianity is often left in parenthesis in modern theological and ecclesiological studies. The encounter between Middle Eastern Christianity and Western Christianity,[45] set against contemporary geopolitics, continues to give force to the relevance of this divide.[46] Pope John Paul II, who was deeply aware of the political consequences of the divide between Eastern and Western Christianity in modern European history, posited that today, the universal Church needs to learn to breathe with "two lungs."[47] Although ecumenical dialogue has made a start in reconstituting the Christian world,[48] profoundly different sensibilities separate Western Christianity, which has a Latin tradition, from its Eastern equivalent, which is deeply indebted to Greek and Semitic culture.[49] It is Christianity in the Middle East, through its presence and character, which sustains the possibility of an ongoing dialogue between the Eastern and Western Christianity. The Jesuit scholar of Coptic origin, Fadel Sidarouss, echoes the importance of this assertion:

> The roots of Christianity are decidedly Eastern. Consequently, when the West adopted Christianity, it in fact adopted an "other," something different; this Eastern alterity became constitutive of its Western identity, which

enabled it to be more easily open to difference throughout its long history: we may think, for example, of what we have said about reason, but also its dialogue with modernity, admittedly difficult and onerous. There is thus a qualitative difference between the Church of the West and the Churches of the East, in the sense that they have not, throughout the centuries, experienced a different "other," which has inevitably led them to remain within the domain of an identity without formative contacts with a constitutive alterity; and when they enter into relationship with an other—we think here of Islam—they do so in an apologetic and defensive rather than dialogical manner. Clearly, the Eastern Churches were plural from the time of their origins, and benefited from the support of Greco-Roman culture for the first seven centuries; but with the arrival of Islam they withdrew into a "golden age" which imperceptibly became their "mythical origin" on which they dwelt without further innovation, thus privileging the "pole of identity."[50]

The political-theological context for Christianity in the Middle East is different from nation to nation and also influenced by different Eastern Christian cultures. For example, Coptic Christianity in Egypt has an orientation towards the Nile and Christian Ethiopia, plus relationships with Arab and African Islam. As Sidarouss describes the character of the Coptic Church, "The contemporary Coptic Orthodox anthropology draws its resources from the first centuries of the Christian era. Its sociohistorical foundations reveal: an Apostolic Church, founded, according to tradition, by the Evangelist Mark; a Johannine theology, namely the descending theology of the School of Alexandria; a history of martyrs and minority, all along its history, from the time of the Romans till today; a national Christendom, fundamentally linked with the history of Egypt; finally a unique monastic spirituality, founded by Antony, Pacome, Shenouda."[51]

The Arab Spring of 2011 revealed diversity and change within the Coptic community, as it did within Egyptian Islam and Egypt as a whole. It demonstrated a desire for national unity, common to the vast majority of Copts and Muslims, although unity was undermined by interconfessional tensions rife since the 1970s, the monastic bent of Coptic leadership, and the ambiguous role of the Egyptian state.[52]

The renewal of the Coptic Church has been identified with significant individuals who personified the monastic spirituality and leadership at the heart of this movement—Patriarch Cyril VI (1902–1971), Patriarch Shenouda III (1971–2012), and the monk Matta el Meskin. The two monks who became patriarchs gave institutional strength, structure, and meaning to the monastic renewal. As Edward Watkin observed in his appraisal of Cyril VI: "Not only has a monk become a patriarch, but the Patriarch has remained a monk."[53] The monk who did not become a patriarch, Matta el Meskin, is a spiritual author, as well as the cornerstone of the extraordinary renewal of the monastery of St Macarius in Wadi el-Natroun, in the Scete Desert. He is a major figure in the monastic renewal that the Coptic Orthodox Church has been undergoing since the 1950s. Matta el Meskin's radical focus upon personal faith and monastic enclosures stands in contrast to institutional religion and ecclesiastical authority.[54] This flowering, however, has come at a cost. As Catherine Mayeur-Jaouen describes the character of Coptic revival, "In many respects, this insistence on a threatened identity and on religious values resembles the outpourings of Muslim religiosity of the previous 30 or 40 years from Islamists, Salafists, or traditional Sufis. In Egypt, the repopulation of the monasteries, a phenomenon which has continued since the 1960s, took place at the price of a remarkable unifying and puritanical reform."[55]

During 1990–2000, relations between Egyptian Copts and Muslims were increasingly marked by the growing communal identity in opposition to the other. Islam during this period became the dominant political idiom, especially noticeable in the declaration that Shari'a law was the main basis of legislation.[56] As Meir Hatina has observed, "The status of religion in the state has been one of the burning issues on the Egyptian political agenda ever since Egypt's encounter with the West in the nineteenth century. Egypt may have become more modernized and Westernized than any other Muslim state except Turkey, yet it never renounced the age-old fundamental Islamic unity of religion and state or the dominance of the Shari'a in determining personal status."[57] The growing presence of Shari'a as a marker in Muslim identity has had a profound impact upon Christians and other non-Muslims who live in Egypt. The ignorance of Coptic Christianity within the wider Muslim community in Egypt, accompanied by increasing Salafist discourse in the public domain, further strained Christian-Muslim relations. The question of conversion between the two religions became a point of dissension. There was a "celebrated scandal" when the wives of two Coptic priests converted to Islam, although they were returned to their community. This episode was given as the pretext for the attacks on the Syriac Catholic cathedral in Baghdad in October 2010, which killed many worshippers. The election of a Muslim Brotherhood government in 2012 led to Islamic political activism that Coptic Christians found oppressive. The pushback represented by the

Tamarod movement (the grassroots movement founded to register opposition to President Morsi) in June 2013 was followed by General al-Sisi's taking power. This event provoked an unprecedented level of violence directed at Coptic Christian churches and schools, which shocked the majority of Egyptians. The Copts accepted the maintenance of Article 2 of the new Constitution promulgated in 2014. (Islam is the state religion and Shari'a the principal source of legislation.) However, the Constitution also stated that freedom of belief was absolute, and even Al-Azhar (Egypt's famed university and mosque) produced a text affirming "citizenship as the sole criteria for responsibility within society."[58] In March 2017, Al-Azhar issued a "Declaration on Citizenship and Coexistence" in which relations between Muslims and non-Muslims are defined through the prism of the "Constitution of Medina."[59] However, Coptic Christians in Egypt find their margin for maneuver more limited in a country where religious freedom remains insecure.[60]

In the context of the modern nation-state, some Christian churches can be understood as the "national church"—the Maronite Church in Lebanon, the Church of the East/Chaldean Church in Iraq, and the Coptic Orthodox Church in Egypt. However, Christian churches are increasing their opportunities to work in common to protect their interests in the face of political environments that do not afford them security or allow them full citizenship.[61] This is particularly important in creating political and religious space for Christianity in Middle Eastern societies, a development which would have an impact on the wider culture.[62] The question of religious freedom is crucial, and the Catholic Church in the Middle East has promoted religious freedom through diplomacy and the negotiation of concordats.[63] Sebastian Brock reminds us of the importance of the Syriac Christian tradition: "Several of these Churches have existed, throughout the entire span of their history, as minority religious communities, living under governments that were often hostile. This experience has ensured that they have been free from the sort of triumphalism that has at times disfigured the Latin West and the Greek East."[64] The political-theological issue is particularly significant for the Middle East,[65] where Christians have long interacted with political traditions influenced by Judaism and Islam. However, the plurality of Eastern Christianity, particularly the Orthodox churches in modern history, is complex. Elizabeth Prodromou has suggested that Eastern Orthodoxy's engagement with pluralism is one of discernible ambivalence.[66] In discussing Eastern Christianity's relationship to the state, we need to take into consideration several historical experiences: the Byzantine theocratic legacy; the Ottoman legacy; the colonial-mandate regimes; the legacy of Arab, Turkish, Israeli, and Iranian nationalism in relation to the identity of the nation-state; and political Islamism. The history of the Eastern Orthodox churches also includes the domination of the Armenian Church in the nineteenth century by Orthodox Christian Tsars in the Russian Empire, by the Sunni Muslim Ottoman Empire in the Levant and Persia (Iran), and by Shiites in Iran. As Antoine Courban emphasizes—

[These] … churches, either, Orthodox or Catholic, either Chaldcedonians, non-Chaldcedonians or even Reformed, should rather be seen as an archipelago where each of them has its own specificity, a particular collective socio-cultural identity as well as their own way of establishing relations with the Islamic powers under which they lived throughout history.[67]

The long shadow of the Ottoman *millet* system remains central to the debate regarding the historical dynamic between states and non-Muslim communities, which continues to be relevant for the legal status of Christians in several countries today.[68] However, it would be wrong to state that the "secular" nation-states of the twentieth century (Turkey, Egypt, Baathist Iraq, and Syria) favored the Christians of the East, in contrast to Islamic states governed by Shari'a law. The Turkish republic sought to discriminate in every way possible against non-Muslims remaining in Turkey. The Syrian state was increasingly influenced by forms of communalism, which in essence is a call for a single Arab identity.[69] In Iraq, the harshly repressed Kurdish revolts and the long Iran-Iraq war (1980–1988) brought about the destruction of the Christian villages of Kurdistan. The goodwill shown to Christians by the regime of Hafez al-Assad and that of Saddam Hussein were nevertheless synonymous with subjection. In Nasser's Egypt, the nationalizations of 1958–1961 corresponded to the Islamization of many businesses and led to the departure of non-Coptic Christians, seen as outsiders. After 1970, the regimes of Sadat and Mubarak added to the Islamization of law, and to the Islamization of education, the media, society, and the public space in general. Confessional tensions served to justify these authoritarian practices, which were approved by the Patriarchate of Shenouda III (1971–2012), itself authoritarian. In Lebanon, the confessional system established by the Mandate seemed for a long time to serve Christian interests. However, the Lebanese Civil War (1975–1990) demonstrated the limits of confessionalism, a system that continued to be contested into the 1990s.[70]

The most recent phase, the hoped-for transformation of political governance in state and society associated with the Arab Spring, has encouraged Christian leaders such as Cardinal Raï, Patriarch of the Maronite Church, to call for a "Christian Spring" that would pave the way for an Arab Spring in which the Arab peoples would benefit from a climate of peace, justice, and brotherhood. Cardinal Raï also expressed the hope that the Arab regimes would be "transformed into democratic regimes that should separate religion from the state; strengthening civil liberties and human rights, the right to respect difference, and embrace diversity in unity."[71] Christians in the Middle East desire to harness the "crisis" toward constructive change, rather than submit to a future determined by "murderous identities" born in violence.[72] These ideals are emphasized by Sidarouss:

> When the people betray God's covenant and the values of the Gospel, this merits strong words of disavowal. The church is called to exercise this mission in every domain of human life. However, while the Churches have reacted in individual cases, they have scarcely if ever addressed the "structures of sin," social political, professional, economic—collective sin. This is because they are unused to speaking prophetic words to the *res publica*. The social teachings of the universal Church have not been taken up in the local context, nourished spiritual and moral reflection, or led to action. In the Egypt of today the Churches are called to speak a prophetic word of rejection and disapproval, and to live out the values of the Gospel themselves. Paradigms are changing: from the purely individual to the collective, from the purely ecclesial to the national, from the purely spiritual to the temporal. But a strategy is needed to ensure that this does not remain theoretical but leads to common cause against injustice, the creation of a lawful state, and defence of the poor and oppressed."[73]

Today, it is a challenging task for Christian theologians in the Middle East to respond to the numerous religious, political, and cultural issues that affect the region.[74] Harald Suermann, a German scholar of Middle Eastern Christianity, underlines the close links between Eastern theology and liturgy:

> Speaking of John Damascene and Ephrem the Syrian they wrote in order to contemplate the eternal mysteries, and their theology is considered as "outside time." However, studying the hymns of Saint Ephrem leads to the conclusion that he battled against the various heresies of his region. He was

aware of the currents of thought of his era and built his theology on that thought. As to John Damascene, his theology is also a dialogue with his times: should Islam be considered a religion or a heresy? What is the place of icons in churches? Should we serve the new masters? In short, "the great Eastern theological texts were written in a precise context, responding to the pressing questions of the time." This dialogue was continued later. Following the Muslim conquest, theologians began to express themselves in Arabic, thus also enabling dialogue between Christian theology and Muslim thought. Later, Muslims gained an awareness of Greek knowledge through Christian intermediaries. With the arrival of Western theologians, those in the East sought to assimilate their theologies. Finally, there was a period characterized by "the pure reception of theology and less by adaptation to the demands of time and place." However, the renewal of the Coptic Church and theological thought in the context of Palestine and Israel are striving once again to respond to the burning questions of our time.[75]

Suermann articulates that theology must be closely connected to the questions that concern the Christians in our own time. To emphasize this connection, he enumerates a serious problem with which Eastern theology should concern itself today: the exodus of Christians from the Middle East. Many Christians leave their countries for economic and social reasons. Should the Church not speak prophetically, as did the ancient prophets? Alongside renewal, there is also a form of conservatism that marginalizes the churches and renders them passive and of no consequence on the political and social scene.[76] Many Christian thinkers today urge a new "political-theology" that takes seriously the reordering of religious culture across the region. The former Melkite Archbishop of Beirut Grégoire Haddad is often cited as a proponent of this type of engagement, especially in his arguments for an open *laïcite*.[77] The crisis in the relationship between religion and politics in the region was taken up by the Special Assembly of Bishops for the Middle East, held in Rome in October 2010.[78] Mounchir Basile Aoun interprets Haddad's emphasis on liberation as the key idea in addressing the crisis:

> The word liberation does not figure prominently in the lexicon of Christian communities in today's world. Rather, the key word is survival. This is because Christian faith is seen as inflicting a heavy burden, a requirement for confinement to defending the physical existence of individuals and groups which, in Lebanon and in other countries of the Arab world, continue to depend on the message of Jesus Christ. However, there is a dividing line

between liberation and survival which betrays the state of paralysis into which Christian witness delivered within societies existing in the Arab world runs the risk of falling. The theological originality of Grégoire Haddad has been to recenter this witness on the demands of a liberation which modern Arab man desires with all his heart. Since for him liberation remains the best guarantee of survival. In effect, to physically survive without engaging in the liberation of Arab man resembles more of a spiritual death, since true Christian survival in the Arab world belongs more in the register of evangelical boldness. The Christian thus finds himself invited to expend his energies in order to defend the life of others.[79]

A significant challenge for Christianity in the Middle East has been division, which requires a theological and ecclesiological response that affirms unity in diversity and, according to Antoine Fleyfel, an ecumenical theology whose purpose is to change entrenched attitudes.[80] Jean Corbon, the well-known Catholic ecumenist, wrote: "The Christian Middle East appears as the microcosm of the universal ecumenism: there where the greatest diversity had abounded in division, the grace of Communion in unity has over-abounded."[81]

The reality of Christianity in the modern Middle East is first of all one of numbers. The actual number of Christians, however, is difficult to determine. For some decades, there have no longer been confessional censuses in the countries of the Middle East, where governments are concerned with veiling the multi-confessional nature of their societies. The political consequences of this policy were highlighted during the "Arab Spring" when religious and ethnic minorities, including Kurds, Shiites, Christians, and Druze, challenged the emergence of an Islamist trend, which has sought to dominate political society.[82] The Middle Eastern church families represent approximately 30 million Christians, approximately 15 million of whom reside in the Middle East. For nineteen centuries, the natural rate of increase of the Christians in the Middle East was higher than that of the Muslims, thanks to a lower mortality rate. In the twentieth century, the Muslim mortality rate became the same as that of the Christians, while their birth rate had long since surpassed that of Christians. These demographic changes contributed to a net reduction of the Christian presence in the Middle East.[83]

The Middle Eastern Christian diaspora to North and South America, Australia, and Europe also is a major factor in the reduction of Christian presence.[84] Diaspora contributes to making Christian identity in the

Middle East a contested one, leaving Christians caught between an Arab Christian identity and an Eastern Christian identity.[85] Although the jurisdiction of each church corresponds to a definite territory, emigration of numerous faithful has given identity a broader and yet more personal character.[86] The churches have responded by creating numerous ecclesial structures in the West to help retain the link between the land of origin and these new Middle Eastern Christian spaces. This renewed ecclesiological link overcomes geography, and the Eastern churches in diaspora behave as though they were independent structures, constituting distinct episcopacies on the same territory.[87] Despite continued contacts with their churches of origin, Christians of diaspora focus less upon Middle Eastern identities, whether Arab, Egyptian, Lebanese, Palestinian, or Syrian, when articulating their Christian identities. Spirituality, monasticism, and theological practices associated with early Christianity are increasingly coming to the fore. Over time, many Middle Eastern Christians of diaspora are distanced from day-to-day life in Islamic culture and society, regarding themselves instead as members of a global Christianity. For young people who have grown up abroad, it becomes difficult to associate the country and original language of their parents with religious faith, or to connect individual religious sentiment with attachment to the original community.[88]

Christianity in the Middle East the last hundred years has witnessed a profound series of crises. Displacement by war, genocide, and interreligious conflict, along with loss, emigration, and exile, has been a core experience of Christianity in the modern Middle East. Against this background of displacement, Christians have sought to resettle and build anew. Before the Lebanese Civil war, generations of displaced Christians, particularly Armenians and other Eastern Christians, arrived in Lebanon and helped to make that country a leading cultural and economic space for all Christians in the region.

In Iraq, after the fall of the Baathist regime in 2003, Iraqi Christians became the canaries in the coal mine for the Middle East. The extent to which Christians were tolerated in the new Iraq was closely watched by Lebanese Maronites and other non-Muslim populations of the region. Tragically, Christians in Iraq have been devastated since 2003, with approximately 70 percent leaving the country. The Christians of this diaspora include those who had the resources (human, educational, and financial) to make the journey into exile. Those who remained are much poorer. Thus, the cultural and social profile of Christians in Iraq has changed profoundly, with those who remained pushed to the margins of society. In the new political order, the rights of Assyrians and Chaldeans were mentioned in the 2005 Constitution; however, there was no common ground between an Assyrian Democratic Movement calling for an autonomous region in the plain of Nineveh and Chaldeans advocating Iraqi citizenship. After 2008, the situation of Christians in Mosul, directly threatened by war, accelerated their departure. The fall of Mosul and its surrounding villages to ISIS in the summer of 2014 forced its last Christians into exile.

The long centuries of Ottoman domination fossilized the Eastern Christian churches in their divisions. Modern crises and contemporary ecumenism are beginning to bring down the barriers. In recent times, remarkable developments have taken place in the ecumenical relations between churches in the Middle East, both on bilateral and multilateral levels: agreements that allow partial mutual participation in sacraments, formation of future priests, and catechesis. Three main factors are responsible for these developments: the ecumenical movement of the twentieth century and the establishment (in 1948) of the World Council of Churches, the Second Vatican Council, and the large-scale emigration from the Middle East to Europe, the Americas, and Australia. Although this large-scale emigration has in general been disastrous from the point of view of the indigenous Christian Churches in the Middle East, it has produced two good consequences: emigration to Western countries has provided the possibility of publication without censorship, and has brought the existence of non-Chalcedonian churches into the awareness of the Western churches—thus providing an opportunity and incentive for theological dialogue.[89]

As previously mentioned, the past hundred years have brought a profound change in the configuration of Christian presence in the Middle East. In the last days of the Ottoman Empire Christians made up 20–30 percent of the population. The Armenian genocide, the massacre of the Syriac Christians, and the exchange of populations between Greece and Turkey (there is still debate about numbers, but this exchange involved approximately 1.5 million Orthodox Christians and half a million Muslims) had radical impacts. Today, there are barely 200,000 Christians in a population of 70 million in the modern Turkish republic—although Turkey may contain as many as 2 million people of Armenian heritage, the descendants of Christians, mainly women and children, who were taken as slaves or forced into Islam during the fall of the Ottoman Empire. Each year, a number of these individuals return to their original Christian faith.[90] The percentage of Christians in Syria has declined from 20 percent before the Second World War to fewer than 10 percent in 2011 to approximately 5 percent today.

During the Lebanese Civil War, some 670,000 Christians were displaced, a far larger number than the 160,000 Muslims who were displaced. Lebanon's centuries-old Christian majority is no more. This has allowed the Shia community to emerge as the majority community and its political organizations, such as Hezbollah, to gain power in Lebanon and to challenge traditional Maronite Christian dominance.

Since the beginning of the 1960s and the internal Kurdish-Iraqi war, approximately one million Christians have left their northern Iraqi mountains and homelands to emigrate or move to other parts of Iraq. During this period, Baghdad has gained large numbers of Christians; the Chaldean patriarchate relocated there in 1950. Since 1948, some 230,000 Christians have left the Holy Land. The Christian population of Jerusalem is estimated to have declined from 30,000 in 1948 to 5000 today.

Christian communities in the Middle East have inevitably lost many of their most educated and young members. The churches thus have lost the leadership that should be guiding their communities' futures. In some communities, more men than women have left, changing the gender balance. When Christian women marry Muslim men, this fractures and diminishes the Christian population, with implications for property rights and the education of children.[91]

In conclusion, Christianity originated in the Middle East. Eastern Christians still speak of pluralism and personal liberty, despite the deadly confrontations that today are putting the Middle East to fire and sword. The meaning of the presence of native Christians in the Middle East and their ability to remain there is dependent on these Christians' attaining real citizenship (*muwatana*) in nation-states whose governance seeks the common good.[92] Christianity in the Middle East has a witness beyond itself: let us hope that the churches of both East and West rise rapidly rise to this challenge, for the key to the future of this important region may lie in the hands of the few.

Notes

1. S. M. Kenworthy, "Beyond Schism: restoring Eastern Orthodoxy to the History of Christianity," *Reviews in Religion and Theology*, 15/2 (2008), 171–178.

2. Dyron B. Daughrity, "Christianity Is Moving from North to South—So What About the East?" *International Bulletin of Missionary* Research, Vol. 35, no. 1, 2011, 18–22, 21.

3. See the Pew Foundation report on 'Global Christianity: A Report on the Size and Distribution of the World's Christian Population' in 2011 Online version of *Global Christianity: A Report on the Size and Distribution of the World's Christian Population* at http://pewforum.org/Christian/GlobalChristianity-worlds-christian-population.aspx

The *Report* estimated that there are some 2.18 billion Christians, representing nearly a third of the estimated 2010 global population of 6.9 billion. Christians are to be found across the globe, which today means that no single region can indisputably claim to be the center of global Christianity, which is not the case for other religious traditions. For example, 60 percent of all Muslims live in South or South East Asia, roughly 20 percent in the Middle East, and 20 percent in Africa and other parts of the world. For Christianity this is in contrast to the past when Europe held that position; for example, in 1910 about two-thirds of the world's Christians lived within the continent. Today, however, approximately one quarter of all Christians live in Europe (26%), the Americas (37%), in sub-Saharan Africa (24%), and in Asia and the Pacific (13%). The *Report* noted extraordinary changes in the global configuration of Christianity—in sub-Saharan Africa a 60-fold increase, from fewer than 9 million in 1910 to more than 516 million in 2010; and in the Asia-Pacific region, a 10-fold increase, from about 28 million in 1910 to more than 285 million in 2010.

4. http://www.pewforum.org/Christian/Global-Christianity-orthodox.aspx. A recent study has noted that Eastern Christians in 1910 composed 20.4 percent of the Christian population; however, this had declined to 12.2 percent in 2010. See Todd M. Johnson and Gina A. Zurlo, "Ongoing Exodus: Tracking the Emigration of Christians from the Middle East," *Harvard Journal of Middle Eastern Politics and Politics*, Vol. 3, 2013–2014, pp. 39–45, p. 42. The impact of the Bolshevik Revolution in 1917, the totalitarian Communist system across much of Eastern Europe and Ethiopia after 1974, the genocide of the Armenian and Syriac Christians in the late Ottoman period; famine in Lebanon during WWI, and exchange of populations between Turkey and Greece might all be noted as contributing factors to this decline.

5. Dietmar W. Winkler, "Christianity in the Middle East: some historical remarks and preliminary demographic figures," Syriac *Christianity in the Middle East and India* (Ed) D. Winkler, Gorgias Press, 2013, 107–125.

6. A. O'Mahony, "Christianity in the Middle East: Modern History and Contemporary Theology and Ecclesiology: An Introduction and Overview," *Journal of Eastern Christian Studies*, Vol. 63, no. 3–4, 2013, 231–260.

7. Frans Bouwen, "The Churches in the Middle East," Lawrence S Cunningham, ed. *Ecumenism. Present Realities and Future Prospects,* University of Notre Dame Press, 1998, 25–36.

8. S. H. Griffith *The Church in the Shadow of the Mosque: Christians and Muslims in the World of Islam* (Princeton, 2008), 11.

9. S. Brock, 'The Syrian Orthodox Church in the modern Middle East," A. O'Mahony, 'The Coptic Orthodox Church in modern Egypt," and J. Whooley, "The Armenian Church in the contemporary Middle East," in *Eastern Christianity in the modern Middle East,* eds. O'Mahony and Loosley, 13–24; 56–77; 78–106.

10. R. Mofarrij, "Renewal in the Antiochian Orthodox Church in Lebanon," *Studies in World Christianity,* 15 (2009), 217–235.

11. S. Roussos, "The Greek Orthodox tradition: International politics, ethnicity and theological development in the Middle East," *Bulletin of the Royal Institute for Inter-Faith Studies,* Vol. 7, no. 2 (2005), 141–156.

12. D. Christiansen, "Palestinian Christians," in *The Vatican-Israel Accords: Political, Legal, and Theological Contexts,* ed. M. J. Breger (Notre Dame, IN, 2004), 309–339.

13. D. M. Neuhaus, "New Wine into Old Wineskins: Russians, Jews and Non-Jews in The State of Israel," *The Journal of Eastern Christian Studies,* 57 (2005), 207–236.

14. D. W. Winkler estimates that nearly half of all Catholics who live in the wider Middle East today are expatriate or migrant workers spread across the region but mainly living in the Gulf area. "Katholisch sein im Nahen Osten: Rückblick auf die Sondersynode im Vatikan," *Stimmen der Zeit,* 229/1 (2011), 30–38.

15. A. O'Mahony, "Patriarchs and Politics: The Chaldean Catholic Church in modern Iraq," in: *Christianity in the Middle East: Studies in modern history, theology and politics,* London, Melisende, 2008, 105–142.

16. A. O'Mahony, "Between Rome and Antioch: Syrian Catholic Church in the modern Middle East," in: *Eastern Christianity in the modern Middle East,* eds. A. O'Mahony & E. Loosley, London, Routledge, 2010, 120–137.

17. John Whooley, "The Armenian Catholic Church in the Middle East," *The Catholic Church in the contemporary Middle East: Studies for The Synod of the Middle East,* eds. A. O'Mahony and J. Flannery (London, 2010), 153–184.

18. Ignace Dick, *Les Melkites,* Turnhout, Brepols, 1994.

19. A. O'Mahony, "Latins of the East: The Vatican, Jerusalem and the Palestinian Christians," in: *The Christian Communities of Jerusalem and the Holy Land: Studies in History, Religion and Politics,* Cardiff, University of Wales Press, 2003, 90–114.

20. Herman Teule, *Les Assyro-Chaldéens,* Turnhout, Brepols, 2008.
21. Christine Chaillot, "L'Église assyrienne apostolique en Iraq," *Proche-Orient Chrétien,* Vol. 67, 2017, 62–74.
22. Samir Khalil Samir, *Rôle culturel des chétiens dans le monde arabe,* Beirut, Cahiers de l'Orient chrétien, 2003.
23. Todd M. Johnson and Gina A. Zurlo, "Ongoing Exodus: Tracking the Emigration of Christians from the Middle East," *Harvard Journal of Middle Eastern Politics and Politics,* Vol. 3, 2013–2014, 39–45, 39.
24. Sebastian Kim and Kirsteen Kim, *Christianity as a World Religion,* London, Bloomsbury, 2016.
25. Todd M. Johnson and Gina A. Zurlo, "Ongoing Exodus," 44.
26. Catherine Mayeur-Jaouen, "'Les chrétiens au Moyen-Orient à l'heure de Daesh," *Annuaire français des relations internationals,* Vol. XVII, 2016, pp. 681–695, p. 681. Mayeur-Jaouen is referring to the work by Jean-Pierre Valognes, *Vie et mort des Chrétiens d'Orient. Des origines à nos jours,* Paris, Fayard, 1994.
27. Francine Costet-Tardieu, *Les minorités chrétiennes dans la construction de l'Égypte modern 1922–1952,* Paris, Karthala, 2016.
28. Boutros Labaki, "The Christian communities and the Economic and Social Situation in Lebanon," *Christian Communities in the Arab Middle East: The Challenge of the Future,* ed. Andrea Pacini, Oxford, Clarendon Press, 1998, pp. 222–258; Boutros Labaki, "Les chrétiens du Liban (1943–2008). Prépondérance, marginalisation et renouveau," *Confluences Méditerranée,* no. 66, 2008, 99–116.
29. Bernard Sabella, "Palestinian Christian emigration from the Holy Land," *Proche-Orient Chrétien,* Vol. 41 (1991), 74–85; B. Sabella, "Socio-economic characteristics and challenges to Palestinian Christians in the Holy Land," Palestinian *Christians: Religion, Politics and Society in the Holy Land,* ed. A. O'Mahony, London, Melisende, 1999, 222–251.
30. B. Sabella, "L'émigration des arabes chrétiens: dimensions et causes de l'exode," *Proche-Orient Chrétien,* Vol. 47 (1997), 141–169.
31. Mar Awa Royel, "The Pearl of Great Price: The Anaphora of the Apostles Mar Addai & Mar Mari as an Ecclesial and Cultural Identifier of the Assyrian Church of the East," *Orientalia Christiana Periodica,* Vol. 80 (2014), 5–22.
32. Joseph Yacoub, *Babylone chrétienne. Géeopolitique de l'Église de Mésoptamie,* Paris, Desclée de Brouwer, 1996.
33. Fabrice Balanche, "Un scénario à l'irakienne pour les chrétiens de Syrie, *La vocation des chrétiens d'Orient. Défis actuels et enjeux d'avenir dans leurs rapports à l'islam,"* ed. Robert & M. Younès, Paris, Karthala, 2015, 27–44, 27.
34. Religious discourses of the Syrian conflict are increasingly generalized as they seek refuge elsewhere. Andreas Schmoller, "Now My Life in Syria Is

Finished: Case Studies on Religious Identity and Sectarianism in Narratives of Syrian Christian Refugees in Austria," *Islam and Christian–Muslim Relations* Vol. 27, no. 4, 2016, 419–437.

35. Balanche, "Un scénario à l'irakienne pour les chrétiens de Syrie," 28.

36. Nicola Migliorino and Ara Sanjian, "Les communautes armeniennes du Proche-Orient arabe," *Confluences Méditerranée*, no. 66, 2008, 73–82.

37. Tens of thousands of Iraqi Christians since 1991 have also transited through Turkey via church and familial networks. Didem Danış, "Attendre au Purgatoire: les réseaux religieux de migrants chrétiens d'Irak en transit à Istanbul," Revue *européenne des migrations internationales*, Vol. 22, no. 3, 2006, pp. 109–134, 2006; Didem Danış, "A Faith That Binds: Iraqi Christian Women on the Domestic Service Ladder of Istanbul: Solidarity or Exploitation," *Journal of Ethnic and Migration Studies*. Vol. 33, no. 4, 2007, pp. 601–615. See also for general context, A. O'Mahony, "Christianity in modern Turkey: an overview," *Living Stone Yearbook 2014: Christianity engages with Islam: contexts, creativity and tensions*, London, Melisende, 2014, 41–63.

38. Laure Guirgis, *Les coptes d'Égypte. Violences communautaires et transformations politiques (2005–2012)*, Paris, Karthala, 2012.

39. Paolo Maggiolini, "Christian Churches and Arab Christians in the Hashemite Kingdom of Jordan," *Archives de sciences sociales des religions*, no. 171, 2015, 37–58.

40. B. Sabella, "Palestinian Christians: Realities and Hopes," *Studies in Church History: The Holy Land, Holy Lands, and Christian History*, Vol. 36 (2000), 373–397.

41. Mayeur-Jaouen, "Les chrétiens au Moyen-Orient à l'heure de Daesh," 682.

42. See the historical reflections in contemporary context by Bernard Heyberger, *Les chrétiens au Proche-Orient, de la compassion à la compréhension*, Paris, Payot, 2013.

43. Herman G. B. Teule, "Christianity in Western Asia," *The Oxford Handbook of Christianity in Asia*, ed. Felix Wilfred (Oxford University Press, 2014), pp. 17–29; A. O'Mahony, 'Western Asia,' *Atlas of Global Christianity*. Edinburgh, Edinburgh University Press, 2009, 150–151.

44. Paolo Dall'Oglio, "Eglises plurielles pour un Moyen-Orient plurie," *Mélanges de sciences religieuses*, Vol. 68, no. 3, (2011), 31–46. Dall'Oglio was the principal founder of the contemporary monastic community Deir Mar Musa al-Habashi, which attempted to incubate a new living tradition of Christian engagement with Islam under the influence of Charles de Foucauld and Louis Massignon. Dall'Oglio was kidnapped in Raqqa in July 2013 by Islamic State of Iraq and the Levant, see, P. Dall'Oglio, 'La refondation du monastère syriaque de saint Moïse l'Abyssin à Nebek, Syrie,

et la Badaliya massignonienne," *Badaliya au nom de l'autre (1947–1962)—Louis Massignon*, eds., M. Borrmans and F. Jacquin, Paris, Éditions du Cerf, 2011, pp. 372–374. See also his 'political testimony', *La rage et la lumière: Un prêtre dans la révolution syrienne* avec la collaboration de Eglantine Gabaix-Hialé, Paris, Les Editions de l'Atelier 2013. Massignon is a key-figure in the modern history of Christian-Muslim relations who is credited with defining the terms "The Muslim World" and *Salafiyya*, two ideas which seem to contest the plural religious character of the wider Middle East region. Henri Lauzière, "The construction of *Salafiyya*: Reconsidering Salafism from the Perspective of Conceptual History," *International Journal for Middle East Studies*, Vol. 42, 2010, pp. 369–389; p. 3768–381; A. O'Mahony, "Louis Massignon: A Catholic Encounter with Islam and the Middle East," in *God's Mirror: Renewal and Engagement in French Catholic Intellectual Culture in the Mid-Twentieth Century*, eds. Katherine Davies and Toby Garfitt, Century, (New York: Fordham University Press, 2014), 230–251.

45. Joseph Maïla, "De la question d'Orient à le récente géopolitique des minorités," *Proche-Orient chrétien*, Vol. 47, 1997, pp. 35–58; J. Maïla, "Réflexions sur les chrétiens d'Orient," *Confluences Méditerranée*, no. 66, 2008, 191–204.

46. The reality of Eastern Christianity is often overlooked by Western, and, in particular, U.S. policy, especially in its relations with Islamic political movements and states in the Middle East. This is also noted in evaluating the Russian Orthodox Church's concern for the Eastern Christian churches in the Middle East, which is seen as state-political concern, rather than a new aspect of the post-communist European context. See, Alicja Curanovic, *The Religious Factor in Russia's Foreign Policy*, London, Routledge, 2012. The importance of this particular lacuna, the lack of understanding of Eastern Christianity, is gaining a wide purchase in political circles especially with regard to the present situation in Syria and future of Christianity in the Middle East. *Elizabeth H. Prodromou, 'The Politics of Human Rights: Orthodox Christianity Gets the Short End, Washington, DC. 5/8/2013.* http://www.archons.org/news/detail.asp?id=638

47. John Paul II had the religious division in Europe primarily in his mind: A. O'Mahony, "… again to breathe fully from two lungs: Eastern Catholic Encounters with History and Ecclesiology," *The Downside Review*, Vol. 134, 2016, pp. 107–118; A. O'Mahony, "The Vatican and Europe: Political Theology and Ecclesiology in Papal Statements from Pius XII to Benedict XVI" in: *International Journal for the Study of the Christian Church*, Vol. 9, no. 3, 2009, 177–194.

48. Frans Bouwen, "Unity and Christian Presence in the Middle East," *The Catholic Church in the contemporary Middle East: Studies for The Synod of*

the Middle East, eds. A. O'Mahony and J. Flannery (London: Melisende, 2010), pp. 87–105, who quotes the second pastoral letter of the Catholic patriarchs of the Middle East who state "In the East, we Christians will be together or we will not be," 87.

49. Joseph Yacoub, "La dignité des personnes et des peuples. Apport mésopotamien et syrique," *Diogéne*, no. 215, 2006, 18–37.

50. Fadel Sidarouss, quoted in Thom Sicking, "Théologie orientale ou théologie en orient?", *Proche-orient chrétien*, Vol. 55, 2005, pp. 309–333, p. 320. See Fadel Sidarouss, "Pour une Théologie Contextuelle dans l'Orient Arabe Contemporain," *Quo Vadis, Theologia Orientalis? Actes du Colloque Théologie Orientale: contenu et importance," (TOTT)*, Ain Traz, Avril 2005, Textes et Etudes sur l'Orient Chrétien, no. 6, CEDRAC, Université Saint Joseph, Beyrouth, 2008, 215–237.

51. F. Sidarouss, "Éléments d'anthropologies copte," *Proche-Orient chrétien*, 2011, Vol. 61, no. 1–2, 45–59; 59.

52. Catherine Mayeur-Jaouen, "Les chrétiens au Moyen-Orient," pp. 687–688; Mayeur-Jaouen, "L'Église copte à la lumière de la Révolution égyptienne de 2011," *Istina*, Vol. 59, (2014), 5–20.

53. Edward Watkin, *A Lonely Minority: The Modern Story of Egypt's Copts*, New York, William/Morrow & Co, 1963.

54. Samuel Rubenson, "Tradition and Renewal in Coptic Theology." *Between the Desert and the City: The Coptic Orthodox Church Today,* edited by Nelly van Doorn-Harder and Kari Vogt, Oslo, Novus forlag, 1997, pp. 35–51; A. O'Mahony, "Tradition at the heart of Renewal: The Coptic Orthodox Church and monasticism in Modern Egypt," *International Journal for the Study of the Christian Church*, Vol. 7, no. 3 (2007), 164–178.

55. Mayeur-Jaouen, "Les chrétiens au Moyen-Orient," 689.

56. Edouard S. Sabanegh, "Débats autour de l'application de la Loi islamique (Shari'a) en Égypte," in: *Mélanges de l'Institut Dominicain d'Études Orientales du Caire*, Vol. 14, 1980, 329–884.

57. Meir Hatina "On the Margins of Consensus: The Call to Separate Religion and State in Modern Egypt," *Middle Eastern studies*, Vol. 36, no. 1, 2000, 35–67, 35.

58. Mayeur-Jaouen, "Les chrétiens au Moyen-Orient," 690.

59. Two Christian thinkers have engaged with this text situating it within a contemporary context. Nayla Tabbara, "Une lecture de 'la délarion d' al-Azhar sur la citiyenneté et le vivre-ensemble,' and Antoine Messarra, "La Déclaration d'al-Azhar: Que faire? Tentative d'analyse et proposition d'action," *Proche-Orient Chrétien*, Vol. 67, 2017, pp. 131–135 and pp. 138–146. The model of the so-called Constitution of Medina used in both liberal—moderate and radical Islamic thought to promote notions regarding the possibility of Jews and Christians living within Dar al-Islam,

continues to influence Islamic political thought; see, Harald Suermann, 'Die Konstitution von Medina Erinnerung an ein andreres Modell des Zusammenlebens,' *Collectanea Christiana Orientalia*, Vol. 2, 2005, 225–244.

60. Mayeur-Jaouen, "Les chrétiens au Moyen-Orient," 690.

61. Antoine Audo: "The Current situation of Christianity in the Middle East, especially Syria, after the Synod of the Middle East's Final Declaration (September 2012) and the Papal Visit to Lebanon," *Living Stones Yearbook 2012: Christianity in the Middle East: Studies in Modern History, Politics, Theology and Dialogue*, Vol. 1, 2012, 1–17.

62. Joseph Yacoub, "Les régimes politiques arabes et l'islam politique," in: *Fièvre démocratique et ferveur fondamentaliste Dominantes du XXIe siècle*, Paris, Éditions du Cerf, 2008, 121–140.

63. Rafael Palomino, "The Role of Concordats Promoting Religious Freedom with Special Reference to Agreements in the Middle East," In *CONGREGAZIONE PER LE CHIESE ORIENTALI, Ius Ecclesiarum vehiculum caritatis*, Città del Vaticano, 2004, 893–900.

64. Sebastian Brock, "The Syriac orient: a third "lung" for the church?" *Orientalia Christiana Periodica*, Vol. 71, no. 1, 2005, 5–20, 15.

65. Frans Bouwen reflects upon many of these issues, including religious freedom, in his contribution on the Synod for the Middle East held in Rome October 2010 by the Eastern Catholic bishops of the region: "The Synod for the Middle East: First results and Future Possibilities," *Living Stones Yearbook 2012: Christianity in the Middle East: Studies in Modern History, Politics, Theology and Dialogue*, Vol. 1, 2012, 18–37.

66. Elizabeth Prodromou, "Orthodox Christianity and pluralism: Moving beyond Ambivalent?" in E. Clapsis, ed. *The Orthodox Churches in a Pluralistic World: An Ecumenical Conversation*, (Geneva: World Council of Churches Publications/Brookline, MA: Holy Cross Press, 2004), pp. 22–46 (p. 24). Quoted in Ina Merdjanova, "Orthodox Christianity in a Pluralistic World," *Concilium*, no. 1, 2011, 39–50, 39.

67. Antoine Courban, "Chrétientés au milieu du monde musulman. Le cas des pays du Levant Arabe" *Irénikon*, Vol. 89, 2016, 5–24, 24.

68. Maurits H. van den Boogert, "Millets: Past and Present," *Religious Minorities in the Middle East Domination, Self-Empowerment, Accommodation*, ed. Anne Sofie Roald; Anh Nga Longva, Leiden, Brill, 2011, 25–45.

69. Fabrice Balanche, "Communautarisme en Syrie: lorsque le mythe devient réalité," Confluences *Méditerranée*, no. 89, 2014, 29–44.

70. Mayeur-Jaouen, "Les chrétiens au Moyen-Orient," 685.

71. www.Leorientlejour 21 January 2013. The Maronite patriarchate is an important religious actor in Lebanon. These thoughts are developed further

in Patriarche Béchara Rai, *Au coeur du chaos: la résistance d'un chrétien en Orient—Entretiens avec Isabelle Dillmann*, Paris, Albin Michel, 2016. See also Sami E. Baroudi & Paul Tabar, "Spiritual Authority versus Secular Authority: relations between the Maronite Church and the State in Postwar Lebanon: 1990–2005," *Middle East Critique*, Vol. 18, 2009, 195–230.

72. F. Sidarouss, quoting Amin Maalouf in "The Renewal of the Coptic Catholic Church: Grappling with Identity and Alterity," in *The Catholic Church in the contemporary Middle East: Studies for The Synod of the Middle East*, eds. O'Mahony and Flannery, 139–152.

73. F. Sidarouss, "L'Église d'Égypte, people de prophètes, de rois et de prêtres—lectures théologique de la evolution de Janvier 2011," *Proche-Orient chrétien*, Vol. 63, 2013, 64–84, 67.

74. A. Fleyfel, *La théologie contextuelle arabe, modèle libanais* (Paris, 2011).

75. Harald Suermann, quoted in Thom Sicking, "Théologie orientale ou théologie en orient?" *Proche-orient chrétien*, Vol. 55, 2005, 309–333, 313.

76. Harald Suermann, quoted in Thom Sicking, "Théologie orientale ou théologie en orient?" *Proche-orient chrétien*, Vol. 55, 2005, 309–333, 315–316.

77. A. Fleyfel and G. Haddad, *La théologie contextuelle arabe, modèle libanais* (Paris, 2011), 147–175.

78. Samir Khalil Samir, "Le synode des évêques pour le Proche-Orient," *Nouvelle revue théologique*, 133/2 (2011), 191–206.

79. M. Aoun, "Pour une théologie arabe de la liberation: contribution à l'étude de la pensée de Grégoire Haddad," *Proche-orient chrétien*, 59/1–2 (2009), 52–76, at 52–53. In his recent work builds upon these themes, "actuality of the Christian faith in the current intercultural context of Arab societies. Arab Christianity seeks to express the Christian faith in the categories of openness to Muslim otherness, of existential conviviality and fraternal solidarity. In order to safeguard not only the physical existence of these communities but also and above all the relevance and fecundity of their message of life," *Le Christ arabe: Pour une théologie chrétienne arabe de la convivialité*, Paris, Cerf, 2016.

80. A. Fleyfel, "La centralité de l'œcuménisme pour l'élaboration d'une théologie arabe moderne et contextuelle," *Théologiques*, 2 (2010), 213–238.

81. J. Corbon, "Ecumenism in the Middle East," in *Christianity: A History in the Middle East*, ed. Habib Badr, Beirut, Middle East Council of Churches, 2005) 871–883, at 882.

82. Fiona McCallum "Christian political participation in the Arab World," *Islam and Christian-Muslim relations*, Vol. 23, 2012, 3–18.

83. Statistics are very difficult to obtain in relation to the numbers of Christians in the Middle East; however, see Philippe Fargues, "The Arab Christians of the Middle East: A Demographic Perspective," *Christian Communities in*

the *Arab Middle East: The Challenge of the Future,* ed. Andrea Pacini, Oxford, Clarendon Press, 1998, pp. 48–66; Youssef Courbage, "Démographie des communautés chrétiennes au proche-orient: une approche historique," *Confluences Méditerranée,* no. 66, 2008, 27–44.

84. Ch. Cannuyer, "Les diasporas chrétiennes proche-orientales en Occident," in *L'Œuvre d'Orient: Solidarités anciennes et nouveaux defies,* eds. H. Legrand and G. M. Croce (Paris, 2010), 319–344.

85. The dynamic of an increasingly global reality faced by Middle Eastern churches, due to emigration and a significant growth in a diaspora community, strongly encourages these ecclesial cultures to redefine their identity in such a way as to make it compatible with an ethnic and cultural pluralisation of its congregation. This has been particularly noticeable for the Maronite Church. According to the *Annuario Pontificio* 2016, declared Maronites who relate to the Church number 3,537,690. Latin America has been a significant destination for Middle Eastern Christians, especially for those from Lebanon and Syria, with some 700,000 in Argentina; 481,000 in Brazil and 153,000 in Mexico. Paul Tabor, "The Maronite Church in Lebanon: From Nation-building to a Diaspora/Transnational Institution," *Migration et politique au moyen-orient,* ed. Françoise De Bel-Air, Damascus, Institut françai du Proche-Orient, 2006, 185–201.

86. Georges Labaki, "La jurisdiction territorial du patriarche maronite d'antioche: de l'orient à l'occident," *Christianisme oriental: Kérygme et Histoire,* ed. Charles Chartouni, Paris, Geuthner, 2007, 143–158.

87. A. O'Mahony considers the fate of an earlier migration from of a significant number of Eastern Christians from Ottoman lands into Europe in "Between Rome and Constantinople: The Italian-Albanian Church—a study in Eastern Catholic history and ecclesiology," International *Journal for the Study of the Christian Church,* Vol. 8, no. 3, 2008, pp. 232–251. These Albanian Christians who have lived for four centuries on the Italian peninsula continue hold a historical focus upon Christian-Muslim coexistence as a contemporary experience.

88. Mayeur-Jaouen, "Les chrétiens au Moyen-Orient," 691–693.

89. Sebastian Brock, "The Syriac Churches in Ecumenical Dialogue on Christology," in A. O'Mahony, ed. *Eastern Christianity. Studies in Modern History, Religion, and Politics,* London, Melisende, 2004, 44–65.

90. Laurence Ritter, "La découverte d'une thématique efface et l'importance de la categorisation: Arméniens caches et Arméniens islamisés de Turquie," *La vocation des chrétiens d'Orient. Défis actuels et enjeux d'avenir dans leurs rapports à l'islam,* ed. Robert & M. Younès, Paris, Karthala, 2015, 123–136.

91. H. Teule, "Middle Eastern Christians and Migration: Some Reflections," *The Journal of Eastern Christian Studies,* 54 (2002), 1–23.

92. Mayeur-Jaouen, "Les chrétiens au Moyen-Orient," 695.

CHAPTER 4

Christian Contributions to Art, Culture, and Literature in the Arab-Islamic World

Bernard Sabella

The awakening of Arab culture from its condition of dormancy, which extended from the middle of the thirteenth century through the eighteenth, was characterized by developments in several fields of artistic expression. The multiplication of printing presses facilitated the dissemination of theological, philosophical, literary, journalistic, and theatrical works that were stimulated by contact with Western culture. The field of filmmaking also blossomed. Contributors to this cultural renaissance, both in the Middle East and in the Arab Diaspora, grappled with issues of identity politics, diversity, and secularism. In this chapter I will trace these developments.

The fall of Baghdad wrought by the Mongol Hulagu in 1258 heralded the demise of Arabic and Islamic culture and civilization that developed during both the Umayyad and the Abbasid dynasties. One exception was Ibn Khaldun (1331–1406) and his works, chief among which was the famed *Muqqadimah*, or *Introduction to History*, which presaged modern sociology. Another was Andalusia, not only for its literary and philosophical treatises as well as its architectural splendor and grandeur, but also for creating an environment that promoted acceptance of the other and free-

B. Sabella (✉)
Palestinian Legislative Council, Jerusalem, Israel

© The Author(s) 2018   89
K. C. Ellis (ed.), *Secular Nationalism and Citizenship in Muslim Countries*, Minorities in West Asia and North Africa,
https://doi.org/10.1007/978-3-319-71204-8_4

dom of expression. Apart from these two areas of excellence, the period between the fall of Baghdad in the thirteenth century and the eighteenth century could be characterized as a period of cultural, artistic, and literary decline. In spite of some apologetics on the merits of the Ottoman Empire and its five-century domination of most of the Arab world, the two countries that saw the beginnings of cultural and literary awakening, Egypt and Lebanon, were semi-autonomous and hence immune to an extent from the restrictive environment of Ottoman rule.

Some social theorists argue that culture contact is the primary cause in initiating change in cultures and hence in promoting all sorts of innovations through transfer of accumulated knowledge and expertise.[1] This theory of culture contact could also explain the literary, artistic, and theatrical awakening of the Arab World from the beginnings of the nineteenth century. Hanna Fakhoury (1914–2011) in his famed *Tarikh Al Adab Al 'Arabi* (*History of Arab Literature*), which was first published in 1951 and has had many reprints since, places printing as one factor, together with schools, the press, literary societies, libraries, stage acting, and Orientalism, that contributed to the Arab Awakening.[2] John Haywood in *Modern Arabic Literature 1800–1970* concurs with Fakhoury on the importance of the printing press and cites Father Louis Cheikho's (1859–1917) *Tarikh Fan Al Tiba'ah Fi Al Sharq* (*History of the Art of Printing in the East*). Cheikho points out in his book that the churches and the Christian religious orders were among the first to introduce the printing press in the East.[3] Religious books, catechetical materials, missals for Mass and other religious rites and celebrations were a primary consideration for the church fathers to introduce printing in Arabic. A fortuitous outcome of the church's religious printing press was the growing interest in the Arabic language promoted actively by some church fathers and the early literary figures who were accorded the opportunity to publish their works.

According to Cheikho, one of the first printing presses in the East was the Qozhaya Press in the Valley of Qadisha with its famed monastery dating from early in the seventeenth century. Apparently this was an old press that used rather rudimentary tools to print the Psalms in Arabic in 1585, which made it one of the first Arabic books in print. Cheikho attributes the fame of this press to a Beiruti, Seraphim Huka, who undertook in the nineteenth century to renovate it. The first of the books printed was the *Missal of Divine Mass* (*Al Quddas Al Ilahi*), in 1838, which Bishop Germanous Farhat translated from Syriac.[4] In the beginning of the eighteenth century the Greek Melkite Patriarch Asthenious of Antioch started a press in Aleppo that specialized in printing Christian religious books. The Psalms and the Gospels in Arabic were printed in 1706. The Maronite Press in Aleppo in 1857 specialized also in printing religious books, but in addition it printed Arabic books such as *Mabade' Al Qira'ah* (*Principles of Reading*), *Dalil al Hurriyah Al Insaniyah* (*Guide for Human Freedom*) and the pioneering philosophical novel of Francis Mrash (1836–1873), *Ghabat Al Haq* (*Forest of Truth*), which seemed to some to presage *The Prophet* by Gibran Kahlil Gibran. In 1883 the Maronite Press of Aleppo printed an Islamic calendar, which may have been a first. The Greek Melkite Shweir Printing Press was started by Abdallah Al Zakher in the middle of the eighteenth century and specialized also in religious books. The Greek Orthodox Printing Press in Beirut was established in response to the Shweir Printing Press. In 1882 the Orthodox Printing Press published Nasif Yaziji's (1800–1871) *Sharh Diwan Abi Al Tayyeb* (*Explanation of Diwan Abi Al Tayyeb*) and the novel of Adib Ishaq (1856–1886), *Al Hasna' Al Barisiah* (*The Beautiful Parisian*), as well as the magazine *Al Hiddiyah* (*The Gift*) between 1883 and 1888.[5]

The American Press in Beirut appeared at the same time as that of the Greek Orthodox. The person in charge of the Arabic books was Fares Al Shidyaq (1804–1887) "one of the great architects of the *Nahda*," according to Haywood.[6] (*Nahda* is the noun that designates the Arab Renaissance.) Besides printing religious books, the American Press embarked on publishing books of general interest such as *The Quest in the Knowledge of Arabic* by Bishop Germanous Farhat (1670–1732) in 1836 and *Conclusive Argument in the Origins of the Language of the Bedouins* by Nasif Yazigi, which was printed in 1866. The American Press was known for its American letters and high printing quality. The American Press, like the other Christian religious presses, did not refrain from printing books that attacked each other on religious and theological grounds. Thus the Catholic press in general was wont to print books that warned of the dangers of Protestantism and that criticized the Greek Orthodox and their ways. These were answered by books attacking the Catholics for their presumptuous positions, including the supremacy of the Pope.

It would not have been possible for Butros Al Bustani (1819–1883) to become the literary dean or patriarch of his family, which boasted more than 12 literary figures, authors, and publishers, without the presence of the printing press. Haywood extends to Bustani the title of patriarch to the *Nahda,* although he did not believe that Bustani was "… a major creative writer." Haywood attributes Bustani's major influence to "two contributions to literature; firstly the revival of a knowledge and love of the Arabic language; secondly in his belief that the Arab world could revive only through knowledge of the thought and the discoveries of modern Europe."[7] Bustani mastered Syriac, Latin, Italian, and Arabic, his mother tongue. He helped in the translation of the Bible, initiated by American missionaries in Beirut, a task that necessitated his acquiring knowledge in both Hebrew and Greek. He turned Protestant in 1860 when the strife between the Druze and the Maronites was at its highest. In response, he initiated a two-page newspaper, *Nafir Suriyya*, calling for tolerance and cooperation between the two communities.[8] He worked on *Muhit al Muhit*, a two-volume dictionary that appeared in 1870, and on *Da'irat al-Ma'arif*, an Arabic encyclopedia, which other Bustanis eventually completed. In 1868 he published the Arabic version of *Robinson Crusoe*. He was an enthusiast for the education of Arab women, and in a book that appeared in 1849, he argued—

> Again, how great are the advantages to children which are derived from women's education. For the woman bestows on her children such knowledge, culture and civilization as she herself has. The child receives his first impressions from his mother, because she is the first thing to impinge on his senses and perceptions. So from looking into the light of her face, he obtains his first thoughts...[9]

In 1869 he undertook to compare Arabic with European customs. Bustani, like other early pioneers of the Arabic literary awakening, benefited both from his knowledge of foreign European tongues and his visits to Europe and contact with its cultural and other developments. The early travelers naturally compared the existing conditions in their own societies with what they saw in Europe, an experience that later also influenced some of the great literary figures of Egypt like Taha Hussein. Bustani was well ahead of Qasem Amin, who in 1899 wrote his renowned book *Tahrir Al Mar'ah (The Liberation of Woman)*, which caused an intellectual and social stir that influenced the thinking of generations of Arabs to come. The fact that Qasem Amin studied law in Paris could have influenced him in developing his stance on the issue of women's liberation. Amin believed, as Bustani did, in the need to educate women since, without education, women were without freedom and hence could not contribute to the welfare of society or undertake efficiently educational and nurturing tasks. Most important to Amin was the belief that woman should be set free and should not be veiled.

Haywood refers to the dozens of members of the Bustani, Yaziji, Khoury, and other Christian Lebanese families that made up the vanguard of the literary and cultural awakening in Lebanon and throughout the Arab East. It would be difficult to list the accomplishments of each of these literary figures in this presentation. Suffice it to say that their contributions were essential to exposing a broader Arab audience to the literary riches of the Arabic language and its manifestations in prose, poetry, and the other genres of literary expressions.

Fakhoury believes that both Lebanon and Egypt were the two pioneering countries in Arab awakening because of their contact with the West. He attributes the beginning of Lebanon's contact with the West to Amir Fakhr El Din al Ma'ani, who welcomed Europeans in Lebanon, but also to the interest shown by the Holy See and some European sovereigns in Lebanon and its affairs, as well as to European and American missionaries, especially those who established schools and other educational institutions. Fakhoury mentions the early contacts with the West by Lebanese such as Jibrail al Sihioni, Ibrahim al Haklani, and Bishop Germanous Farhat, who loved Arabic and worked studiously for its development.[10] No doubt contact with the West touched first and foremost the churches and the Christian religious orders that had special relationships with the Holy See and with other parts of Europe. Father Louis Cheikho starts his *History of the Art of Printing in the East* by referring to the Arabic books first printed in Rome and Paris and the effect that the printing presses of Europe had exerted on heads of churches in the East since the early seventeenth century.

Cheikho describes the history and accomplishments of over 17 different printing presses in Lebanon during the nineteenth century, among which was the first Islamic printing press, the Matba'at Jami'at al Funoun Printing Press of al Funoun Society, founded in 1874 by Abdel Qader Al Qabbani (1849–1935), who brought its letters from London. Most of these printing presses, with the exception of a couple that were dedicated to printing official proclamations and decrees, belonged to the different churches and had an initial focus on religion that eventually spread to secular topics of interest to a broader audience.[11]

The Napoleonic campaign in Egypt at the end of the eighteenth century could not have contributed to the cultural contact between Egypt and the West without the presence of the cohort of scientists and learned men that Napoleon brought with him as well as two printing presses, the library, and the establishment of schools and the scientific council Al Majma' Al 'Almi, which the French had set up. Two newspapers in French were printed in Egypt during the Napoleonic campaign, with occasional articles and tribute poems in Arabic, especially those by local authors that praised Napoleon and the French.[12] But the contact that had a more lasting effect on Egypt was the initiative taken by Muhammad Ali (1769–1849), an Albanian in origin, who sent study missions to Europe, and to France specifically, and who encouraged literary movements. Khedive Ismail (1830–1895), who himself was impressed throughout his study stay in France with the developments taking place in France and Europe in general, followed in the footsteps of his grandfather. If Lebanon and Egypt took the lead in culture contact with the West, it is primarily because of their unique semi-autonomous relations with the Ottoman authorities, which allowed for openness to the West in a relatively unhindered manner.

Palestine and Iraq were not in the same position as Egypt and Lebanon even though Palestine church printing presses such as the Franciscan Printing Press appeared in 1846, the Armenian Printing Press in 1848, and Matba'at Al Qaber Al Muqqadas, the printing press of the Holy Sepulcher, founded by the Greek Orthodox Clerical Brotherhood of the same name in 1849. Indigenous Palestinian Christians took the lead in establishing their own printing presses. In 1892, as reported by Suleiman, a member of the Doumani family established the Doumani Press with Arabic, Turkish, and French fonts. Alphonse Antoine Alonzo, a Roman Catholic Palestinian, established Al-Wataniyyah Press, using Arabic, Turkish, French, and Russian fonts. Jurji Habib Hananiya, of a Greek Orthodox Palestinian family, established a modern printing press and used Arabic, Turkish, and Russian fonts. He founded the newspaper *Al Quds* in 1908, the first Arabic newspaper in Palestine.[13] But the general environment in Palestine was not ripe for the establishment of a movement of literary, cultural, and artistic awakening similar to what happened in both Egypt and Lebanon during nineteenth century and the beginning of the twentieth century. Palestine was more or less a secluded country except for visits by pilgrims and tourists.

Of note regarding the Russian font used by the Palestinian printing presses was the connection to the Russian Teachers' Training Center in Nazareth, which was founded in 1886. Russian pilgrims in the late nineteenth and the early twentieth centuries arrived in droves to visit the holy sites in Palestine; imperial Russia had an interest in promoting its presence in the region through the establishment of religious and educational institutions. Among the students at the Russian Teachers' Training Center were Khalil Baidas (1874–1949) and Mikhail Nu'eimah (1889–1988). Baidas, one of Palestine's foremost intellectuals, wrote novels and translated Tolstoy and Pushkin into Arabic. He started a magazine, *Al-Nafā'is al-ʿasriyyah* (النفائس العصرية, *The Modern Treasures*), which was well respected throughout the East and in the Diaspora. Nue'imah was one of the foremost intellectuals and authors of the *Nahda* with scores of impressive publications. He graduated from the Russian Teachers' Training Center, where he met Baidas, and went on to the United States, where he founded Al Rabita Al Qalamiyah in New York City together with Gibran and other Diaspora literary figures. He later returned to Lebanon, where he settled in his village of Shakhroub near Biskanta.

As for Iraq, Cheikho mentions the printing press of the Dominican Fathers, which was founded in 1860 in Mosul with the help of the Franciscan Friar Yusef from Jerusalem. Among the scores of mostly religious books printed there were some literary books, such as *Kalila Wa Dumna*, translated by the Syriac Father Yusef Daoud and printed in 1869, and a mathematics book in 1865 as well as the Psalms in Chaldean in 1890. Another church printing press was the Chaldean Press, established during the tenure of Patriarch Yusuf Udo, with its fonts in Chaldean, Arabic, and French brought from Paris in 1863; however, it did not last long because of the death of its founder. A couple of other printing presses are mentioned by Cheikho, but apparently they were limited in their imprint.[14]

Christian Arabs as well as Arab Jews played an important role in the Arab Awakening between the end of the nineteenth century and the beginning of the twentieth century. Not only did they play this role as a result of pioneering cultural contact with the West, but are also important because they were rooted in their respective societies, Iraq and Egypt, and are prime examples of the contributions of Arab Jews both in political nationalist formations and in artistic and financial matters. While Syria seems to be often subsumed by or lumped together with Lebanon, it is worth mentioning Rizqallah Hassoun (1825–1880) from Aleppo, who hailed from an Armenian Persian background and who, besides Arabic, knew Armenian, Turkish, French, Russian, and English. In 1854 he was the first to establish a newspaper, *Mir'at al Ahwal*, in Istanbul and was in favor of liberty and reform in the Ottoman Empire.[15] Another Damascene who played a role in the *Nahda* was Adib Ishaq (1856–1886), who founded the weekly Cairo newspaper *Misr* (*Egypt*) in 1877 and then moved on to Alexandria, where he founded the daily newspaper *Al Tijarah* (*The Commerce*). He was influenced by Jamal Eddin Al Afghani as he attended his learning circle.

In Egypt, the literary awakening was characterized by the prominence of well-established poets such as al Baroudi (1838–1904), Ahmed Shawqi (1868–1932), Hafez Ibrahim (1872–1949), and Khalil Mutran (1872–1949), who hailed originally from Lebanon. Haywood believes that Mutran foreshadowed poetical modernism in Egypt and indeed throughout the Arab world. In spite of the fact that Mutran was a Maronite he was a supporter of Islamic solidarity and Arab independence. His ode on the Arab Awakening affirms his rootedness and that of his fellow literary figures in their Arab identity:

> O noble company of Arabs, ye
> My pride and boast, o'er every company,
> Long have I chided your carelessness and sloth,
> Yet not as one that might despair or loathe,
> But candidly, as if to wake a friend
> Unconscious of vast perils that impound.[16]

The Mutran ode reminds one of another famous ode that was used as an epigraph to George Antonius's famed *Arab Awakening* of 1938. Ibrahim al Yaziji (1847–1906), a Greek Catholic poet, grammarian, and man of letters, wrote the ode "Arise, ye Arabs, and Awake" (*tanabbahu wa istafiqu ayuha al-arabu*) in 1883. This ode, as the following verses indicate, is a call for resistance to Ottoman rule:

> Your status in the eyes of the Turks is debased,
> And your right by the hands of the Turks is usurped,
> You possess no known status or honor,
> Nor any existence, or name or title,
> O to my people and my people are none but the Arabs.[17]

In addition to incitement the ode sang of the achievements of the Arab race, of the glories of Arab literature, and of the future that the Arabs might fashion for themselves by looking to their own past for inspiration. The ode denounced the evils of sectarian dissensions, heaped abuse on the misgovernment to which the country was prey, and called upon the Syrians to band together to shake off the Turkish yoke.[18] One practical innovation credited to Ibrahim was his creation of a "greatly simplified Arabic font. By reducing Arabic character forms from 300 to 60 he simplified the symbols so that they more closely resembled Latin characters. It was a process that contributed to the creation of the Arabic typewriter."[19]

Lebanese literary figures were indisputably pioneers in planting the roots of literary renovation, reform, and renaissance in the Arab world. These roots presaged the writings of Jamal al Din al Afghani (1838–1897), Muhammed Abdo (1849–1905), Qasem Amin (1863–1908), Ahmed Amin (1886–1954), and Kheir al Din al Tunisi (1820–1890). No doubt that the study missions initiated by Muhammed Ali to Europe, and to France in particular, bore fruit. The issues raised by the likes of Afghani became issues of general and public interest that influenced the academic and social exchanges among the literary, political, and social elites of Egypt and elsewhere in the Arab world for decades to come. Do we take from Europe, and what should we take? What is the relationship of religion to progress and vice versa? Are women entitled to education? How would women's education reflect positively on family and society? We should place these questions and challenging issues raised and discussed by Afghani and his group of intellectual pioneers within a context that saw between 1870 and 1914 the publication of hundreds of short stories in both Egypt and Lebanon.[20] If the Lebanese and other literary avant-gardists foreshadowed the introduction of the *Nahda*, the Afghani group addressed the core issues that touched on the nature of the *Nahda* and that questioned in earnest the future vision of Arab Eastern society in keeping with the times. The rise of the Afghani group was concomitant in Egypt with three important publications: the *Al Ahram* daily newspaper and printing press established in 1875 by the Lebanese Bishara and Salim Takla[21]; *Al Hilal*, a cultural monthly magazine established in 1892 by the well-known Jurji Zeidan[22]; and *Al Muqtataf*, a scientific, literary, and cultural magazine originally founded in Beirut by Yacoub Sarrouf (1852–1927) and Fares Nimr in 1876 and moved to Cairo in 1888.[23] What role did these publications play in promoting the discussions on the issues of the *Nahda*? What impact did these publications have on the wider audience of Egyptians and Arabs as they tackled literary, cultural, and scientific topics? These are questions that definitely require a separate examination.

The spread of schools had a definite influence on the beginnings of acting and the theater in the Arab East. Private Christian schools were among the first to encourage students and teachers alike to stage school plays that were mostly adapted from French or other Western sources. Schools were influenced by the pioneering theatrical activities of Maroun Al Naqqash (1817–1855). These schools did not cater to Christian students only, as they were open to all students irrespective of religion. Maroun al-Naqqash was the foremost pioneer of Arab theater; indeed, he is credited with introducing this genre of literary art into the Arab world. One of his first plays in Arabic, *Al-Bakhil*, was an adaptation of *L'Avare*, or *The Mean Man*, by Molière. Naqqash built his own stage, which was the first in the Arab world and which was turned into a church after his death as per his will.[24] In Damascus, Ahmed Al Qabbani hosted a stage in his grandfather's home, and although there was no immediate connection with Naqqash, the latter nevertheless had had an influence on him and on members of the Qabbani family who became also interested in the theater. The nephew of Maroun, Salim, cooperated with Adib Ishaq (1856–1885) in the staging of some Arabic plays in Alexandria. Adib Ishaq was of Armenian origin, and his name was Adib Zalmatian. Born in Damascus, he was educated at the Lazarian school there. His newspaper, *Misr*, alluded to above, was issued together with Salim al Naqqash in 1877, and *Al Tijarah* (*The Commerce*) in 1878, followed by *Al Mahrousah* in 1880. The contributions of Ishaq to the theater were modest, but he was a prolific newspaper writer and wrote in support of the "shura system and representative government for the sake of people's rights."[25]

If Naqqash was the pioneer of Arab theater, George Abyad (1880–1952), a Syrian by origin who lived in Egypt, became the "dean of Arab theatre." He spared no efforts to promote the theater in Egypt and throughout the Arab world, with attention to quality productions, particularly after World War I. Khedive Abbas II took a liking to his work and sent him to Paris to study acting, which he did with the famous French actor Sylvain. When he returned to Egypt in 1910, he started his own acting troupe and staged *King Oedipus*, translated by Farah Anton (1874–1922), who also composed plays and operettas and other translated works that were staged. Abyad staged Shakespeare plays and one play by Delavigne on the life of Louis XI translated by Elias Fayyad. According to Landau, Abyad "... had the mold of a fine tragic actor, but no more. Even though he remained 'the dean of the Arab theatre' in Egypt in post-war years and received well-deserved applause in his tours of Syria, Lebanon, Palestine, Tunisia and Tripolitania."[26] Landau states that Abyad's Christian background was not in his favor, particularly after Egypt gained independence and sectarian sensitivities surfaced between Muslims and Copts. Abyad nevertheless is credited with "awakening the consciousness of the Arab theatregoer ... and in educating collaborators and pupils to new artistic values ... and the need for exact translation of foreign dramas and serious preparation for every play."[27]

If Abyad was the "dean of Arab theatre," then Naguib Elias Al Rihani (1889–1949) was the "Father of Comedy." Son of a Chaldean father and a Coptic mother, he attended the Frères School in Cairo. He was married to the famed actress and entertainment figure of the early twentieth century, Badiah Al Masabini. Rihani put up French plays adapted to the Egyptian context and ventured as well into filmmaking. Among his most popular plays were *Kesh Kesh Bey in Paris* and *Al 'Ishrah Al Tayyibah (The Good Company)*, performed in 1920 with the renowned Sayed Darwish composing its music. In 1936 he produced *Hukum Karakosh (The Rule of Karakosh)*, and in 1945 *Hassan, Murcus and Cohen*, which later on was made into a film.

Hassan was the handsome, confident, cultured, well dressed Muslim front for the drug concern, but he had no expertness in anything except how to make friends and establish relations with the government. Cohen was the conservative, careful financier who was the treasurer of the company, but he had little front. Murcus was the Coptic member of this drug company, a slightly dowdy chap, a practical operator. His know-how for getting things done in the community was what made the concern a success. When Murcus made a diplomatic engagement for Hassan, Hassan always appeared and did his job well; when Murcus needed funds for some operation he convinced Mr. Cohen and the funds were forthcoming; but neither Mr. Hassan nor Mr. Cohen could quite get along unless they consulted Mr. Murcus.[28]

This comedy, with its three "religious" characters, portrayed the stereotypical views that people of Egypt and the Near East held of the different religious and ethnic groups living among them. The stereotype of the Muslim who meshes well with his community, that of the Jew who is in control of finances, and that of the Christian go-between who nurtures the diplomat within him are all stereotypes that do not necessarily reflect the whole reality and its complex relations. On a professional level, Fouad al Muhandes, one of the foremost comedians in Egypt and the entire Middle East, pays tribute to the influence that Rihani had had on him and on the development of comedy in Egypt, and to Rihani's style of comedy, which impacted his own style.[29]

Another author of historical plays, a literary genre that became popular post-independence, was Yusuf al Haik, who published in 1932 *Laila, Al Nu'man's Daughter and the Chosroes*. By defining the people interested in the theater, he summarized the qualities of the theatergoers of his time: "those with a natural penchant towards acting, those yearning for the memories of their forefathers, those moved by their fathers' sentiment, those hoping to revive their ancestors' heroism and those desiring to feel the truth of the events."[30] Landau mentions the Palestinian Arab theater under the British Mandate (1920–1948) and two of the early local playwrights, Jamil Habib Bahri and Nasri al Jauzi. Clearly, however, the influence of the Egyptian theatrical troupes that visited Palestine at the time, such as those of Abyad, Rihani, and Kassar, was important in the development of theater in the country. The private Christian schools had had an important role in encouraging the staging of school plays. This was imitated by national secular schools. Some claim that there were up to 30 troupes in Jerusalem alone during this period but that they failed to attract audiences outside of their own neighborhoods and localities.

Various clubs, civil associations, and the Jerusalem broadcasting station "Huna Al Quds" ("Jerusalem Calling") also played a role in promoting theater. One of the obstacles faced, as in Egypt and elsewhere, was the prohibition on women appearing on stage. This was overcome in Palestine as in Egypt by Jewish and Christian actresses who took the roles of women. Of note is that Jamil Habib Bahri composed 12 theatrical plays, among which were *The Beloved Country* in 1923, *The Traitor* in 1924, and *The Pursuit of Honor* in 1926. Jamil, Saliba, and Farid al Jouzi, Greek Orthodox Palestinians, played roles in establishing the Palestinian broadcasting station side by side with their acting in plays and comedies. Among the other Palestinians who had roles in the theater were Archimandrite Stephan Salem from Nazareth and Asma Touba, who wrote the play *Christmas Tree*, performed in 1942. Asma was active in the Women's Union in Acre, and when she left Palestine for Beirut in 1948, a book of hers on Palestinian women was at the printer, but she could not retrieve it because of the war. Jamil Bahri was quite active in Haifa's literary circles, and he often welcomed the visits of the Abyad troupe from Egypt and one unforgettable visit of the famed Yusef Wahbeh in the 1930s.[31] One can sense that those days were relatively free, as the conditions, in spite of both the British and French mandates and the troubles in Palestine, allowed people to move back and forth and thus enabled various literary and artistic activities and exchanges, including plays and musical concerts performed by visiting troupes and singers in a number of Middle Eastern countries.

Theater and literature prospered in the Arab world as spirited and industrious artists, literary figures, actors, and novelists insisted on introducing their writings and staging the plays. The broadcasting stations in Palestine and elsewhere started playing a role in increasing the interest of the public in plays heard over radio as more and more households were introduced to the radio, a luxury for many at the time but eventually a popular possession that influenced and shaped perceptions of developments at home and abroad. Among those spirited, industrious artists and intellectuals were many Christian Arabs who naturally opted to explore the wealth of their language and the possibilities that its development would offer in an age of exciting transition.

Filmmaking is a topic in its own right, and a brief overview of two contributions should raise interest in a more detailed account of the rise of the film industry in the Arab world and its contributions to the *Nahda*. When the Lama brothers, Ibrahim and Badr, originally from Bethlehem, decided to return home from Chile to Palestine in 1924, they disembarked at Alexandria and fell in love with the city. Enthusiastic about filmmaking, they set up their own Condor Film Company. Influenced by Rudolf Valentino's films, they wrote, directed, and acted. Badr, the younger brother, took the lead role in *Qoublah fi-il-Sahra'* (*A Kiss in the Desert*). In 1930 they established the Lama Studio in Qoubbeh Gardens, Cairo. In 1941 they produced a historical film on Saladin that was poorly designed. In 1963 Yousef Chahine (1926–2008) made it into the spectacular *El Nasir Salah Eddine*.[32]

Yousef Chahine was born in Alexandria of a Lebanese father and a Greek mother. Both Alexandria and Cairo would feature prominently in his films. "The introvert is often associated with Cairo," noted *Film Comment*—

> with its narrow streets and cramped dwellings—while the extrovert is associated with Alexandria, which remains the golden city of Chahine's work, a cosmopolitan Utopia where Europe and Africa peacefully coexist, where Christians (Chahine's family was Roman Catholic), Jews and Muslims could once live together, providing a model for a now lost Middle Eastern harmony. The image of the port, open to the world, becomes an image of acceptance and synthesis.[33]

Chahine is accredited with launching the international career of Omar Sharif in 1953, when Sharif acted in the film *Sera'a fil Wadi* (*Struggle in the Valley*).

For those who opted to leave for the United States or South America—many of whom were prominent authors, literary figures, and promising media prospects—the emigration that took place in the late nineteenth and the early twentieth centuries to a foreign land did not obliterate their ties and links to their homeland and to the people they left behind to face a multitude of challenges. One of the signs of this attachment to the homeland was the welcoming of visiting theatrical and musical troupes from back home. These performances were frequented by almost all members of the emigrant community, who showed by their attendance a strong link to their countries of birth. In 1920 Al Rabita Al Qalamiyah was founded in New York, at the head of which stood Gibran Kahlil Gibran. Among those who formed the Rabita were Mikhail Nu'eimah, Abdel Masih Haddad, Nadra Haddad, Elias Atallah, William Katsivalis, Nasib 'Areidah, and Rashid Ayoub. Later on they were joined by Wadi' Bahut and Elia Abu Madi.[34] According to Omar Dakkak, the primary preoccupation of the members of Al Rabita was "real renewal away from tradition and the regurgitation of the past so that literature would become a reflection of the soul and a mirror for life." The members of Al Rabita published their writings and reflections in the newspaper *Al Saeh*, which had been founded by Abdel Masih Haddad. In 1921 Al Rabita published a volume of the works of their members, which left a great impact in the Diaspora and back home. The individual members of Al Rabita made their own contributions, which influenced Arabic literature at home and left a lasting impact on the thought and intellectual life of a wider society. Gibran's *The Prophet* continues to be a bestseller in English, and his writings in Arabic are read and often quoted among young and old Arabs.

In South America a spirited group of authors and literary figures decided to form Al 'Usbah Al Andalusiah on the model of Al Rabita Al Qalamiyah of New York. Shukrallah al Jar, publisher of the magazine *New Andalus*, together with Michel Ma'alouf, started Al 'Usbah in 1932, joined by Natheer Zeitoun and Habib Mas'oud. Their goal in establishing the 'Usbah was "to follow the rich heritage left by Arabs in Andalusia." Later on, Rashid Salim Al Khoury (Al Shaer Al Qarawi) and Elias Farhat joined the 'Usbah. The magazine started by the 'Usbah under the same name was published for over 20 years between 1934 and 1954. Apparently the Greek Orthodox Church played an important role in maintaining ties between the Diaspora communities and their homelands. It was pointed out by a Muslim blogger that the—

Eastern Church was the home of the Almighty for all and it was the home of Arabism for the emigrants. It provided a strong link for these emigrants to their original homeland.... This Church made it part of its mission to spread the language of the Qur'an (i.e., Arabic) and to elaborate on the heritage and glories of the Arab homeland. This approach has endeared

Brazilians of Arab origin to their Church as they hurriedly congregate in the Church where they see in the faces and composures of the priests loved memories from the land of Christ and reflect as well on the pride of the priests that bears a refreshing touch to the ancient East.[35]

One of the Diaspora's leading figures was Amin al Rihani, who in 1911 wrote *Kitab Khaled* (*The Book of Khaled*), a philosophical, reflective book, the first ever by an Arab author in English; in the previous year he had published his *Rihaniat*. Karam al Helou, in his review of the study by Nijmeh Hajjar on Amin al Rihani, maintains that the same issues that preoccupied the pioneers of the Arab renaissance are still with us. Among these issues we still face, according to Helou, are feelings of sectarian fanaticism, tribalism, and localism over those of belonging to the nation and homeland. Rihani was dreaming of a new spirit and a reform movement that would unify the Arab nation and that would emphasize its civilizational role. According to Rihani, "Arab unity based on nationalism and not on religion is a holy unity that I bequeath to you. Know that there is no salvation to minorities except through their unity with the Arabs and their integration with the majority on intellectual, literary, and spiritual realms so that the homeland is neither majority nor minority."[36] Rihani stressed the importance of having an intellectual revolution for the rejuvenation of the Arab nation; this same emphasis was voiced half a century later by such thinkers as Abdallah Al 'Ara'oui, Mohammed Abed al Jabiri, Adonis, and Hisham Sharabi.

Helou, in his review of Hajjar's study, argues that her statement that Rihani's Arab journey had reinforced his transformation from a Maronite from the Mount of Lebanon, afraid of the threat of Arabs, to an Arab nationalist in service of their causes does not do justice to Butros al Bustani, the Maronite and the son of the Mount of Lebanon, who was the first to speak proudly of his Arab nationalist identification. Helou reminds Hajjar of the fact that the Maronites of the Mount of Lebanon were those who preserved the Arabic language and literature as they published dictionaries and encyclopedias, and started newspapers and literary magazines. But Helou is cognizant of the challenges that confronted the Rihani national secular awakening project, which failed, and ponders whether there is still hope for such a dream for the future.[37]

A national secular awakening project would not be possible, according to Farah Anton, if it were not based on *Al Tasamoh* (forbearance) *wal Tasahol* (and open-mindedness or leniency) towards the other. To illustrate his idea on *Tasamoh*, his novel *Urashalim Al Jadidah* (*The New Jerusalem*) addresses the Arab takeover of Jerusalem in 638 CE as an example of for-bearance. Anton insisted in his writings on the need not to misjudge others because of their religious beliefs and to allow people the freedom of belief. Anton believed in a state that separates civil authority from religious authority, thus guaranteeing equality to all citizens and encouraging acceptance of differences, which is something that could promote knowledge, different interpretations, and the courage to think innovatively.

The issues posed by the likes of Rihani, Anton, and the other pioneers of the Arab Renaissance are still with us today. They have become in fact more poignant as religion and religious identity take precedence over other common human identities and preoccupations. The questions that need to be addressed are what future there can be for the Arab East and what lessons we can learn from the illustrious literary figures that shaped the *Nahda* and that argued for a society open to all. While Arab nationalism figured predominantly in some early writings, the realities at present have distanced us from the nationalist ideal. The preoccupation with religion and religious identity has also contributed to gaps, dislocations, and divergences that apparently are very difficult to reconcile. Yet Arab Christians, like other like-minded Arabs, still believe in a common future—witness the writings, artistic performances, political affiliations, and other personal and public manifestations that continue to attest to the possibility of a joint vision of living together. The challenge for all of us is how to mold this vision, given the destruction that has been wrought of late to intercommunal and interreligious relations. If reconstruction and rehabilitation of Arab society are to be part of our future vision, then what contributions can we make as individuals and communities? Going back to the past is clearly impossible; once the mirror is broken, it cannot be fixed again. How, then, can we, with our different identities, religious and ethnic values, political affiliations, and historical narratives, come together again, with *Tasamoh* and *Tasahol?* Is it possible to come together again, or are we destined to disband and to each seek our own salvation, so to speak? How does the heritage of our forefathers weigh on us, or is it passé and do we need to search for new and different alternatives?

NOTES

1. See, for example, Raphael Patai's "On Culture Contact and Its Workings in Modern Palestine," *American Anthropologist*, Vol. 49, Number 4, Part 2 (The American Anthropological Association, 1947).

2. Hanna Al Fakhoury, *Tarikh Al Adab Al 'Arabi*, or *History of Arab Literature* (Beirut: Dar Al Yousef Lil Tiba'ah Wal Nashr Wal Tawzi', n.d.), 901.

3. John A. Haywood, *Modern Arabic Literature 1800–1970: An Introduction with Extracts in Translation* (Lund: Humphries, 1971), 27.

4. Louis Cheikho, *Fan Al Tiba'ah Fil Sharq*, or *History of the Art of Printing in the East*, 2nd ed. (Beirut: Dar Al Mashreq, 1995), 30–31.

5. Ibid., 45.

6. Ibid., 19.

7. Haywood, *Modern Arabic Literature*, 61.

8. Ibid., 62.

9. Ibid.

10. Fakhoury, *Tarikh Al Adab Al 'Arabi*, or *History of Arab Literature*, 884.

11. Cheikho, *Fan Al Tiba'ah Fil Sharq*, or *History of the Art of Printing in the East*, 25–156. The extensive second chapter in his book is on "Fan Al Tiba'ah fil Sham," or "The Art of Printing in Al Sham," which is mostly devoted to the Lebanon with the last few pages to printing presses in Damascus and Aleppo.

12. Haywood, *Modern Arabic Literature*, 30.

13. Suleiman, Mohammed Basil, "Early Printing Presses in Palestine—A Historical Note," *Jerusalem Quarterly*, Number 36, p. 85. See also Cheikho's chapter on "Fan Al Tiba'ah fil Quds Al Sharif," or "The Art of Printing in the Noble Jerusalem," in his *Fan Al Tiba'ah Fil Sharq*, or *History of the Art of Printing in the East*, 157–169.

14. Cheikho, *Fan Al Tiba'ah Fil Sharq*, or *History of the Art of Printing in the East*, 171–187.

15. Haywood, *Modern Arabic Literature*, 64.

16. Ibid., 98.

17. Quotation of translated ode "Arise, Ye Arabs, and Awake," in Yaseen Noorani, *Culture and Hegemony in the Colonial Middle East*, Palgrave Studies in Cultural and Intellectual History (New York: Palgrave and Macmillan, 2010).

18. Al Hakawati. http://al-hakawati.net/english/Arabpers/ibrahim-al-yazigi.asp

19. Ibid.

20. Haywood, *Modern Arabic Literature*, 127.

21. Nader Habib, "Meeting the Taklas," *Al Ahram Weekly*, Issue Number 1201, June 12, 2014. http://weekly.ahram.org.eg/News/6506.aspx

22. See the Zeidan Foundation Enhancing Intercultural Understanding. www.zeidanfoundation.org/ZF_Website_AlHilal.html

23. In his book *The Arab World: Society, Culture and State*, Halim Barakat refers to an article published by Sarrouf and Nimr in the May 1885 issue of

the magazine *Al Muqtataf* on "Learning and Universities," in which they argued that knowledge cannot be achieved by any university unless it rids itself of religious fanaticism.

24. Haywood, *Modern Arabic Literature*, 60.
25. Fakhoury, *Tarikh Al Adab Al 'Arabi*, or *History of Arab Literature*, 1049.
26. Jacob M. Landau, *Studies in the Arab Theater and Cinema, Preface by Professor H. A. R. Gibb* (Philadelphia: University of Pennsylvania Press, 1958), 78.
27. Ibid., 79.
28. Haywood, *Modern Arabic Literature*, 89. Acknowledgment for the translated quotation is due to the Middle East Institute, Washington, DC.
29. See *Al Nahar* newspaper piece on Fouad Al Muhandes and his admiration and learning from Naguib al Rihani for the last two years of the life of Rihani, Issue Number 1022, August 15, 2010.
30. Landau, *Studies in the Arab Theater and Cinema*, 115.
31. Ibid., 102–103.
32. http://www.bibalex.org/alexcinema/cinematographers/Ibrahim_lama.html
33. http://www.youssefchahine.us/index2.html
34. Omar Al Dakkak, *Shatharat Forum of Arab Intellectuals and Researchers*, "Al Rabita Al Qalamiyah". http://www.shatharat.net/vb/showthread.php?t=11439
35. http://iloveallahmohamedislam.blogspot.co.il/2012/10/blog-post_229.html, "Al Sahafa Al 'Arabiyah fil Brazil," or "The Arabic Press in Brazil," October 27, 2012.
36. Karam Al Helou, "Review of Najma Hajar's *Amin Al-Rihani et le Renouvau Arabe Etude*," *Al Hayat* newspaper, Thursday, November 8, 2012, Langue et Culture Arabes. http://www.langue-arabe.fr/spip.php?article1127
37. Ibid.

CHAPTER 5

Christians in Arab Politics

Tarek Mitri

The Regional Context

The Arab uprisings or revolutions of 2011 initiated, in an unanticipated manner, transformations in a region that seemed resistant to change. For some time, expectations and hopes energized the process of transformation. Today's disillusionment, though understandable, is often rushed and at times engineered. It serves the purpose of justifying attempts to reverse transition, divert its course, and withdraw into defensive and regressive identity politics.

Overstating failures is the other side of the exaggerated enthusiasm evoked by the widespread use of the "Arab Spring" metaphor. Such usage brings to memory many short-lived springs, in our region, in Eastern Europe, and in nineteenth-century Europe. Their end seemed to overshadow their long-lasting effects.

Disillusionment, uncertainty, and fear notwithstanding, the yearning for dignity, freedom, and political participation that motivated revolutions against patrimonial authoritarian regimes cannot be dismissed as ephemeral. The broad-based social demand for democracy, no matter how vaguely conceived, is often ignored by those who precipitously opt for an essentialist and culturalist explanation of the difficulty, or even the

T. Mitri (✉)
Issam Fares Institute, American University of Beirut, Beirut, Lebanon

© The Author(s) 2018
K.C. Ellis (ed.), *Secular Nationalism and Citizenship in Muslim Countries*, Minorities in West Asia and North Africa, https://doi.org/10.1007/978-3-319-71204-8_5

impossibility, of transitioning towards a democratic polity and society. The weakness of state institutions that are grounded in the rule of law, and the fragility of national cohesion and identity are exacerbated further by the rapid and unanticipated collapse of the old order. These developments favor a tendency to over-emphasize the strength of primordial lies in comparison with civic ties that are constitutive of a modern democratic society. President Obama affirmed in a sweeping statement that the organizing principle in the Middle East is tribalism.[1] True, one cannot ignore the resurgence or reinvention of sub-national identities and the centrifugal forces at work in many Arab countries. Many members of communities, not only minorities, seem to have lost their aspirations to form a state for all. They beg for a power structure that can protect them from another community. Weakened states and political and electoral strategies of mobilization accentuate communalism and encourage the surfacing of narratives of victimhood, which are often emotional and aggressive.

Identity Politics: Actors and Victims

Ethnic groups, and ethnicized religious groups, are both actors and victims of identity politics. Throughout the twentieth century, their members struggled to assert themselves, and be recognized, as citizens. But many retreated and became minority-centered communities, "enclaved" when possible. If power relations permitted, some opted for autonomy and advocated federalist or separatist solutions to the weakened states and fragmented societies. Such expressions of identity politics are intertwined with post-uprising conflicts. Many leaders across the region do little more than tap into the persecution felt by communities without offering them alternatives to fear and uncertainty. Many are victims, but ethnic and religious minorities, Christians included, claim extraordinary victimhood, no matter if some, such as the Yezidis, have suffered far more than others.

The very conflicts that undermine what is left of the state become, for many rulers of the region, a source of legitimacy, a cause for further entrenchment and a distraction from addressing problems that they are not capable or unwilling to solve, such as in Syria, Iraq, Libya, and Yemen. It is not therefore a surprise to see violence becoming a policy by default.

Some would argue that the United States' political decision to retreat from the Arab world meant, in actual fact, endorsing the very forces fueling the Arab nations and states' self-destruction. One cannot ignore the extent to which the United States, despite its tendency to disengage, remains at the heart of Arab politics. Friends and foes alike continue to construct their narratives and define their courses of action on the basis of what they guess to be Washington's intention. A striking example is the Syrian regime, which while pretending to confront the United States, keeps an eye on its response as it crosses every possible red line. Russia would not have launched its war on Syrian soil and led the hesitant political process, were it not convinced that the Syrian opponents of the regime, unlike the Afghans of the 1980s, had no real support from their American rival.

In Europe, hesitant and incoherent attempts to pursue democratization in the Arab world, sanctioning human rights abuse, engaging moderate Islamists, developing humanitarian responses, resorting to diplomacy, and articulating a refugee policy are being overshadowed by or even subdued to one idea: accepting any power structure or initiative that might protect against *Daesh*,[2] the Islamic State, and the continuing spillover of a massive refugee movement.

Looking back at the endogenous transformations in the Arab world, one has abundant reasons to fear that for quite some time, many countries will continue to descend into disintegration, violence, and chaos. The state system has fallen in Iraq. In Lebanon, state institutions have become largely dysfunctional. In Palestine, the two-state solution is increasingly more elusive. There is no peace process; it has a process with no end game in sight. No less disastrous is the difficulty of reconstructing a cohesive national entity in view of Hamas' tight control of Gaza and unwillingness to mend relations with the Palestinian authority in Ramallah.

In the Arab Maghreb, Libya has not succeeded in re-emerging from its multiple civil wars. Tunisia is often regarded as a relative success in the post-uprising region. It has followed the path of a peaceful political transformation, bridging the gap between Islamists and secularists. A compromise transcending the political and ideological divide produced a progressive constitution and a government better placed, even if not fully effective, to face security threats, economic problems, and social disparities.

Egypt is still prey to a polarization between army and Islamists depicted indiscriminately as terrorists, including violent confrontations triggered by a reversal of the political process augured by the 2011 uprising.

In Syria, a peaceful and rather secular uprising was militarized by necessity, once the civilian population was repeatedly targeted by bloody repression. Calls for decisive protection of civilians remained unanswered, as the international community had no appetite for action. The Western military intervention in Libya, initially meant to protect civilian population in Benghazi and at the same time serve national interests of some European countries, failed in stabilizing Libya and facilitating its transition to democracy. This failure was invoked as an argument for the justification of passivity in Syria.

The regime's survival, largely attributed to Iranian support and in recent times, to Russian support, reveals an asymmetry that determines the course of a conflict which, more than anywhere else in the region, has extended beyond national borders. The massive influx of refugees into neighboring countries and its spillover into Europe, as well as the control of Daesh over swaths of territory, are illustrations of regionalization and internationalization of an internal conflict.

FROM *DHIMMA* STATUS TO THE PACT OF CITIZENSHIP

The Christians of the Arab world have been recognized as communities in law and public conscience since the birth of Islam. The statute, or rather the pact of the *dhimma*, while expecting their loyalty to the Islamic state, has protected them. Nevertheless, it also implies a measure of inferiorization, both civil and political. This recognition was a form of acceptance, or even legitimization, of religious plurality at a time when it was deficient elsewhere. But such pluralism, in the sense of an acceptance of plurality, was in its way a hierarchical pluralism.

In several regions, the Christians became a minority in terms of power relations before becoming a numerical minority, such as in Syria, where they outnumbered the Muslims until the twelfth century. Despite this, their contribution to the formation of the Arab-Islamic civilization cannot be treated as marginal. There were obvious limits because they were asked to be instrumental in building a society in which a religion that was not theirs was the cornerstone of legitimacy. Their role, however, was not confined to science, art, philosophy, and serving state institutions. Nor were the ideas that fashioned the thinking and institutions of the "Islamic Order" unfamiliar to the Christians. Nevertheless, their undeniably important role was weakened once the task of building a society had been completed.

Beginning in the early sixteenth century under the Ottomans, the *dhimma* system organizing pluralism reached its highest point of codification. The *millets*, which were both nations and religious communities, enjoyed relative autonomy. During the nineteenth century the picture changed. The ideologies and political and legal structures developed in Europe progressively penetrated the Arab-Muslim world. On the one hand, the European powers, tempted by the Ottoman Empire's weaknesses, and having adopted an imperialistic attitude, developed relations with various minority communities. On the other hand, the leaders of these communities were not unresponsive to the proposed "assistance." In fact, hierarchical pluralism was exploited in favor of the needs of external domination. The Christians were often faced with difficult choices that differed according to their character, religious affiliation, their social condition, and the political fluctuations they experienced. But on the whole they aspired to a "citizenship" freed from direct or indirect domination from abroad. While their fight for political and civil equality opposed them to the increasingly moribund Ottoman Empire, it united them with the Muslims in a national struggle for independence. For the majority of Christians, this struggle was to continue against the European nations after they had shared the spoils of the First World War.

The stakes of the struggles for national liberation were not just the future of the majority communities, but also the relationships between majorities and minorities. In the search for a new socio-political framework it was not enough to divide, or accept the division, of a geographic area and the distribution of different ethnic and religious groups throughout the territories. Collective identities had to be proposed in a way acceptable to different communities. Thus, the *Nahda*, or renaissance, movement largely initiated and sustained by Christians, was primarily cultural, as it paved the way for the emergence of political movements.

The role of the emerging national states was, in fact, reinforced even though the states were questioned in the name of a vision for unity of an Arab *umma*, an inclusive entity defined in cultural-linguistic terms rather than those of ethnicity or religion. This vision was considerably attractive. But neither the states nor the Arab nationalist movements, which had the same ideology as some states such as modern Iraq and Syria, succeeded in achieving national integration; nor could they modify radically the various traditional identities.

In the latter part of the nineteenth and in the early twentieth centuries, Christians played a role in shaping a new social and political order that far outweighed their numerical importance. Their contributions, more in cultural than political activity, attempted to shake loose their minority status and identity. More than a century later, it remains uncertain whether their post-*millet* consciousness survived the tragedies, failures, and disappointments of the twentieth century.

In the nineteenth century, secessionist tendencies grew as the local elites expanded their autonomy. It had also become evident that the non-territorial *millets* were not immune to foreign intervention. European support for different Christian communities gradually modified the balance of power within the Ottoman Empire. At the same time, projects of national revival and emancipation were at work among Christians. The diffusion of Western education through missionary schools accentuated differences between communities. Christians were opened to a new type of culture to which Muslims had a limited access. This acculturation provided the hitherto weaker Christians with a new means of self-affirmation. For them, Western influence was also frequently a source of economic prosperity and subtle forms of political power. Majority–minority relations were thus modified. New political opportunities permitted some Christian communities, or fractions of communities, to move rapidly, some would say abruptly, from passive acceptance of the *millet* system into a rather militant nationalist and, in certain cases, separatist strategy.

The nation-states that emerged from the empire, including modern Turkey, came as a rejection of the Ottoman past. Muslims faced a more serious problem than the Christians. A nation depends to a significant extent on the memory of great and mystified historical events or on the achievements attributed to it alone. Ruled by the Ottomans, Muslims shared their history. Emerging nation states in the Middle East, on the contrary, lacked a distinctive national experience.

A large number of Christians, however, were opposed to the separatist tendencies of some of their co-religionists. They opted for modern nationalist and universalizing ideologies. They emphasized their common ethnocultural identity with Muslims as the basis of independence and modern nation building. The patriotic bond cemented opposition to the Ottoman central and oppressive power and later to the dominating European powers. Accordingly, in the struggle for independence (and its achievement), the pact of citizenship was established, superseding the former *dhimma* pact. The revolution of 1919 in Egypt was a case in point. In Palestine, the pact of citizenship was affirmed as Christians and Muslims suffered together dispossession and ethnic cleansing.

The Resurgence of Communal Identities

But the attitudes of the *millet* system did not fade away. In the search for independence and liberation, Islamic self-awareness was intensified. A sometimes violent self-assertion gained visibility and appeal against the failure of modern, more or less secular, independent, and authoritarian governments.[3] In some instances, this led to anti-Christian feelings. It was said, and believed, that the colonial powers, and later national governments, gave preferential treatment to Christians and used them to benefit their domination. No matter how questionable these perceptions were, there will always be people, today as yesterday, who cannot, or do not dare, oppose those who make them angry. They look unconsciously for substitutes and often find them.

In short, the opening of the twentieth century suggested that a new society was in the making, yet it was ruled by an old state. More than a hundred years later, we see old societies in new states. Primordial ties, those of kin, ethnicity, and religion, seem to command more loyalties than civic relations. Some will argue that the revolt in Egypt may change the rule but it remains to be seen if the new constitution, and the subsequent political dynamics, will confirm anticipated confidence.

The force of communal identities among Christians is not a problem that Christians wrestle with alone. One ought to remember that loyalty to one's religious community deserves careful scrutiny. It is certainly a function of a combination of historical memory and spiritual impulse. But it is strengthened in times of pressure, or oppression against one's identity. Loyalty to a given religion, however, should not be assessed only in relation to critical situations. The strength of the bond that binds a religious community is determined by a long-term tendency to seek comfort and security in abiding by traditional beliefs and customs; it has a protective function against abrupt and risky change.

But religious identity and communal identity are not one and the same. Religiously identified institutions are influential in playing social and political roles even when fewer numbers of people believe or practice the religion that such institutions represent. In some extreme cases, people fight in the name of religions in which they have ceased to believe. There are tensions and conflicts that have a religious past, but their religious content is of no significance. Religions in which people have little or no faith continue to define communities, in which people have much faith.

Everywhere, and the Arab world is no exception, meaningful identities are multiple. Nevertheless, when various needs, material or spiritual, are being met or expressed in one identity, borders between communal loyalties are mutually enforced rather than mutually balanced. They create closed communities with exclusive memories, either activated or reinvented. Difference in community size becomes an issue of a minority threatened by a majority. Insecure communities in one place are tempted to seek protection from others elsewhere who are perceived to share a common identity, in order to achieve political empowerment, inviting external attention to, and support for, minority rights. Rather than strengthening such empowerment, external support often runs the risk of weakening further the minority communities it purports to rescue. National governments and political movements that are part of a majority community see their suspicion towards minorities justified and deepened.

POLITICAL UNCERTAINTIES AND CHRISTIAN FEARS

Breaking this cycle is not easy. The fears of Christians can be exorcised only by a nuanced analysis of Islamism or by the dialogue of informed elites. This is even more difficult, because despotic regimes—as we have seen in the era of popular uprisings—overplay fears and instrumentalize them. Moreover, some Christian politicians exacerbate fears for the purpose of dominating their communities while pretending to protect them. These same leaders, intensifying mistrust vis-à-vis the Muslim majority and decrying its supposed indifference to the Christians, make their coreligionists prisoners of an essentialist duality of opposing minorities and majorities.

For their part, those who manifest minority-centered attitudes, as well as disappointed secularists, have little taste for discernment. They hesitate less and less in rejecting political activism and react more and more to the threat—be it real or imagined—with resignation, leading to emigration or withdrawal. The latter implies internalization of marginality or, in many cases, an attempt to break its yoke by searching for success in the areas of economic activity or mastery of science and technology.

Christians have been constantly warned that the alternative to dictatorial regimes is Islamic fundamentalism or, even worse, chaos. Receptive to the alarmist discourse of despotic rulers or accustomed to succumbing to their pressure and occasional favors, a number of Christians from different walks of life have chosen to passively support what they perceived as secular authoritarian regimes. They thought that stability ensured their survival as "minorities" while the popular uprising carried the risks of open-ended instability and the threats of an uncertain future. Fearing the possibility of their marginalization, they seemed to retreat into a process of political self-marginalization and moral resignation. Conversely, we find among various Christian communities in the Arab world many individuals whose concerns could not justify shying away from the yearning for freedom and democracy and from active participation in the movements for change.

To a limited extent, both attitudes have polarized Christians since the demise of the Ottoman political and juridical order. There were times where the minority-centered consciousness of some Christians was transcended by others who advocated causes cutting across communal barriers, and in so doing tried to shake loose their minority status. Their role in the making of a new social and political order outweighed by far the numerical importance of Christians in the region. The disproportionately influential contribution of Christians in the modern movement of Arab awakening might explain, although only partially, why its promises seem in retrospect more far-reaching than what has been possible to achieve. Furthermore, the often justified disappointment of many paved the way, for some, to a bitter withdrawal into preservationist conservatism.

Christians aspired to full citizenship liberated from direct or indirect domination, external or internal. While their fight for political and civil equality made them opposed to the moribund Ottoman Empire, it united them with their Muslim compatriots in a national struggle for independence. For most of them, this combat was to continue against the European nations after those nations had shared the spoils of the First World War. Thus the stakes of the struggles for national liberation were not just the future of the majority communities, but also the relationships between majorities and minorities. Collective identities had to be proposed in a way acceptable to different communities. However, at the end of the twentieth century, the disillusionment of Arab peoples provoked by the failures of both national governments and nationalist political movements was quasi-general. For Christians in particular, such feeling was permeated with anxiety, arising from the effects of their dwindling numbers, accumulated economic difficulties, thinning political participation, and anguish in the face of mounting Islamism. However, this community-specific anxiety could not overshadow the fact that the worries of Christians are lived and expressed, *mutatis mutandis*, by a considerable number of Muslims. A number of Muslim voices acknowledge that, while Christians have their own reasons for disquiet, their difficulties reflect problems within the society as a whole. To be sure, the liberation of Christians is a necessary condition for the liberation of the Muslims. While accepting the particular character of Christian apprehension, many Muslims recognize an unease of their own. For most often, it is not the relationship between the Muslim majority and the Christian minority that is at stake but justice, political participation, human rights, and national dignity.

It remains true, however, that the Christian perception of relations between the majority and the minority is clouded by hostility toward Islamism and in particular toward its violent and radical movements. More often than not, the way many Christians look at their future is blurred by their perception of Islamism as monolithic. Some of them risk the dangerous pitfall of considering Islamism to be the most authentic expression—however excessive—of Islam itself.

Christians cannot be oblivious to the fact that self-assertion movements in the name of Islam gained visibility and appeal against the failure of modern, more or less secular, independent and authoritarian governments. In some instances, the success of these movements has led to anti-Christian feelings. It remains true, however, that the Islamist opposition to secular tyranny could be seen, as in a commonly used metaphor, as a wave; however big waves seem to be, they are diminished once they have used up their initial driving force. It may still be premature to suggest that the Arab uprisings may augur an era where many Islamist movements we presently know will have to reinvent themselves or lose part of their appeal.

For many decades, church leaders have tried to accompany their faithful along an arduous road. More often than not, they privileged what Jean Corbon called the risk of existing over the fear of disappearing.[4] They refrained from overplaying minority militancy and identity politics. The notion of Christian presence was their antidote to both aggressive communalism and withdrawal from public life. The role of church institutions was defined not only in terms of their functions of preservation but by the gospel-rooted imperative of witness and service to the neighbor. Churches never perceived Christians and Muslims as two monolithic blocks facing each other, nor did they oppose rights of the minority to aspirations of the majority.[5]

Today, Christians and church leaders are reminded by compatriots of their own recent history. No matter how legitimate their anxiety in the present times of uncertainty, they need not succumb to a sort of engineered fear. Exaggerated fear is commonly provoked and manipulated by despotic rulers, taking hostage the Christian minorities, linking their fate to their own and terrifying them about their future. Descending into engineered fear may endanger the ability of Christians to contribute toward shaping the future of their nations and of their own future. In addition, it alienates them from the majority of their people if they resign their ethical obligation to condemn oppressive violence and injustice.

The popular uprising in Syria was early on portrayed as a confrontation between the secular and the Islamists. The secular character of the Syrian regime is overstated while its communal and despotic features are ignored. The Syrian uprising is over-Islamicized, and the plural character of the Syrian opposition is denied. The loss of memory favors generalizations. One of these is the claim that Christians support Assad and recognize in him their protector from fanaticism and discrimination, failing to see the sad reality that Christians have become, in the political and literal sense, his human shield. Be that as it may, Christians do not hide their deep concern about what has been witnessed in Syria, nor do they deny their fears about the future. Such fears are induced, directly or indirectly, by minority-centered attitudes, rooted in historical memory, whether real or imagined. They are also grounded in the absence of Christian participation in public life and a degree of social isolation, imposed by the dictatorial regime for 50 years. Christian communities may well have retrogressed to a sort of *millet* condition, where they are granted certain rights and Churches limited freedom and prerogatives in managing some of their "internal affairs," in exchange for total loyalty and acquiescence to the deprivation of their political rights and parts of their civil rights. A culture of silence has prevailed, out of apprehension or caution, along with the internalization of fear from state repression and from enmities created by the regime. This culture has favored the tendency to lower expectations and accept minimal rights and perceive them, in certain cases, as privileges, leading to an overestimation of policies and measures in the areas of religious freedom and free economic activity.

Reclaiming Citizenship

In conclusion, in contrast with the paths walked by those who opt for an exclusively minority-centered militancy and by those who choose the silence of fear or resignation, there is a third way. This path is opened by the reinvention, through political participation, of the pact of citizenship that binds Christians and Muslims together, and by the renewal of the role that Christians played during the early-twentieth-century *Nahda* movement. To be sure, a new political and social order is in the making. The pact of citizenship that was a determining factor in various independence movements is to be reclaimed and enacted in the present longing of Arab peoples for freedom, dignity, and democracy.

Needless to say that the future of Christians in the Arab world does not only depend on the contributions they are capable of, but also on the attention that fellow Muslim co-citizens may give to them. Christians deserve, but also need to be worthy of, an attention that is not condescending but motivated by the sense of common good, along with recognition of the wealth of religious and cultural plurality whose preservation could spare the Arab world the sad face of uniformity.

Progress on the arduous road towards democratic transformation cannot be achieved by adopting a presumably universal model of transition. A paradigm for political change has to be suited to the realities of today, not the lingering hope of an earlier era. In the past, haste in moving forward did not adequately recognize the strength of sub-national identity assertion, nor cultural resistance to new norms of political practice. Not enough time was given to the first and crucial phase of transition, which is supposed to establish rules for public life accepted by all, ensuring the widest political participation and underlining inclusivity as an energizing principle. This principle is considered too costly for those in power, especially those who claim to be representing majorities. They refrain from reaching out to the fearful minorities—whether ethnic, religious or political. Equally, their inability to be inclusive contributes to the radicalization of the excluded.

Finally, we should not forget that times of uncertainty and fear are also times of change. The tension of turning victims into actors may not be resolved in the near future. Perceiving the present fragmentation and communalization as inevitable and designing political systems that mirror them, however, assumes they are never-changing realities. Voices suppressed today will not be silenced forever. In the midst of chaos and destruction, the emergence of forces striving toward equal citizenship and national unity may become, rather than an impossible dream, a principle of hope.

Notes

1. "One of the most destructive forces in the Middle East, Obama believes, is tribalism—a force no president can neutralize. Tribalism, made manifest in the reversion to sect, creed, clan, and village by the desperate citizens of failing states, is the source of much of the Muslim Middle East's problems, and

it is another source of his fatalism." See Jeffrey Goldberg, "The Obama Doctrine: The U.S. president talks through his hardest decisions about America's role in the world." *The Atlantic*, April 15, 2015. http://www. theatlantic.com/magazine/archive/2016/04/the-obama-doctrine/ 471525/

2. "DAESH is a transliteration of the Arabic acronym formed of the same words that make up ISIS in English: 'Islamic State in Iraq and Syria', or '*al-dowla al-islaamiyya fii-il-i'raaq wa-ash-shaam*'." Depending on how it is conjugated in Arabic, the word can mean "to trample down and crush." But it can also mean "a bigot." ISIS has reportedly threatened to cut out the tongues of anyone it hears using the term. Government officials choose the term to avoid using other, more common, names for the group. Using "Islamic" and "State" together offers legitimacy to the group, some believe. See: Patrick Garrity, "Paris Attacks: What Does 'Daesh' Mean and Why Does ISIS Hate It?" ABC News, November 14, 2015. http://www. nbcnews.com/storyline/isis-terror/paris-attacks-what-does-daesh-mean-why-does-isis-hate-n463551

3. "Classical Islamic law considers that only Muslims are full citizens of an Islamic society. As for the *kitabiyyin* (the 'Peoples of the Book'), they continue to benefit from their 'privileges' (their own law), under the protection of the Islamic State, but remain in the status which is subordinate from a political and civil point of view." Bernard Botiveau, "The Law of the Nation-State and the Status of non-Muslims in Egypt and Syria," in Andrea Pacini, ed. *Christian Communities in the Arab Middle East: The Challenge of the Future* (Oxford: Clarendon Press, 1998), 112.

4. "Middle Eastern Churches were not able to inherit a developed political culture, as they never had any experience of power. In the modern nations of the Mashreq, Lebanon alone has offered them the opportunity for it, which explains the stumbling pace and the tragedies of the last fifty years." Jean Corbon, "The Churches of the Middle East: Their Origins and Identity, from their Roots in the Past to their Openness to the Present," in Andrea Pacini, ed. *Christian Communities in the Arab Middle East* (Oxford: Clarendon Press, 1998), 99.

5. "When the Council of Middle Easter Churches was established in 1974, the first aim listed in its constitution was the survival of the Churches. For the same reason the seven Catholic Patriarchs sent a pastoral letter to their faithful on *Christian presence in the East: witness and mission*: 'We have chosen *presence* as an element of faith, which means that our presence in society in which we live is a sign of God's presence in the world. We are therefore called to be 'with', 'in', and 'for' society, not 'against', 'outside', or even 'on the margins of it.' This is an essential requirement of our faith, or vocation and our mission." Corbon, op. cit., 106.

CHAPTER 6

Christian Contributions to Education and Social Advancement

Sami El-Yousef

INTRODUCTION

The Christian presence in the Holy Land and across the Middle East has always been a diverse one, as it covers a wide ... variety of churches and is older than many neighboring nation states. Jerusalem, for example, is the seat of 13 heads of churches, including the Orthodox, Catholic, and the Evangelical churches. There are also over 125 Catholic religious congregations with presence in the Holy Land (Israel and Palestine).[1] Some are monastic in nature, while others are apostolates of service especially in the fields of education, healthcare, and social services. For the past few centuries, these communities have operated under many governing authorities, from the Ottoman Empire to the British Mandatory Administration and the modern states of Jordan, and lastly Israel and the Palestinian Authority, which has some influence on the population. As a matter of fact, people of my generation have a unique history, with each successive generation being born under a different governing authority. In my own family, my grandfather was born in 1890 during the tail end of the Ottoman Empire;

S. El-Yousef (✉)
Latin Patriarchate in Jerusalem, Jerusalem, Israel

© The Author(s) 2018   121
K. C. Ellis (ed.), *Secular Nationalism and Citizenship in Muslim Countries*, Minorities in West Asia and North Africa, https://doi.org/10.1007/978-3-319-71204-8_6

my father was born in 1921 during the Palestinian mandate; I was born in 1960 during Jordanian rule; and my four children were all born after 1967 and hold birth certificates issued by the State of Israel! Four generations born in the same city, and yet each generation has a birth certificate issued by a different authority. Despite this unstable situation, what has been a constant safety net in many people's lives has been the Church and the institutions of the various churches that provide services in education, healthcare, and social services. Thus, this presentation highlights this unique relationship between the living stones and the Christian institutions with focus on their contributions and challenges.

HISTORY OF RELIGIOUS CONGREGATIONS IN THE HOLY LAND

The region has a very rich history of the presence of religious congregations. The Orthodox presence certainly predates the Catholic one, but given that the Catholic institutional presence is more diverse and present in much greater numbers, the concentration here will be on the developments within the Catholic Church. In 1099, the Latin Patriarchal Diocese of Jerusalem was established with the Crusaders, though there was no residing Patriarch to govern the Church. Due to this void, Pope Clement VI asked the Franciscan Friars in 1342 to act as the guardians of the holy places and assure the presence of the Latin Church in the Holy Land and ensure the growth of the local church. This lasted for approximately 500 years. In 1847 Pope Pius IX reestablished the Latin Patriarchate, which marked the return of many religious orders and congregations to the Holy Land that we see today.[2]

There are 30 other religious orders and congregations of men maintaining convents, monasteries, schools, hospitals, academic institutions, and social programs. Among the most numerous are the Salesians of Don Bosco, the Monks of Bethlehem, the De La Salle Brothers, the Benedictines, the Dominicans, the Cistercian monks, the Incarnate Word Missionaries, and the Missionaries of Africa. Three of the congregations are Eastern rite (one Greek Catholic and two Maronite). There are 73 women's religious orders and congregations in the Holy Land. The largest is the Congregation of the Rosary Sisters, founded in 1880 by a Christian Palestinian from Jerusalem, Blessed Marie-Alphonsine Ghattas. This congregation runs many schools and other institutions, and the Sisters serve in many of the Latin parishes. The first congregation of women to arrive in the Holy

Land, in 1848, was the Sisters of Saint Joseph of the Apparition, serving in schools, hospitals, parishes, and a retreat house in the diocese.

Further, among the other congregations there are Franciscan Sisters of the Immaculate Heart of Mary, Teaching Sisters of Saint Dorothy, Nuns of Bethlehem and of the Assumption of the Virgin and of Saint Bruno, Franciscan Missionaries of Mary, Daughters of Charity of Saint Vincent de Paul, Benedictines, Religious of Nazareth, Sisters of Our Lady of Sion, Carmelites, Little Sisters of Jesus, Salesian Sisters, Sisters of Saint Elizabeth, Comboni Sisters, Missionaries of Charity of Mother Teresa, Sisters of Saint Bridget, Daughters of Saint Anne, Servants of the Lord and the Virgin of Matara, Franciscans of the Sacred Heart, and Adorers of Most Holy Sacrament. Eight of the congregations are Eastern rite. In addition to these orders and congregations, there are 20 institutes of consecrated life in the Holy Land.[3]

The beginnings of the educational aspect of these religious orders can be traced back to the sixteenth century, when the Franciscans opened a school in Bethlehem around the year 1518; this was followed by schools in Jerusalem and Nazareth. However, due to the prevalent political climate, the work of such congregations was limited in nature until the nineteenth century. Towards the end of the Ottoman rule, most services provided to the Arab communities in education, health, and social services were indeed offered by these religious congregations given the neglect of the governing authorities. As a matter of fact, the official records of the Department of Education for the years 1913–1914 demonstrate that 90 percent of all elementary school students in historic Palestine were educated at congregational schools, while a mere 10 percent were educated at public schools.[4]

Such religious congregations intensified their work in the second half of the nineteenth century with the establishment of schools, hospitals, clinics, orphanages, and old-age centers; during that period various churches were involved, including the Orthodox, Catholic, and Evangelical (Protestant) churches. The work of such religious congregations was dramatically expanded during the British Mandate of Palestine given the encouragement and support provided by the British government. A number of additional schools, special needs centers, and orphanages were started in addition to the expansion of existing institutions such as schools, clinics and hospitals. This expansion continued after the 1948 war in both Israel and Palestine and became an integral part of the services provided in these sectors. With the passage of time, a small number of institutions closed down due to reductions in external funding, but most other institutions continue to provide their services until today. What has further characterized the work of these church institutions is the quality of services provided, especially in education and health, as these institutions were staffed by religious people who had vocations in these disciplines.

STATISTICS ON THE CHRISTIANS IN THE HOLY LAND

In 1947, the Palestinian population of historic Palestine was 1,845,559, including 1,076,783 Muslims, 608,225 Jews, and 145,063 Christians.[5] That translates to the Christian population's being 7.9 percent of the total population, or 11.9 percent of the Palestinian population. Today the combined population of Israel and Palestine is approximately 13.3 million. Had the Christian population been maintained, there would be approximately one million Christians in the same geographical territory as in 1948. However, current reality proves otherwise.

Israel today has 8.52 million people, 74.8 percent of whom (or 6.38 million) are Jewish; 20.8 percent are Arab (or 1.77 million people), with the rest (4.4 percent, or 374,000) classified as "Other," most of whom are non-Arab Christians or members of other religions. Of the Arab population, the indigenous Christians constitute 165,000 people, or just under 2 percent of the population of the State of Israel.[6]

The Palestine scene paints an even bleaker picture, where Christians constitute at best about 51,760 to a population[7] of 4.82 million (2.94 million in West Bank including East Jerusalem and 1.88 million in Gaza).[8] This is a mere 1 percent of the population, and that number is gradually decreasing. If we review the statistics for Bethlehem, the birthplace of Christ, the number of Christians back in 1947 was about 85 percent but by 1998 the figure declined to 40 percent, while today that number is estimated to be 18 percent.[9] If we also look at the figures for the Gaza strip, the Christian population there is a mere 1313[10] or 0.07 percent of the population, compared to 3000 people just a few years ago.

The reasons for these sharp declines in the Christian presence are many and varied. The main reason is the political instability and the repeated conflict between Israel and the Palestinians, leading to harsh economic conditions, lack of freedom and security, and more recently, the spread of fanatic Islamic movements across the Middle East.

With these declines in the Christian population, we can see why these trends have become very important, especially in that they do not match the Christian institutional presence in our region and its value and active contribution to the service sectors.

CHRISTIAN INSTITUTIONAL PRESENCE: DISPROPORTIONATE CONTRIBUTIONS

To be able to truly appreciate the Christian contributions in Israel, we must note that today there are 47 Christian schools serving a total of 33,000 students of all faith traditions including Christians, Muslims, Druze, and Jews.[11] In addition, there are approximately 40 kindergartens serving the Arab population. These schools serve 50 percent of all Arab students in Nazareth: 80 percent of this group in Haifa and 40 percent in Jaffa.[12] As far as the health sector is concerned, there are four major hospitals and numerous clinics and dispensaries, with five institutions catering to the needs of people who are physically or mentally challenged. As for other institutions, there are no less than four institutions that provide safe havens to the youth as well as 15 community centers that cater to the general public. Finally, one of the striking presences is in the large number of scout troops that belong to the two largest churches, where there are 18 Catholic scout troops and 14 Orthodox.[13] Not only are scout troops visible during religious and national celebrations, but more importantly, embody the value set of volunteerism and community service that is instilled in the upbringing of the youth in addition to the traditional scouting principles.

As for the Palestine scene, among the bright stars in this Holy Land are the institutions of the various churches providing services in the areas of education, health care and social services. According to a study by Diyar Consortium in Bethlehem conducted in 2008, there are 261 institutions of the various churches in Palestine, including 121 working in education such as schools, colleges, vocational training centers, and higher education; 29 providing services in the health sector, such as hospitals and clinics; 30 providing social services, including orphanages and old age centers; and 73 working in a variety of other sectors including sports, youth, environment, and culture. Further, and according to the same study, this constitutes some 45 percent of the non-governmental organizations (NGO) sector in Palestine.[14] This certainly is a disproportionate contribution of service to the community, where the demographics of our region is such that indigenous Christians number around 210,000 people, or 1.6 percent of the population, in Israel and Palestine combined. It should be stressed that the services provided are in all instances open to all segments of society, with no discrimination of any kind, in most instances targeting the marginalized and poor. In some geographic areas—and I point to Gaza as a very clear example where about 1300 Christians live in a population of close to two million Muslims—the recipients of the services of the Christian institutions are predominantly non-Christian. This is an example of how the Christian community influences society without discrimination.

CATHOLIC SCHOOLS

Out of all the Christian institutions, the largest network of schools operating in the Holy Land is by far the Catholic schools network followed by the Greek Orthodox schools. As for the Orthodox schools, there are 19 schools serving the Holy Land (2 in Israel, 7 in Palestine, and 10 in Jordan). In total, 6883 students attend these schools.[15] By comparison, there are 108 Catholic schools serving in the same territory, providing a quality education to 56,594 students and employing 6762 teachers and support staff. The overall percentage of Christian students is 48 percent. However, this percentage varies greatly from location to location. The schools that cater to students with special needs have a particularly low percentage of Christian students (about 1 percent). In other locations where the Christians are in the majority, in a rural setting, for example, the percentage is in the 90–100 range. As for the trend in enrollment in Christian schools, there has been an overall slow but steady decline in Christian student enrollment of 4 percent with the highest decline in Palestine, amounting to 7 percent. Table 6.1 provides key statistics for the Catholic schools.[16]

Table 6.1   Key enrollment trends in catholic schools in the holy land

	Number of schools	Total number of students	Percentage Christian	Student trend in 5 years	Christian students decline (5 year trend)	Christian students range	Personnel (teaching, admin and support)
Israel	29	18,035	61%	−3%	−4%	13–91%	2052
Palestine	31	15,975	36%	+5%	−7%	1–84%	1775
Jordan	48	22,583	45%	+3%	−2%	4–100%	2935
Total	108	56,594	48%	+2%	−4%		6762

Unfortunately, similar statistics for the other Christian schools are hard to come by, but the profile is similar to the Catholic schools. In many of the geographical areas where these schools operate, the majority of the student population is a non-Christian population, and the statistics confirm the fact that these modern-day schools do not exist to serve the Christian community, but rather society at large. What is noticeable is the five-year trend in enrollment, which witnessed a general decline of 3 percent in Israel at a time when the general Palestine enrollment increased by 5 percent, while in Jordan it increased by 5 percent. Thus the most dramatic case is the one in Palestine where the Christian enrollment declined by 7 percent at a time when the overall enrollment increased by 5 percent. This is quite significant and is an indication of the continued emigration of Palestinian Christians due to a variety of reasons, the most obvious one being the continued occupation and the political deadlock gripping the region. However, other studies suggest that in some locations, Christian students' enrollment is on the decline due to economic reasons, as fewer Christian families can afford the cost of private education or the cost of transportation. One example is Gaza, where a study of the Christian community there revealed that only 54.2 percent of the Christian students attend a Christian school, while 36 percent attend public schools, and 9.8 percent attend United Nations (UNRWA) schools as registered refugees.[17] This was certainly a striking finding, as one would have expected a much larger percentage of the Christian students to be attending Christian schools given that there are five such schools in Gaza and given the unique circumstances of Gaza. This example demonstrates that the Christian community in many instances faces the same challenges of the larger society in which they are fully integrated.

CHRISTIAN VALUES

The guiding principles of the Christian community and the Christian institutions are the value set that is practiced within Christian families. Thus, Christians apply these traditions and instill them in the mission and work of the Christian institutions. These values are more needed today than ever before, values that Christians not only live by and teach to their children, but also teach to anyone who becomes affiliated with them. Thus, the church instills the much-needed values of faith in God, respect, self-control and moderation, honesty and integrity, kindness and compassion, contentment and thoughtfulness, patience and perseverance, peace and humility, and loyalty and commitment.

In my own line of work, as the regional director of the CNEWA-Pontifical Mission for Palestine office in Jerusalem, a temporary agency of the Holy See set up in 1949 to do humanitarian and development work in service of the poor and weak in the countries where we operate, I am frequently on field visits to various institutions and communities throughout Israel and Palestine. In many instances, such services are directed to non-Christians. In all my field visits and encounters with recipients of our institutional services, I have yet to come across a person who has not been touched in one way or another by our Christian values. Some will come out and say it in very clear terms that they cherish the value set they are privileged to encounter. In others, you see the value set in the attitude and behavior! One of the most touching encounters I have ever had in my life was when I assumed the duties of my current work at the Pontifical Mission some seven years ago, and was asked to go to Gaza, of all places, to check on the work that was just concluded rebuilding a clinic belonging to the Near East Council of Churches that was reconstructed and fully equipped after it was completely demolished by an Israeli F-16 jet in the last days of the first war on Gaza in January 2009. As one of my very first duties I reluctantly went to Gaza questioning our involvement in Gaza given that there are only 1300 Christians there, none of whom is a recipient of the services of this clinic, which is located in one of the poorest neighborhoods of Gaza City, the Shajaia neighborhood. I walked into the clinic and it was packed with Muslim women along with their children, since this is a mother and child clinic. Out of curiosity, I went straight to two of the women and I asked them a very simple question: why do you come to this clinic for services while there are other clinics nearby offering similar services, all of them are free of charge. The two women answered without any hesitation: *"This is the only place where we come to receive a service and we are treated as human beings, with full respect while preserving our dignity!"* Even though I have lived in this land throughout my life and worked for Catholic institutions for over 30 years, never before had I gotten such an unqualified response on how much the value set is instilled through our Christian institutions.

Interfaith Dialogue: The Lived Experience

Another dimension where Christian institutions shine is in the area of interfaith—with three core values: understanding, respect, and dialogue. As mentioned previously, in many instances, our institutions offer services to beneficiaries of different faith traditions. In Palestine, this clientele is mostly Christian and Muslim beneficiaries. In Israel, in some instances, depending on the location and the type of service, the beneficiaries are Muslims, Christians, Druze, and Jews. One can only imagine the interfaith dialogue that is "*lived*" rather than being taught or discussed in academic conferences or between religious hierarchs including Muftis, Rabbis, and Bishops ... students of all faiths that study together, grow up together, learn to respect each other, and form lifelong relationships inspired by Christian values end up developing into solid citizens of the country and forming the next level of leaders. What better interfaith appreciation and dialogue than what goes on in the classroom, or in a hospital room where patients regardless of their faith tradition learn to appreciate each other as equal human beings believing in the one God. Even when there is violence on the streets and societies are completely polarized, these institutions remain immune to the calls for hatred and revenge that you hear on the streets.

Humanitarian Support and Response to Crisis: The Case of Gaza

In 2005, Israel unilaterally withdrew from Gaza, evacuating all Israeli settlers in the process and gradually isolating the area. In 2006, the Palestinians had open and free elections that favored Hamas, a fundamentalist Islamic party, and gave them a landslide win in the Legislative Council. In 2007, Hamas led a coup against the ruling Fatah party and took over the Gaza Strip, forming its own government and imposing fundamentalist Islamic rule over Gaza. Needless to say, this heightened tensions, as the Christian community and institutions had to face new realities. One of the most controversial moves was the decision by the Ministry of Education to segregate students and teachers by sex. This would have impacted all five Christian schools serving a total population of over 3000 students, most of them Muslims. All Christian schools in Gaza offer a co-educational experience. Ultimatums were given to the schools that unless they segregated, they would be shut down. In addition, Christian symbols became clearly unwelcome, and even Christmas trees were not allowed on public display. Christian women students studying in some universities in Gaza had to conform to the traditional Islamic dress code. In short, this was a dramatic shift in lifestyle for the Christian community and for the Christian institutions involved. This tension lasted for a few years without any major change.

On the other hand, Gaza witnessed three wars in a span of six years. The first one lasted for 20 days between December 2008 and January 2010, the second one was shorter but no less devastating and lasted for eight days in November 2012, while the last one was the most intense and lasted for 51 days in July and August 2014. The amount of physical destruction in all sectors spanning from education to health, infrastructure, and the economy was simply beyond imagination.

What was noticeable was that the first responders during each active war were the Christian institutions. Convents, Christian schools, and community centers opened their doors as temporary shelters to receive the internally displaced, as over 50 percent of the land of Gaza was declared a closed military area. At the height of the conflict, an estimated 485,000 people—28 percent of the population of Gaza—were internally displaced.[18] The sole Christian hospital as well as the clinics remained operational despite bomb raids, electricity shortages, and limited supplies, providing critical lifesaving medical services; hygiene and food packages and clean water were distributed by the major Christian humanitarian organizations in addition to local Christian organizations. In short, the few Christian organizations in Gaza were the shining stars in a sea of desperation. This certainly did not go unnoticed by the local government and by the community at large. Appreciation was shown immediately after the war as the tension that had developed in relation to the Christian community receded dramatically. The first Christmas bazaar took place a few months after the last war, and Christmas trees were no longer forbidden. The highest political figures in the Hamas hierarchy met with the religious leaders and Christian dignitaries to congratulate them for Christian feasts. The Greek Orthodox scout troop is making a comeback in Gaza, and the gender segregation issue at the Christian schools has been shelved for the time being.

Life in Gaza continues to be a great challenge, and I do not wish to paint a rosy picture for the Christian community or for Christian institutions there, as they continue to face many challenges; but I wish to stress the role Christian institutions play in an emergency setting and what impact this has had on changing the perception and attitudes toward Christians.

Conflict formally started in the region 69 years ago (as of this writing), with the establishment of the State of Israel in 1948, and solidified in 1967, or 50 years ago, with the illegal occupation of the West Bank, including East Jerusalem and the Gaza Strip. Thus, the continuing occupation coupled with the breakdown of negotiations between the two sides have led to repeated conflicts, some of them major ones, including the first Intifada (1987), the second Intifada (2000), and three successive wars for various periods on Gaza in December 2008, November 2012, and July

2014. But apart from labels, one must acknowledge that the current situation is a very dangerous one indeed, where we see total polarization between two peoples practicing three faiths who are supposed to live as good neighbors side by side in peace and harmony. Governments on both sides seems to demonize each other and spread hatred and suspicion of the other. The separation wall, which has been under construction for over ten years, has created not only a physical barrier, but a psychological barrier, since the human face is lost between the two sides. Most of the younger generations of Palestinians and Israelis do not interact with each other, and stereotypes are entrenched. For any Palestinian child, after the construction of the wall, their only encounter with Israelis is with soldiers conducting raids at night and arresting their friends and neighbors, or with settlers stealing more land and constructing more Jewish-only settlements. For them every Israeli is their jailor, as Israel created the largest open air prison in the world with the construction of the wall, denying the Palestinian masses most of their basic human rights.

Likewise, for every Israeli child, the construction of the wall was a necessary evil to "*protect*" them from the Palestinians, who are all labeled "potential terrorists" who only wish to harm Israelis and ultimately destroy Israel; the implication is that the Palestinians have brought this harsh life upon themselves! Where is the human face in this sad reality? I believe when Pope Francis visited Bethlehem in May 2014 and departed from his regular tour and asked to stop by the separation wall, got out of his car, touched the wall, and prayed for its removal, his Holiness knew very well the great psychological damage it is creating as well as the destructive impact it is having, especially on the younger generations on both sides. In this regard, as the message on the streets is one of hatred and revenge, the only places where you experience the message of peace, love, respect, coexistence, acceptance, and tolerance are Christian institutions. This should never be underestimated, as eventually this message filters through, leaving an impact on those who are affiliated with these institutions.

CHALLENGES FOR THE CHRISTIAN INSTITUTIONS: CONTINUED FUNDING

In Israel, Christian institutions providing services in many sectors, including education, health, and social services, receive subsidies from the various relevant ministries for taking a load off public institutions. With the exception of schools, such subsidies cover most of the operating costs; the challenge then becomes capital development projects and equipment needs. All these institutions are subject to reviews by government inspectors who demand that such institutions meet certain codes or face fines and eventually closures. Since most such institutions are housed in old buildings that are in some instances 150–200 years old, meeting modern building codes is very expensive and extremely challenging. A case in point is Saint Louis Hospital in Jerusalem, built in 1879 and run by the Sisters of Saint Joseph of the Apparition. In 2010, the inspectors of the Israeli Ministry of Health found many deficiencies and gave a long list to hospital management of repairs needed in order to maintain their license. In light of the fact that the repairs would require major structural work in the building, the hospital was given five years to complete the work and meet the codes. Given the good connections of the hospital administration and a very energetic young director, a multi-million-dollar five-year plan was devised which ultimately saved the hospital from being shut down. Though this was a clear success story, other institutions were not as lucky, and some of their operations were suspended. The operations of the St. Vincent de Paul orphanage in Jerusalem were suspended, as the Sisters could not secure the funding in time to do the renovations and meet the deadline set by the inspectors of the Ministry of Social Affairs.

In the sector of education, the challenges are different, as the trend in recent years has been to cut the subsidies to the 47 Christian schools in Israel serving 33,000 students of all faiths. Over the past several years, the cuts amounted to 45 percent—at the present time a mere 29 percent of the operating costs of the schools are covered by the government.[19] This has created a serious financial crisis, as not only do the schools have to worry about much needed-renovations and equipment upgrades, but also a large percentage of their operating costs must be fundraised from external sources. Thus the whole sector of Christian schools in Israel is in crisis mode and must try to find alternate sources of funding, and thus some major decisions will have to be made in the very near future.

In Palestine, the situation is completely different, given that the private schools, including all Christian schools, do not receive any government subsidies and are mostly on their own. Luckily the Latin Patriarchate network of schools relies on the Equestrian Order of the Holy Sepulcher of Jerusalem to provide funding for their schools, the Custody of the Holy Land provides funding for the Terra Santa Franciscan network, the Greek Orthodox Patriarchate supports their network of schools, etc. This is by no means an easy task given that as economic conditions worsen from year to year, parents' ability to pay tuition becomes more challenging. As far as international donors are concerned, the scenario is all too familiar: they do not provide funds to cover operating costs. Despite the many financial obstacles they face, these schools until now have continued to make ends meet and provide quality services under extremely challenging conditions.

GREATER RESPONSIBILITY FOR CHRISTIAN INSTITUTIONS AND THE NEED TO SUSTAIN THEM

The construction of the separation wall and the continuing occupation has created a situation that only fosters more polarization, demonization, hate, and fear of the other. Thus, more emphasis must be placed on the Christian institutions to work harder than ever before to instill a message of hope and faith in the people under their care. This will help the younger generation see the human face in the other and adopt the Christian value set that is so desperately needed today more than at any time in the past. Our Christian institutions have been through similar trying conflicts and crises, as some of them predate all the recent troubles with some schools and hospitals established over 150 years ago. Thus, the accumulated experience of earlier conflicts coupled with emphasis on the value set should empower our institutions to help the population at large deal with this conflict, as they have done repeatedly before. This assumes that the external environment will not dramatically change, as it has in some of the neighboring countries such as in Syria and Iraq.

Christian contributions to education, healthcare, and social advancement are huge in comparison to the size of the Christian presence and constitute a disproportionate contribution to the building of the various social services. This institutional presence is the pride of the Christian witness, as services are provided to all segments of society with no distinction as to religion, ethnic group, gender, or nationality. Further, Christian institutions constitute the backbone of the Christian presence in the various countries where they are present. Generation upon generation has been able to carry on this tradition and keep these institutions open and thriving. However, with the changing face of the Middle East as a whole and the Holy Land in particular, will we be able to maintain the tradition and keep this Christian witness alive? Will the living stones remain or will they emigrate, leaving a Holy Land consisting of churches and monument holy sites staffed by a few religious men and women? This is the challenge facing all of us as we move forward.

NOTES

1. "Directory of the Catholic Church in the Holy Land." *Assembly of the Catholic Ordinaries in the Holy Land* (Jerusalem: Latin Patriarchate Printing Press, 2014), 6–10.
2. Bathish, Bishop Kamal. "Latin Patriarchate of Jerusalem," 2005. Accessed November 12, 2016. http://www.lpj.org/Nonviolence/Patriarch/LP.html
3. Claudia, *Churches in the Holy Land-Religious Congregations in the Holy Land*. Jerusalem, March 19, 2014. http://popefrancisholyland2014.lpj.org/blog/2014/03/19/orders-and-congregations-in-the-holy-land/
4. Farah, Fouad. *The Living Stones—Christian Arabs in the Holy Land* (Nazareth: Al-Hakeem Press, 2003).
5. Ibid.
6. *Israel Population on the Eve of the 68th Independence Day*. Media Release (Jerusalem: Central Bureau of Statistics in Israel, 2016). www.cbs.gov.il/hodaot2016n/11_16_055e.pdf
7. Collings, Rania A, Rifat O Kassis, and Mitri Raheb, *Palestinian Christians in the West Bank Facts, Figures and Trends* (Bethlehem: Diyar, 2010).
8. *Estimated Population in the Palestinian Territory Mid-Year by Governorate, 1997–2016*. Statistical Report (Ramallah: Palestine Central Bureau of Statistics, 2016). http://www.pcbs.gov.ps/Portals/_Rainbow/Documents/gover_e.htm
9. Pacini, Andrea, *Socio Political and Community Dynamics of Arab Christians in Jordan, Israel and the Palestinian Territories* (Oxford: Clarendon Press, 1998).
10. Murad, Rami, Ali Abuzeid, and Ali Bandi, *Survey of the Christian Community in the Gaza Strip*. Survey (Gaza: Young Men's Christian Association, 2014), 29.
11. The Office of Catholic Schools in Israel, *Statement of Christian Schools in Israel* (Jerusalem: Latin Patriarchate in Jerusalem, August 31, 2015). http://en.lpj.org/wp-content/uploads/2015/08/31-8-statment.pdf
12. Farah, op. cit.
13. Mansour, Johnny, *Arab Christians in Israel Facts, Figures and Trends* (Bethlehem: Diyar, 2012).
14. Collings, Kassis and Raheb, op. cit.
15. The Greek Orthodox Patriarchate of Jerusalem, *Administrative Structures/Educational Centers*. Accessed November 12, 2016. http://www.jerusalem-patriarchate.info/eng
16. The Greek Orthodox Patriarchate of Jerusalem, *Administrative Structures/Educational Centers*. Accessed November 12, 2016. http://www.jerusalem-patriarchate.info/eng

17. Murad, Abuzeid and Bandi, op. cit.
18. United Nations Office for the Coordination of Humanitarian Affairs. 2014. *Occupied Palestinian Territory: Gaza Emergency Situation Report (as of 4 September 2014, 08:00 hrs)*. Emergency Situation Report, United Nations. http://www.ochaopt.org/content/occupied-palestinian-territory-gaza-emergency-situation-report-4-september-2014-0800-hrs
19. Ambroselli, Miriam, *Israeli Ministry of Education classifies Christian schools among the best in the country*. Jerusalem, August 22. Accessed November 12, 2016. http://en.lpj.org/2016/08/22/israeli-ministry-of-education-classifies-christian-schools-among-the-best-in-the-country/

PART II

Human Rights, Combating Persecution, and the Responsibility to Protect

CHAPTER 7

The Arab-Christian Predicament Before and After the Rise of the Islamic State

Elie Chalala

In the past, in both my professional and academic careers, I have avoided directly addressing the religious or sectarian question in Lebanon and the Arab world at large. As someone who spent his formative years in Lebanon and never lost interest in that country, I did not feel the need to address religion or sectarianism themes. Theoretical and personal reasons exist for my lack of interest in this area, and perhaps my secular background also dissuaded me from this discussion. However, the empirical situation in contemporary Lebanon, and in the Arab world, has now convinced me to confront these issues. While sectarianism obviously predates today's events, a multitude of changes have awakened dormant sectarian tendencies towards intolerance, producing dark forces of unprecedented magnitude which permeate many aspects of Arab life. This crisis threatens the very existence of Lebanon, as well as other Arab countries, and and has led to endless conferences convened in order to protect and preserve Christianity in the Middle East, particularly in Lebanon.

Specifically, reviews of *The Survival of Christians in the East is a Muslim Choice* (published in Arabic by Dar Saer Al Mashreq, 2016, 2nd ed.), written by Lebanese historian and TV host, Antoine Saad, inspired me to weigh in at this particular time. The work reflects Saad's near-authoritative

E. Chalala (✉)
Al Jadid Magazine, Cypress, CA, USA

© The Author(s) 2018   139
K. C. Ellis (ed.), *Secular Nationalism and Citizenship in Muslim Countries*, Minorities in West Asia and North Africa,
https://doi.org/10.1007/978-3-319-71204-8_7

status on Lebanese Christians. He has written biographies about Patriarch Nasrallah Boutros Sfeir, previous head of the Maronite Church, and former Lebanese foreign minister Fouad Boutros, as well as works about other religious and political Lebanese figures. *Survival* addresses the Christian presence in the Middle East, exploring both its historical and contemporary contexts, leading up to the post-Arab Spring period. It expresses the author's great concern about the persecution and declining numbers of Christians in the Middle East, which has caused him to fear for their very survival.

Saad contends that Christians in the Mashreq and in Lebanon have lost whatever influence they once enjoyed and calls upon Muslim elites to help them regain that influence, lest Christians fall victim to extreme religious groups. His main argument concerns his belief that, in general, Christian Arab survival depends upon Arab Muslims' intervening to maintain sectarian diversity in the region and thus choosing to allow Arab Christians to stay. As for Lebanese Christians, their survival depends on their own elites, but that represents a discussion reserved for a later time. In this chapter, I will focus on Saad's thesis concerning Arab Christians in Iraq and Syria.

According to Samir Nassif, who reviewed *Survival* for *Al Quds Al Arabi* newspaper, Saad indulges in too much generalization, not specifying which Christian and Muslim social classes he refers to, and thus lumping everyone together. While Nassif incorrectly renders the current conflict in Lebanon only in terms of class antagonisms, making his focus a bit pointless, he does correctly identify Saad's limited traditional methodology, citing his emphasis on improving the plight of the Christians through the creation of more opportunities for them, rather than by calling for change in the infrastructure of Mideast societies.

Despite such valid criticisms, Saad unquestionably offers many valuable contributions to the literature on Arab Christians in the Middle East. Still, the problematic aspects of Saad's thesis remain threefold: the idealistic nature of his solutions, Christian passivity, and the exoneration of Christians from responsibility for their quandary. He also provides a misguided historical account of Christian roles under authoritarian regimes like Iraq and Syria.

While Saad correctly states that Muslims must be the ones to amend the injustices visited upon Iraqi and Syrian Christians, his idea of appealing to the conscience of Muslim elites for a solution, while also telling them what would be in their own best interests, hardly constitutes a practical resolution, and implies a rationality in the decision-making process that may not always be present. Even if, for the sake of argument, we assume Saad's proposal to be both sensible and rational, it assumes capacity and willingness to dedicate time and resources towards the problem, while also requiring an environment that will allow both Muslim groups and Christian elites to pursue their long-term interests without constraint from the limitations of their own minds or, crucially, from external forces over which they have no control. Yet Muslims find themselves locked in an almost existential war, where Christians remain marginal players, with any harm that befalls them easily dismissed as collateral damage. Whether in Iraq or Syria, an ongoing sectarian war rages between Shiites, Alawites and their allies, on one hand, and Sunnis and their supporters, on the other. Looking at these countries, it's hard to imagine that Muslim moderate elites, retreating before the advance of extremists, will have time and resources to spare for the Christian crisis.

This, however, does not relieve Muslim elites of responsibility for the well-being of Christian communities in the countries where these elites still exercise power. In fairness, historians, including Saad, do credit such Muslim elites in the post-independence period with having given Arab Christians more substantive roles in politics than those granted by praetorian regimes that succeeded them. Still, more needs to be accomplished in this area.

Another limitation of Saad's argument lies in portraying Arab Christians—he excludes Lebanese Christians—as passive players, unable to influence the course of events. He correctly recognizes that Christians lack a major armed force or presence capable of influencing the balance of power, in the manner of Hezbollah. Nonetheless, many Iraqi Christians did lend their support to the Baathist regime, something that cannot be explained in strict confessional terms. Were we to return to the interwar period, we would find also Christians in the Levant quite receptive to the nationalist appeal of totalitarian and extreme nationalist parties, some of which overtly sympathized with Nazi Germany. With the death of the Ottoman *millet* system, the state protection of non-Muslim minorities ended. Christian intellectual elites across the Levant had to choose between the liberal, democratic political parties and a nationalist, socialist-communist one. The rationale for many of their choices derived from idealistic beliefs that nationalist states would guarantee minorities equality despite their sects and numbers, while communist states would ensure them equality regardless of both sects and class. This meant that students of Arab politics found significant segments of their intellectual leadership emerging from minoritarian backgrounds—Christians, Kurds, Jews, Alawites, and others. These minorities feared elections and the notion of a majority rule. For many minority groups, including Christians, "majority" meant Muslim. Thus, to avoid the potential tyranny of the majority, they sought salvation in regimes inspired by nationalist, Baathist, and communist parties.

Although far from the characterizations of Saad's passive players, choices like these have often failed to benefit Arab Christians, nor have they resulted in political appointments with as much influence as appearances would have suggested. In Iraq, Christians sided with Saddam Hussein, but this alienated the Shiite majority, which suffered persecution at the hands of the Baathist regime. Nor did Saddam's appointment of an Iraqi Christian foreign minister, Tarik Aziz (1936–2015), indicate a significant political role for Iraqi Christians. By most accounts, Aziz and others like him held what amounted to ceremonial positions and did not represent Christian constituencies in any real way. In fact, these appointments represented rather cynical messages to Western powers, with the Assads hoping to hide their extreme sectarianism by emphasizing the secular nature of their regime. Baathists even attempted to cultivate Iraqi Christian support for the regime as a buffer to opposition by both the Shiite majority and the substantial Kurdish minority.

Other outside factors have also impacted life for Iraqi Christians. Recently, print, electronic, and social media outlets revealed vivid images of what befell Iraqi Christians, but failed to mention that their difficulties began immediately after the 2003 U.S. invasion. U.S. policies under the Bush administration and the de facto authority in cooperation with the Shiite political parties in occupied Iraq showed a pronounced indifference to religious freedoms and human rights and failed to prioritize issues such as the demographic Christian flight towards the Kurdish areas in northern Iraq.

The rise of ISIS resulted in the worst kinds of atrocities towards Christians. Former Sunni Baathist officers, working in collaboration with other foreign non-Iraqi Sunnis, constituted a sizable proportion of this murderous organization's rank and file. While Shiite paybacks and persecution of Christians caused them to flee to Kurdish areas, ISIS barbarities forcefully pushed them back to the north, and outside the country, away from lands which they had called home for centuries.

Clearly the close alliance of Iraqi Christians with Saddam backfired. Saad does correctly point out that Christians fared better under the post-independence constitutional and non-military regimes; but the damage was done, and the demographic hemorrhage has continued. No matter the cause, the total numbers prove alarming insofar as the future of Christians in Syria is concerned. Throughout the 1970s and part of the 1980s, the consensus suggested that Christians made up between 9 and 10 percent of the population. Today, it has fallen to between 4 and 5 percent. Thus, two questions confront us: Where did the Christians go and why? Lebanon, with a sizable Christian community, could not become a permanent destination for so many, as circumstances have caused Lebanese Christians to immigrate in large numbers, with Syrian Christians following suit. So Arab Christians, have, for the most part, immigrated to different parts of the world, including a substantial number who first moved to Lebanon, but then made their way to the Gulf, Europe, North America, and Australia.

Only those who bought the regime's line of secularism and commitment to minority rights find the reasons behind the large number of emigrating Syrian Christians perplexing. Ironically, when invoking the question of Syrian Christians, the discussion becomes suspiciously ahistorical, focusing exclusively on the post-Arab Spring period and the rise of ISIS. Still, the origins of the Syrian Christian ordeal go back to the 1960s and even to the Syrian–Egyptian union period between 1958 and 1961. Due to historical circumstances, certain segments of many Mideast minorities, including Syrian Christians, tend to come from relatively wealthy and entrepreneurial middle-class backgrounds, in comparison with the broad Syrian population. This class status has made them targets for Nasserite and Baathist socialist policies of nationalization and land confiscation throughout the UAR and Baathist periods, forcing many to leave with whatever capital they could smuggle out of the country.

Other political factors proved equally disruptive. When the Syrian military juntas consolidated their grip on power, laying down the basis of a narrow Alawite sectarian regime, they quietly marginalized Christians in favor of Druze and Ismaili officers, while subjecting Sunni officers to continuous demotion. This behavior increased in 1979, after Muslim extremists attacked Alawite military cadets in Aleppo Artillery School, followed by the regime's massacre of Hama in 1982. Never sizable, the presence of Christian officers in the army often became cynically co-opted in order to legitimize the regime among Christian communities and to cement strong alliances with the hierarchies of their churches, alliances which appear to have endured to the present. Like Tarik Aziz in Iraq, another Christian,

Dawoud Rajiha, held a similar position in Syria, serving as Syrian minister of defense from 2011 to 2012, until he was assassinated along with other senior military officers.

As Syria's Arab Spring unfolded, some Christians joined in, and a few even reached top levels of the opposition leadership. However, as in the rest of the Middle East, secular and progressive activists and intellectuals represent a small percentage of most communities, while the church and traditional leadership continues to hold sway over their supporters and parishioners. Following the regime's bloody response to peaceful protests, Syria's Arab Spring gradually descended into violence, rending the fabric of Syrian society along the seams of religious and sectarian divisions. In war, reason often becomes the first casualty, obscured behind the growing piles of bodies. A classic example, Homs, Syria's third largest city, known as the "capital of the Syrian revolution," contained three major groups—Sunnis, Alawites, and Christians—which had largely inhabited three separate neighborhoods or enclaves. With violence rampant across the city—now in ruins, thanks to the regime—the sectarian identity of the person shooting at you became a matter of speculation. Before the almost total destruction of the city, press reports indicate that regime forces deliberately attacked Sunni areas from Christian neighborhoods in order to incite Sunni retaliations against Christians. This left the Christians no alternative but to join forces with the regime and join regime-sponsored militias or *shabiha* (thugs).

As the alliance between the Churches and the regime intensified, they began to shift the image of neutrality that some Christians had worked so hard to cultivate, with grave repercussions to many Syrian Christians. Church leadership pushed the community into siding with the Assad regime to the detriment of their own parishioners.

The Christian Maronite community in Syria, relatively small in comparison with other Eastern Christian communities whether in Syria or Iraq, received another blow when numerous sources reported in 2011 that Patriarch Bechara al-Raï, the head of the Maronite Church in Lebanon and Syria, repeated the Syrian official propaganda line word-for-word while in France. Al-Rai justified this as necessary "to give Assad a chance to implement the reforms he already announced," describing Assad as "an open-minded person who studied in Europe" but cautioning that "he cannot make miracles." These provocative statements about the Syrian regime lacked wisdom, to put it mildly, and many observers describe them as damaging to both Lebanese and Syrian Christians. After all, that "open-minded person" al-Raï championed has caused the death of nearly half a million Syrians.

Striking parallels exist between the positions of Iraqi and Syrian Christian intellectuals, with the Syrians, like their Iraqi counterparts, largely predisposed to join Baathist, communist, and nationalist parties (in pan-Arab and pan-Syrian configurations). Their attraction to these parties can generally be understood as motivated by the sheer survival instinct to stake out positions close to power. Even when a majority of Arab and world opinions has condemned the Assad regime's brutal destruction of the Syrian people as a crime against humanity, none of the "anti-imperialist," nationalistic intellectuals have uttered a hint of protest.

Claims and counterclaims aside, examining Syrian policies helps clarify forces that influenced almost half of Syria's Christians to leave the country before the Arab Spring and the rise of ISIS. As far back as the 1960s, specific policy directives have influenced the migration due to their sectarian undertones, whether in development, demography or recruitment into the military service. While the obvious goals of these policies centered on discomfiting the Sunni majority, Christians did not necessarily benefit from a system increasingly tilted towards the benefit of Alawite communities. Undoubtedly, nepotism, favoritism and corruption played a role in benefiting those Christians closely allied with the regime, but such tactics only privileged a small cadre of Christians and didn't trickle power down to the masses.

Syria's political economy has also contributed to the dwindling Christian presence in the country. As with most command economies, the political portion of the equation, rather than economic good sense, largely determines the "logic" of Syria's economy. As an example, the system does not use merit as the standard for recruitment of Syrians into the civil service. Instead, one's sectarian allegiance to the regime attains to the level of a job qualification. Christians in Syria tend to have relatively higher levels of education and more skills than the rest of the population due to historical forces such as education in Western-sponsored missionary schools. However, without a merit system, their employment outlook remains bleak.

The failure of such public policies, erroneously described as socialist, have undermined not only the economic opportunities for the Christian community, but ultimately have also damaged the nation as a whole.

Since Assad's first shots against his own people, and the murderous ISIS cult's emergence from the chaos, the already deteriorating conditions for Syrian Christians have worsened. While escaping the atrocities ISIS inflicted on their Iraqi coreligionists (rape, exile, captivity, destruction of churches), some Syrian Christians had to submit to ISIS demands like paying *jizya* (taxes), while others instead relocated or left the country. Still, ISIS alone did not push Syrian Christians out of their homes. Regime-sponsored militias and loyalists made life unbearable for many in coastal towns like Lattakia and in Christian neighborhoods in Damascus (Bab Sharqi, Qassaa, Al Qusour, Jaramana, Douma and Bab Touma), harassing and attacking Christians for refusing to fight against the opposition or enlisting in local militias. Lawlessness, widespread drug and alcohol abuse and random shooting by armed groups have prompted many Christians to try to sell their properties in order to relocate from areas like Old Damascus. Syrian Christians have also witnessed sectarian cleansing, including population transfers, mainly between Alawites, Shiites, and Sunnis. Recently, this involved the forced resettlement into rebel-controlled areas in northern Syria of large groups of Sunnis from besieged Homs, Zabadani, Daraya and other towns.

Considering all this, we should not blame Arab Christians for their predicament, but at the same time we should not acquit them of all responsibility. A critical examination of intellectual and political choices, past and present, remains in order, as their choices of allying with totalitarian parties and authoritarian states reflect faulty readings of prevailing ideas and realities. Even when viewed as a dispassionate exercise in understanding recent history, excavating cause and effect can appear callous. Although it might prove easier with ancient history, the effects of expedient alliances continue uninterrupted to the present day.

Dismissing what they derogatorily call Western ideals—concepts like constitutions, parliaments, elections and the rule of law, regardless of how flawed these institutions might have been, has not served Arab Christians well. Yet their interwar hostility toward political systems based on freedom, economic liberalism and democratic pluralism continues.

Arab Christians have not reconsidered the foundations upon which they have built their ideological mansions, despite totalitarian regimes crumbling before them. The Nazi and Soviet models collapsed, but not before causing more than 40 million deaths. Even the Syrian genocide failed to elicit condemnation of Assad's butchery or force Arab Christians to rethink their politics and alliances. Little hope will remain if historical lessons can't alter the decades-old lens through which Arab Christians view questions of nationalism and despotism.

CHAPTER 8

A Human Rights Perspective on the Protection of Christians and Other Minorities in the Middle East and North Africa

Fateh Azzam

This chapter provides a legal and human rights perspective on the issues of protecting Christians and other minorities. The human rights framework advances a set of standards with levels of details to monitor, inform and offer the needed protection for minority groups for peoples of the Middle East and North Africa. For it to succeed, however, political will is needed, and therein is the rub. Important and clear as it is, the human rights perspective does not stand on its own nor do human rights generally implement themselves. They exist within the broader political and institutional context of the region as well as the global frameworks for the protection of rights, which are, unfortunately, very weak. Although human rights are in fact international legal obligations—certainly for the states that have signed and ratified the relevant treaties—the decision to act in implementation of those legal obligations is a political one.[1]

The human rights edifice as we have it today is built on a few very basic premises that cut across all of its treaties and conventions and indeed can

F. Azzam (✉)
Georgetown, ME, USA

© The Author(s) 2018
K. C. Ellis (ed.), *Secular Nationalism and Citizenship in Muslim Countries*, Minorities in West Asia and North Africa,
https://doi.org/10.1007/978-3-319-71204-8_8

147

be said to form fundamental pillars of customary international law. These include the recognition of the common worth and dignity of all, and the principle of equality and non-discrimination on any basis. The very first article of the Universal Declaration of Human Rights of 1948 (UDHR) simply states, "*All human beings are born free and equal in dignity and rights. They are endowed with reason and conscience and should act towards one another in a spirit of brotherhood.*"[2]

The UDHR proceeds in the second article to describe that all the rights and entitlements enumerated in the Declaration are to be enjoyed "*without distinction of any kind, such as race, color, sex, language, religion, political or other opinion, national or social origin, property, birth or other status.*"

The rights of racial, ethnic, religious and other minorities are specifically protected in international human rights law, including the right of all peoples to practice and teach their faith, preserve and teach their language, and to maintain their cultural identity. We find this articulated, for example, in Article 27 of the International Covenant on Civil and Political Rights, which guarantees to persons belonging to ethnic, religious, or linguistic minorities the right to "*enjoy their own culture, to profess and practice their own religion, or to use their own language.*"[3]

For the protection of minorities, human rights instruments rely on general provisions prohibiting discrimination and racism. Chief among those is the Convention on the Elimination of All Forms of Racial Discrimination, which prohibits in its first article "*any distinction, exclusion, restriction or preference* ...." Similarly, the International Covenant on Economic, Social and Cultural Rights stresses that those rights are to be "*exercised without discrimination of any kind as to race, color, sex, language, religion, political or other opinion, national or social origin, property, birth or other status*" (Article 2.2); and the Convention on the Rights of the Child also guarantees that any child member of a minority group "*shall not be denied the right ... to profess and practice his or her own religion, or to use his or her own language*" (Article 30). There are many other such instruments, such as International Labor Organization conventions and declarations that use similar language on discrimination. UNESCO's declarations on cultural preservation have important protections as well.

The most important instruments relevant to the protection of minorities are three. First, the Genocide Convention, which was adopted one day before the Universal Declaration of Human Rights, sets out to protect the very existence of minority groups, and prohibits not only genocide but "serious bodily or mental harm" and "*the deliberate infliction of conditions of life calculated to bring about* [the group's] *physical destruction in whole or in part."*

Secondly, the 1992 Declaration on the Rights of Persons Belonging to National or Ethnic, Religious and Linguistic Minorities,[4] which sets out in quite some detail the rights specific to such minorities and the special protections to which they are entitled, including protection of their very existence as well as their right to culture, language, association, free expression and many other rights.

The third, and the only one designed as a legal enforcement instrument, is the Rome Statute of the International Criminal Court. The ICC has the authority to investigate and prosecute individuals for crimes of genocide, war crimes, and crimes against humanity. The list of crimes prosecutable by the Court includes forced transfers of persons belonging to minorities, forced sterilizations, and rape as a war crime.[5]

Except for the International Criminal Court, which targets only individuals suspected of such crimes, the system has few teeth to deal with abusive policies beyond naming and shaming in the discussions of the Human Rights Council and the General Assembly or through the reports of human rights organizations. Yet the sad reality is that naming and shaming rarely works, and usually only with states that may—at least occasionally—feel some shame, which are very few.

The legal and political responsibility to protect the rights of minorities lies with the state, which has the authority and is the responsible party to be held accountable. The scope of legal obligation here goes beyond respecting minorities' rights, that is, refraining from violating them, but also to protect them from violation by others. Of course, states are hard-pressed to do so when the party that is the aggressor against minorities is an armed group that exercises de facto jurisdiction over some territory and people but does not have legal recognition as an entity by the international community. In such a case, the obligation must remain squarely on the shoulders of the state to protect minorities against the vagaries of such groups. However, when a state is unable or unwilling to do so or is ineffective in providing such protection, the responsibility falls upon the international community of states as a whole. We are seeing this play out today in the case of the international coalition combating the self-declared Islamic State of the Levant (ISIL), which has taken over territory by force in both Iraq and Syria.

When it comes to the multiplicity of minority communities in the richly diverse Middle East and North Africa, we are witnessing a serious failure to discharge such legal and moral responsibility. A low-intensity level of discrimination exists in a number of countries, although few have perpetrated such dire abuses as the genocidal acts perpetrated by ISIL in Iraq and Syria.[6] The treatment of religious and ethnic minorities in the region is a complex legal and cultural phenomenon and, in my view, cannot just be ascribed to assumed sectarian hostilities and age-old blood rivalries. Rather, I would point to the endemic instrumental use of sectarianism—globally and by national autocratic leadership in the quest to maintain control, power and wealth.

In the mid-1800s, the Ottoman *Tanzimat* copied European constitutional and civil law in the effort to modernize and create a citizenship-based system, while continuing to strike a balance between giving Caesar what is Caesar's—that is, demanding loyalty to the empire—and continuing to allow the different religious and ethnic communities (*millets*) a significant degree of autonomy over their religious and civil affairs. This resulted in a schism that was inherited by Arab states, between penal law and civil laws, especially the provisions that deal with most matters of personal status such as marriage, divorce, inheritance and adoption among others. This created a duality of respecting minority differences and allowing the exercise of community prerogatives on the one hand, and on the other, differentiating the legal status of individual members of those communities at the expense of equality of citizenship. It created obstacles in many aspects of daily life, including inter-communal marriages and adoptions, and affected the laws of nationality in all states of the region. This system persists today throughout the region; the best example is Lebanon, with its 17 or 18 legally recognized confessional communities and the absence of a civil law for marriage.

After the First World War and the collapse of the Ottoman Empire, the victorious late-period colonial powers viewed the region with a sectarian lens, even as they worked to progressively structure their own societies back home on the basis of the rule of law and equality of citizenship. They often pitted communities against one another, favoring one over the other, and threatening the delicate tapestry of inter-cultural and inter-religious coexistence that kept a modicum of peace and relative security, imperfect and problematic as it was. Dividing the entire Arab Gulf in accordance with perceived tribal homogeneity and loyalties, the creation of a "Jewish" Israel and the ruination of a diverse Palestine, the Sykes-Picot treaty, the French attempt to create a "Christian" Lebanon, and allotting the Kurdish region to three separate states are but a few examples.

The early process of state formation in the Arab region produced kings and emirs who governed their nascent states in an authoritarian and autocratic way as though by divine right, and they continue to do so today. Peoples who did revolt against colonialism and overthrew both colonial powers and their client monarchies, as they did in Iraq, Egypt, Syria and Algeria, also produced governance systems and presidents of the new republics that governed in much the same way as the kings and emirs did. Like the colonial powers before them, they publicly espoused an Arab nationalism that rejected diversity and multiculturalism in favor of an assumed Arab/Islamic unity. At the same time, they continued to use tribalism and sectarianism to maintain their power and authority as the previous colonial powers did before them. In both republics and monarchies, such divisions were used to concentrate power and wealth in the hands of a few at the expense of equality and equal access to resources.

Another factor that some point to is the assumed contradiction arising from the uneasy relationship between the constitutional and legal constructs of a state in the modern era, and the Islamic concept of the *Umma* and its attendant laws based in *Shari'a*. Indeed, the constitutions of most states in the region state clearly that Islam is the religion of the state and that *Shari'a* is the primary—if not the only—source of legislation. *Shari'a* laws, however, are as variously interpretable as there are states, as are the perceptions and treatment of non-Islamic minorities. This uneasy relationship has resulted in long-standing questions of belonging and citizenship, which Parolin describes as three overlapping circles of belonging: to bonds of kin, to the religious communities and to the nation-state.[7] There is plenty of evidence to suggest that this has resulted in discrimination against minorities; and I would mention here, by way of example, the Egyptian and Saudi limitations on the building of churches and the non-recognition of the Baha'i communities and their periodic persecution.

Such endemic discrimination, however, does not sufficiently explain the magnitude of recent events around the region. These must be seen in the context of decades of authoritarian rule, sharp curtailment of all citizens' civil and political rights, and failed development policies coupled with the global neoliberal economics that have reduced the role of governmental services, all but eliminating social safety nets.[8] Initially directed at Arab and global leadership, the uprisings in early 2011 have opened a Pandora's box of authoritarianism and sectarianism by both governments and armed groups in Syria, Iraq, Libya, Yemen and elsewhere. Indeed, the Christian minorities are in danger in the Levant; but so are, in various degrees, the Shi'a in Bahrain and Saudi Arabia, the Yezidis in Iraq, the Sunnis in Iran and Iraq and the Baha'is, who have historically suffered significant discrimination everywhere in the region. They are all in need of protection, and the human-rights approach demands that all of the minority groups be protected equally and without discrimination.

Particular attention to the protection of Christians more than others can be problematic as it sets them apart and privileges them more than other persecuted minorities. It furthers sectarian divisions within those societies and undermines the fundamental principle of achieving equality and equal rights for all. The danger is that such discriminatory protection, if we can call it that, confirms for many in the region that the international community that espouses equality, non-discrimination and respect for human rights in fact has a double-standard, and believes that some people are indeed "more equal than others." Everyone needs protection, and every minority that is persecuted needs to be protected or saved equally.

This is not to deny that at different times, different minority groups are victimized in particularly vicious or brutal ways, like the Tutsis of Rwanda in the 1990s or more recently the Christians and Yezidis in Iraq, or the Rohingya Muslims of Myanmar. But I would stress that in advocating for the protection of each particular community, we don't lose sight of the overarching human rights requirement that all must be protected. If the international community mobilizes to protect the Christians of Iraq, for example, it cannot be just because they are Christian, and it should not exclude Yezidis and others, or wait until it's the Yezidis' turn to be protected. Another example is Palestine, where the number of Christians has been rapidly diminishing, but that is because of a military occupation that brutalizes all Palestinians, Muslim and Christian alike. The protection of Christians there must be seen in the context of protecting all Palestinians.

No one people in the world has a monopoly on racism and ethnic and religious discrimination, and sectarianism is not a phenomenon limited to the Middle East or unique to it, but a global one. There has been ample historical documentation of persecution of and discrimination against religious and ethnic minorities all over the globe, from genocide against the indigenous populations of North and South America to that of the Jews and the Roma in Europe to religious and ethnic "cleansing" in the Balkans and Rwanda to the persecution of the Rohingya Muslims of Myanmar, which is happening even now. We are also seeing a frightening rise in Islamophobia in Europe and North America, which is going hand in hand with anti-Semitism and rejection of all minorities there, including refugees.

Human rights principles and their treaties and conventions offer an approach that seeks to provide protection of religious and other minorities on the basis of the inherent dignity of all humanity. International advocacy can rely on human rights texts and on the mechanisms available in the international legal system. However, we can't fall victim to the illusion that simply because we have those agreements that states and armed groups will implement them. They certainly will not do so against their will. With those principles as goals, what is needed is mobilization and advocacy that uses a holistic approach to include an understanding of the political economy of repression and brutality, a long view of history and a clear vision of a future where all can be equal and equally protected.

NOTES

1. See Vienna Convention on the Law of Treaties (1969). Article 26 requires implementation "in good faith," and states may not invoke domestic laws in violation of the treaties' binding provisions (article 27). http://legal.un.org/ilc/texts/instruments/english/conventions/1_1_1969.pdf
2. Universal Declaration of Human Rights, adopted by the U.N. General Assembly on 10 December 1948.
3. For texts of all human rights treaties see Office of the United Nations High Commissioner for Human Rights: http://www.ohchr.org/EN/Professional Interest/Pages/CoreInstruments.aspx
4. Adopted unanimously by U.N. General Assembly resolution 47/135, 18 December 1992. Although such declarations are not binding legally, they are an expression of a moral and political commitment on the part of states to implement them in good faith.
5. The Rome Statute of the International Criminal Court was adopted in 1998 and entered into force on July 1, 2002; see U.N. Document A/CONF.183/9 (17 July 1998). For a full text of the Rome Statute see: https://www.icc-cpi.int/nr/rdonlyres/ea9aeff7-5752-4f84-be94-0a655eb30e16/0/rome_statute_english.pdf
6. See Office of the U.N. High Commissioner for Human Rights, "Human Rights Council opens Special Session on the Human Rights Situation in Iraq," September 1, 2014, at http://www.ohchr.org/EN/NewsEvents/Pages/DisplayNews.aspx?NewsID=14984&LangID=E#sthash.QWCxVCv1.dpuf
7. See Parolin, Gianluca P., *Citizenship in the Arab World: Kin, Religion and the Nation-State* (Amsterdam: Amsterdam University Press, 2009).
8. "The Challenge of Minority Rights in a Changing Arab World," discussion hosted by the Brookings Doha Center, Qatar, June 26, 2013. Audio of the discussion is available at: https://www.brookings.edu/events/the-challenge-of-minority-rights-in-a-changing-arab-world/

CHAPTER 9

The Persecution of Minorities in the Middle East

Alon Ben-Meir

INTRODUCTION

Christians have lived in the Middle East—the birthplace of Christianity—for nearly 2000 years. Christianity was one of the major religions of the Middle East from the fourth century reforms of Roman Emperor Constantine until the Arab-Muslim conquests of the mid-to-late seventh century. Muslim rulers regarded and treated Jews and Christians as *ahl al kitāb*, "People of the Book," that is, followers of Abrahamic religions. They granted them *dhimmi* status, which was meant to protect not only the life and property of non-Muslims, but also the freedom of religion and worship. Unfortunately, the statute also implied a certain civil and political inferiority, and there was a view among some jurists that the *dhimmi* should be made to feel humiliated and disgraced; they were required to pay the poll tax, or *jizya*.

Christians are not the only minority being discriminated against in this region, but their plight is more visible in many places, beyond the regular discrimination faced by minorities such as Yazidis, Druze, and Kurds.

A. Ben-Meir (✉)
World Policy Institute, New York University, New York, NY, USA

© The Author(s) 2018
K. C. Ellis (ed.), *Secular Nationalism and Citizenship in Muslim Countries*, Minorities in West Asia and North Africa,
https://doi.org/10.1007/978-3-319-71204-8_9

155

Yazidis in particular have been massacred, enslaved, and driven away from their ancestral lands in northern Iraq—all at the hands of the Islamic State (ISIS). The 2003 invasion of Iraq, and its ramifications throughout the region which led to the Arab Spring of 2011, challenged the old order; and the long-standing protection of minorities was threatened when several Middle Eastern dictators were deposed. A century ago, 20 percent of the population in the Middle East was Christian; today, Christians constitute no more than 3–4 percent of the region's population.[1]

This chapter explores the persecution of minorities in the Middle East, with a particular emphasis on Christian minorities. It will identify the root causes, followed by a strategy to combat the persecution of religious minorities. The difficulties that impede progress toward mitigating persecution will also be explored. The chapter will conclude with the observation that since minority persecution can be allayed only partially, this phenomenon will remain present for the foreseeable future. Unfortunately, Christians and other minorities may not be able to restore the status quo ante and live in harmony with their largely Muslim neighbors, despite any and all efforts to rectify the bleak situation. As Abraham Joshua Heschel rightly observed, the exercise of religious freedom must be constant—proactive, not reactive to development of events. "The problem to be faced is: how to combine loyalty to one's own tradition with reverence for different traditions."

ROOT CAUSES

There are several factors contributing to the persecution of religious minorities in the Middle East. The upheaval currently sweeping the region in the wake of the Iraq war, the Arab Spring, and the rise of ISIS has resulted in instability and widespread violence. Under such hostile circumstances, minority groups seek to fend for themselves, becoming increasingly insular. On the other hand, the reigning turmoil has galvanized hostility toward minorities, and in particular we are seeing an increase in attacks on non-Muslims as well as on Muslims who do not subscribe to a certain sect or set of beliefs. As a case in point, the 2003 U.S. invasion of Iraq was one of the main instigators behind the rise of many extremist groups, especially ISIS, unleashing a torrent of sectarian violence between Sunnis and Shias and against other religious minorities, including Christians.

As the Middle East is disintegrating, minorities—in efforts aimed at self-preservation—become protective of themselves only; there is a broad withdrawal from political life and the public sphere in general. This political self-marginalization tends to foster a narcissistic approach aimed at building tribal cohesiveness. To a certain extent, perhaps, this can turn the eventual disappearance of Christian communities in many Arab states in the Middle East into a self-fulfilling prophecy. This unraveling is creating new vulnerabilities—and it is within these spaces where any out-group becomes a threat (or an undesirable entity).

THE RISE OF RELIGIOUS EXTREMISM

The rise of Islamic orthodoxy has been a singular driving force in the plight of religious minorities, fueling a growing desire—or what some might call a "need"—to resort to religion as a palliative. The resurfacing of religious division vis-à-vis the Sunni–Shia conflict is creating a societal mindset that posits other religious groups as "the enemy." To take an extreme example, groups like al-Qaeda and ISIS demonstrate a fundamental intolerance for religious and inter-religious out-groups, with the latter taking such fanaticism to new and barbaric heights.

The highest concentration of autocratic states or majority-Islamic countries is in the Middle East and North Africa, where secularism has little influence and religious freedom is limited. In 2014–2015, more than 7000 Christians were killed in these countries and in central Asia because of their beliefs; the number is expected to increase because of the growing rejection of other religious minorities. Furthermore, in many countries non-Middle Eastern countries, like Ethiopia, Nigeria, and Bangladesh, which claim to have some form of secularity and religious freedom, Christians are persecuted and often killed with near impunity.

Generally, persecution and discrimination against religious minorities, especially Christians, manifests itself in a combination of discriminatory laws, political persecution, and outright restriction of religious practices. This includes limitations on public preaching, evangelism, and distribution of religious literature, lack of constitutional protections, and harassment of those who adhere to Christianity. In addition, there are many other restrictions imposed on Christians, in particular, denial of permits to build new churches and increasing regulation of religious spaces. Committing larceny against Christian schools or places of worship is common; mob violence and honor killings often go unpunished. According to a Pew survey, Christians face religious persecution more than any other religious minority, and the rise of ISIS made this a glaring reality.

The threat emanating today from groups such as ISIS, al-Qaeda, and other Islamic states is inspired by religious teachings, distorted under the guise of defending purist Sunni Islam (Shia in the case of Iran), which ultimately aims to infect susceptible Muslim youths to whom religion provides an escape and a sense of belonging. Violent extremists wage a war on Western cultural and religious precepts, and wish to see their acts fused into the identity of their own Muslim community so they can be recognized as the representative of the larger community, especially by the media. Given the ties between the Western world and mainstream Christianity, it becomes a "natural" target for these groups that seek to frame their conflict as one of epic religious proportions.

Albert Einstein put this succinctly when he said, "A man who is convinced of the truth of his religion is indeed never tolerant …. The faithful adherent of a religion will try first of all to convince those that believe in another religion and usually he goes on to hatred if he is not successful. However, hatred then leads to persecution when the might of the majority is behind it."

Islamic extremism, by its very nature, is against any other faith or political faction. In this ideological framework, Islam encompasses one's entire life, and even non-conforming Muslims become "legitimate" targets, as witnessed in the ongoing bloody Sunni–Shia conflict, where extremists on both sides deny the legitimacy of the other to practice the same faith. This intense animosity between the two sects could not have been expressed more vividly than when Saudi Arabia's Grand Mufti recently told the *Makkah Daily* that "we must understand that these [Iran's Shiites] are not Muslim, they are children of Magi and their hostility toward Muslims is an old one, especially with the people of Sunna." And whereas Christians were viewed and treated as a protected community under the Ottomans, the rise of Salafist and Wahhabist Islam has put this community in the cross hairs, with ISIS threatening taxation, conversion to Islam, or death for the few Christians left in the territory it controls.

RADICALIZATION

The wanton persecution of religious minorities is compounded by the threat of radicalization—particularly among the youth—which threatens social cohesion and combines religious doctrine with fanatical violence. Generally speaking, as individuals become more radical, their tolerance for other views and religious beliefs correspondingly falls, often leading to violent results. As Blaise Pascal noted, "Men never do evil so completely and cheerfully as when they do it from religious conviction."

When there is so much uncertainty in the Middle East—many Arab youth lose perspective on who they are and see little prospect for a hopeful future—they are driven to join extremist groups, which provide, however nebulous and criminal, a sense of identity and purpose. If one believes ultimate salvation can be found only through religious means, every other sect becomes an "enemy" to be countered through doctrinal or violent measures. When there is greater religious sectarianism taking place throughout the region (as well as globally), a corresponding greater intensity of religious persecution is often not far behind.

SOCIOECONOMIC DETERMINANTS

The prevailing frustration, pain, and agony in the region as a result of socio-economic despondency is leading to a spike in discrimination, as under these conditions groups try to fend for themselves first—if the government fails to step in and mitigate the situation, there is a tendency to find a "sacrificial lamb" to blame one's ills on.

Rampant unemployment, scarcity of housing, limited opportunity for higher education, and tens of millions of Muslims living in poverty all evoke a sense of resentment against other minorities, even if such minorities do not necessarily enjoy a relative higher standard of living. Out of nearly 400 million Arabs, more than 200 million are under the poverty line; about 200 million young men and women under the age of 25 feel that they have no future.[2]

This naturally leads to discrimination, often expressed through persecution at the local and federal levels. However, improving the socio-economic position of millions of Egyptians, for example, could simultaneously improve the security of Christian Copts, as the economic pain associated with attacks against minority groups would be less of a condition felt in Egyptian society.

Unfortunately, many Arab governments, in an effort to appease the majority, often look the other way when acts of persecution occur against minorities for the sake of appeasement or, even worse, agreement.

ARAB NATIONALISM AND THE ARAB SPRING

Arab nationalism was reinvigorated in the wake of the Arab Spring; as a result, discrimination against Christians was sharpened in certain areas. Whereas Arab states that were ruled by despots—such as Egypt under Mubarak and Qaddafi in Libya—protected freedom of religion, the Arab

Spring that precipitated revolutions in these countries changed the intra-dynamic of religious relations. For instance, during the Egyptian uprising against the Mubarak regime, Egyptian Copts (10 percent of the population, or approximately 8 million people) faced greater acts of discrimination. The rift between Copts and the majority Muslim population was already deep prior to the revolution, but with the swift rise to power of the Egyptian Muslim Brotherhood, new fault lines were exposed. As the revolution was underway, this divide was amplified during the Maspero Massacre in October 2011, when Coptic demonstrators protesting the destruction of a church in Aswan were crushed by armored vehicles and shot.[3]

Given the persecution of Egyptian Copts, it may be hard to recall that there was a time when fraternal feelings between Muslims and Copts was quite strong—so strong in fact that in 1930 Sinot Hanna, a leading Coptic Wafd member, took the knife blow when an attempt was made on the life of Prime Minister Mustafa Nahhas.[4] Copts, Jews, Baha'i, and atheists were free from persecution and discrimination in general; until 1952, Copts enjoyed full rights.

But as in so many countries in the Middle East, the gradual introduction of Islam into the state framework created cleavages between religious minority groups. Christians, and to a lesser extent other religious minorities, were increasingly viewed less as a protected class and more as a privileged one, able to retain a certain position among the elite despite their dwindling numbers. In countries like Egypt and Jordan, Christians tend to be relatively wealthy and better educated than their Muslim counterparts, firmly ensconced in the middle and upper classes.[5]

BLASPHEMY LAWS

The prevalence of blasphemy laws in Muslim countries adds another complex layer to religious discrimination. In Pakistan, for example, Christianity is technically legal, yet Christians experience more violence there than virtually anywhere else. One of the persistent sources of this persecution are blasphemy laws, which are frequently abused to settle personal scores, and carry with them a mandatory sentence of death. Allegations of blasphemy are often presented with no evidence, because to reproduce the evidence would be to reproduce the blasphemy. The U.S. Department of State's annual International Religious Freedom Report of 2014 stated that the government of Pakistan promoted an "environment of impunity" by failing to investigate, arrest, and prosecute abusers.[6] We may add that such an environment makes atrocity-producing situations more likely to occur in the form of mob violence or collective revenge.

Further, the police are doing next to nothing to protect not just the Christian community, but also Ahmadi Muslims as well. Ahmadi Muslims, of whom there are some 20 million worldwide, are one of the only Muslims sects who reject *takfirism*, the declaration of one Muslim that another is *kafir* (a non-believer). *Takfirism* is an inherently discriminatory and violent religious instrument and serves as a justification for persecution; the rejection of *takfirism* by Ahmadis is something to be applauded and set as an example for others in the region.

Blasphemy laws effectively function as a license to kill and torture Christians, as in the 2014 case of a Pakistani couple who were tortured and burned to death in an industrial kiln after being accused—but not convicted—of burning a page of the Qu'ran. Afghanistan also enforces blasphemy laws for things such as condemning the treatment of women or condemning crimes committed by persons acting in the name of Islam; even to belong to the Baha'i faith itself is an act of blasphemy. These laws, which are enforced in Malaysia, Indonesia, Sudan, Iran, and Saudi Arabia, and other predominantly Muslim countries, generally conflict with and weaken universally recognized human rights with respect to religious freedom. Such laws are easily abused via false accusation and often exploited for the sake of personal vendettas, which frequently leads to mob violence. We should also add that they tend to shield religious beliefs, institutions, and leaders from necessary criticism and inquiry.

THE COLONIAL LEGACY

A widely held perception in the Middle East today is that many of the region's socio-economic problems are attributable to the legacy of the post-World War I and II colonial eras and the exploitive regimes of those times. Though many of the newly independent states immediately turned to autocratic rule, the pre-existing state structures were largely kept in place to the relief of religious minorities. According to Belge and Karakoc,[7] following the demise of the Ottoman Empire many of the newly independent states "granted some kind of cultural autonomy to non-Muslims in the areas of religion, family law, and education," thus preserving many aspects of the governing Ottoman-era *millet* system.

But the Arab Spring put this political order to the test—the demand for democratization made many religious minorities uneasy, worried that legal protections carried over from the Ottoman era would fall to the wayside if majoritarian rule replaced authoritarianism. Iraq offers a stark example of this development, where the Christians bore the brunt of a backlash, as they were seen as being representative of the West.

REMEDIES AND COUNTERMEASURES

The following section offers numerous remedies and countermeasures that can be taken by states and organizations alike to counter the rising tide of religious discrimination in the Middle East:

1. End Raging Regional Conflicts: To mitigate the uncertainty held by millions across the Middle East which impacts on religious discrimination, one clear way forward is a concerted and sincere push at the political level by the international community led by the major powers to end many of the raging regional conflicts. A mutually acceptable resolution to the Israeli–Palestinian conflict, for example, would substantially reduce tensions in much of the region, whether by improving relations between Israelis and Palestinians through reconciliation, bringing Israel closer to the Sunni Arab world, or depriving extremist groups such as Hamas and Hezbollah of their *raison d'etre*. A solution to the Syrian conflict would stabilize what is left of the fractious nation and could help toward improving the status of the remaining Christian community in particular, which has seen many of its holy sites defaced or completely destroyed at the behest of radical Islamist militias such as ISIS. The Shiite–Sunni conflict, spearheaded by Iran and Saudi Arabia, respectively, is another major flashpoint that feeds into the frenzy of extremism and must also be mitigated, even if it takes years, if not decades.

It is critical for the West to work to avoid the tendency to engage in wishful thinking. Many of these conflicts are extremely intractable and there is no ready-made recipe for a solution. There should be no illusions—the search for a solution should not be undertaken just because it feels "right." Proposed solutions must be grounded in the prevailing political circumstances and take into account specifically the historical and religious dimensions of these conflicts. There are many considerations, especially internal sectarian combustion, which must be carefully considered as they directly impact the level of persecution, including the varying situations throughout different countries.

2. Preventive Diplomacy and Timely Intervention: Preventive diplomacy is critically important any time there is a sign that acts of persecution might take place, or there appears to be a gradual emergence of an environment that could lead to persecution—measures taken in a timely fashion would prevent such developments from occurring. Needless to say, constant monitoring—especially of those countries which are prone to persecution of minorities—and exposure by UN agencies, Western embassies, and other local human rights agencies, could prevent persecution or maltreatment of minority groups.

Furthermore, in responding quickly to atrocities against religious minorities, the West—particularly the United States—needs to interject itself more forcefully before conflicts spiral out of control, as was the case in Syria, where the Obama administration had the opportunity to punish Assad for his use of chemical weapons and ultimately decided against such a course of action. There is evidence that suggests intervention, however limited in scope, can prevent further calamities against religious minorities. When ISIS was attacking the Yazidis in Iraq with genocidal intent, the United States intervened and saved tens of thousands of Yazidis who were trapped on Mount Sinjar. Similarly, the destruction of the predominantly Kurdish city of Kobani in Syria was prevented when the United States air support helped local Kurdish forces repel ISIS and take back the town.

3. Monitoring and Exposure: At the political level, it is incumbent on governments and nonprofits alike to rigorously monitor and report on infractions committed against religious minorities throughout the world. For example, the Office of International Religious Freedom in the U.S. State Department's Bureau of Democracy, Human Rights, and Labor regularly issues reports on religious freedoms, used by a wide range of government agencies to "shape policy; conduct diplomacy; and inform assistance, training, and other resource allocations"[8] in combating religious discrimination. "Naming and shaming" countries for violations against religious minorities, could in and of itself have a deterrent effect by potentially compelling countries who engage in such practices to rethink their approach, especially if their interests are tied up in a significant way with those of the United States. There needs to be absolute transparency when violations occur—not only should other nations be informed of any violations, but the infraction should be circulated extensively, with specific and descriptive coverage from the media wherever possible.

The U.S. Congress has a central role to play, as it regularly holds hearings on religious freedoms. The frequency of these hearings, especially at this juncture, must be increased to ensure the issue remains at the forefront of Congressional attention. Furthermore, protocols can be established to enable Congress members, specifically those traveling abroad, to alert host governments of violations even when the trip is unrelated to enforcing religious freedoms.

4. Incentives: The global community as a whole must do more than just offer ideological support in combating religious discrimination. As is often the case, significant funding is needed for religious programming so that citizens of a given country can develop legal practices and cultural tools which offer training and instruction in religious tolerance. In order to address these issues, federal agencies including USAID must enforce their mandates, and so must nonprofits whose mission is to promote religious freedom initiatives. When these states modify their existing practices, they can be "rewarded" financially or otherwise, depending on the special needs of a given country; tangible results need to be seen before any incentives are granted.

As a corollary, initiatives aimed at protecting religious freedom should be interwoven into trade deals; whether or not a given country has committed any violations, these considerations should nevertheless be incorporated as a preventative measure. With the correlation between economic status and treatment of minorities, it is vital that religious freedom discourse be introduced into the sterile world of trade negotiations.

5. Coercive Diplomacy: To drive the point home, violators need to fully understand that their transgressions will have consequences. With their tremendous global influence, the United States and the EU can go as far as leveraging international trade or other political deals with a demand of ending violations against religious minorities. While there are often human rights provisions in such deals, negotiators should begin to turn that attention toward infractions committed against religious minorities. Violators can be punished through sanctions—restricting travel of senior officials, limiting trade, etc.—which could compel violating countries incentives to stop discriminatory practices.

However, approaches to addressing violations against religious freedom cannot be generalized. Each country is different, and the same measures cannot be applied across the board. In some countries, the Christian community is firmly entrenched and the situation can be significantly improved because of their long-standing ties and significant numbers.

In Lebanon, for example, Christians still constitute 40 percent of the population and even hold positions of political power.[9] In the Palestinian territories, the presence of Christians dates back to the inception of their faith; many, like their Muslim counterparts, are committed to a free and independent Palestinian state. In war-torn Syria, where there were some 2 million Christians, tens of thousands have been forced from their homes by Islamist rebels and Salafi-Jihadists; as few as 500,000 may remain today.[10] In Egypt, the significant Christian minority, though likely to continue suffering from discrimination, will by and large remain in their country, and their conditions can be improved through coercive/incentive diplomacy.

In other countries, such as Saudi Arabia, Christians are forbidden from openly practicing their faith—items and articles belonging to religions other than Islam (such as Bibles and crucifixes) are prohibited. In Iran, while there are hundreds of churches and a steadily growing number of Christian converts, "Christians continue to be arbitrarily arrested and interrogated because of their faith-related activities."[11]

The objective is to apply different measures to different situations in order to send a clear message that there is a relationship between punishment and reward when it comes to religious freedoms.

6. Education: We cannot underestimate the importance of education in promoting and fostering religious tolerance and inter-religious dialogue. Hatred against religious minorities is all too often taught in public school curricula. According to Egyptian textbooks, for example, there is only one true religion—namely, Islam: "students are not to accept and respect other religions, and references to other religions tend to be subjective, inaccurate, and sometimes derogatory."[12] As long as this remains the case, we can be sure that violence against minorities will persist unabated.

Modifying textbooks and learning about religions other than one's own can be an invaluable experience, if it is approached without belittling, disparaging, or simply dismissing views that are different from the ones we happen to hold. Positive exposure to other religions can deepen the understanding and appreciation we have of our own faith; historically, religions grow out of and in dialogue with other traditions that generally come to inform the various beliefs and practices that are characteristic of any religion. As Gandhi observed, "It is the duty of every cultured man or woman to read sympathetically the scriptures of the world. If we are to respect others' religions as we would have them respect our own, a friendly study of the world's religions is a sacred duty."

Any country that is open to introducing education *about* religion (not preaching) can point out how much more is held in common than is often realized. Classes about ethics of religion are needed, as well as comparative religious studies. For example, in Israel and Palestine, classes that teach

Judaism and Islam can be juxtaposed to one another—the reconciliatory benefits would be immense. To be sure, Western democracies, which generally see eye-to-eye on religious freedom, must be encouraged to undertake programs aimed at promoting religious freedom initiatives in tandem. In so doing, the impact of their activities will have a far greater impact.

7. **Quiet Diplomacy**: There are innumerable instances where a country, due to a preexisting alliance or for the sake of self-interest, will not admonish a partner nation for its violations against religious freedom. Saudi Arabia and other Gulf states are on top of the list in discriminating against Christians, but one does not hear the United States raising this question publicly due to political considerations. Saudi Arabia has been the chief exporter of Wahhabism, a fundamentalist branch of Sunni Islam, which poses a direct threat to Christianity in the region. Wahhabi associations, with the support of the Saudi government, have and continue to spend billions of dollars to promote and propagate their ideology through children's madrasas and Muslim academies, not to mention in books, scholarly journals, fellowships, and thousands of mosques. This is a major source of the extremism that has contributed toward exclusionary policies.

If the United States seeks to make its objections clear to allied nations, it must open a quiet dialogue—particularly with Saudi Arabia and Pakistan—and speak to them quietly to compel them to correct their records on religious freedom.

Difficulties That Impede Progress

There are a number of factors which will continue to hamper any progress toward ensuring the protection of religious freedom and reducing discrimination against and persecution of religious minorities.

The Failure of the United Nations: Through its global agencies, the United Nations has a multilateral role to play in advancing religious freedoms. The office of the Special Rapporteur on Freedom of Religion or Belief in the UN can provide another source of amplifying religious violations and working to compel violating countries to correct their record. Unfortunately, the UN has failed miserably in its less than sincere efforts to combat persecution of religious minorities.

Moreover, the UN Security Council is overly politicized, and a resolution to stop the persecution of minorities is rarely passed; even then there is no enforcement mechanism upon which all Security Council members agree. The UN General Assembly is far less effective, as any resolution passed by this global representative body is non-binding and serves as no more than a show-and-tell, largely ignored by its own members.

The irony is that a country like Saudi Arabia, one of the most egregious violators of human rights, is a member of the UN Human Rights Council. This makes a mockery of the UN's obligation to monitor and punish member states who grossly violate with impunity one of the most important principles of the UN.

The Pervasiveness of Arab Nationalism: Regional instability is further aggravated by the pervasiveness of Arab nationalism and the promotion of a specific branch of Islam as the only legitimate religion, where those who do not follow find themselves squeezed out of the social milieu, if not singled out as unbelievers deserving to be excluded if not outright persecuted.

Denial of Wrongdoing: Countries who regularly engage in persecution of minorities, especially of Christians (such as Pakistan, Saudi Arabia, and Iran), deny altogether that they are engaging in the persecution of other minorities to justify their refusal to provide access to monitors, and intimidate witnesses to any transgression against minorities.

Obstacles to Identifying Culprits: Given the nature of these societies, it is increasingly difficult to identify the culprits behind the persecution of minority groups, especially when the respective governments look the other way and refuse to cooperate with any domestic or international monitoring agencies.

Rejecting Interference in Domestic Affairs: Many countries engaging in religious violations insist that it is an internal issue and outsiders do not have any business getting involved, even though the Arab League charter requires that all member states undertake legislative steps or any other measure required to enforce the charter's provisions.

Finally, as Al-Ghazali eloquently suggested, it is the environment in which we live and often our inability to discern the real enemy that makes it difficult to effectively combat persecution of religious minorities: "Declare your jihad on thirteen enemies you cannot see—egoism, arrogance, conceit, selfishness, greed, lust, intolerance, anger, lying, cheating, gossiping and slandering. If you can master and destroy them, then you will be ready to fight the enemy you can see."

CONCLUSION

The decline of Christians, and other minorities, in the Middle East may well be irreversible. The Christian community that lived in northern Iraq and the Nineveh Plains for nearly 2000 years may not able to recover from the brutal regime of terror that ISIS has waged against them. And even after the defeat of ISIS, "the fate of religious minorities in Syria and Iraq remains bleak."[13] For Iraq's Christian community, it would take a benevolent government to fix the situation there, but this will not happen under a Shia majority which is expected to indefinitely dominate Iraq's governing authority. The violent instability in the region is unlikely to subside. In the past 100 years, the regional Christian population has plummeted,[14] aggravated by the long-term Sunni–Shia conflict which terms "everyone else" as an "enemy" to one side or the other.

We are looking at a gradual, diminishing presence of Christians and other religious minorities, insofar as there is no prospect for restoring a stable order, one replete with tolerance. With the rise of populism, tribalism is becoming a visible global phenomenon. We are witnessing the growth of nationalism not only in the Middle East but in Western Europe and the United States as well, along with a desire for social homogeneity and a tendency to blame others for one's plight.

There is a temptation to suppose that Christian–Muslim solidarity may in time reverse the trend towards increasing exclusivism. In Egypt, which is demographically homogenous, the prospects for renewed Christian–Muslim dialogue may appear somewhat brighter than in other countries of the region. While it is important and desirable to encourage solidarity and mutual recognition, this will not ultimately work in the long-term.

The strategies that have been enumerated for addressing religious persecution of minorities in the Middle East do not constitute a silver bullet that will bring a halt to discrimination and abuse. They are measures which, if seriously applied, may allow Christians to maintain a foothold in the Middle East, but the rebirth of a thriving, flourishing Christian presence in the region can only be a goal for the distant future. This is extraordinarily unfortunate for a number of reasons—not only in terms of the loss of indigenous cultures and their way of life, and the historical and archeological treasures which define so much of the region—but it is also a tragedy for Western Christians, who will only grow more distant and estranged from the land that saw the birth of their faith and imbued their religion with its indelible character.

It is indeed a tragedy for the world when any group of persons—whether they be Christians, Muslims, Yazidis, or Druze—are denied their human dignity and the basic human freedom to believe and worship as they please. The freedom of religion and the dignity of each and every individual will be fully restored when those who now are consumed with hatred for the other, recall and take to heart the words of Matthew 25:40: "Whatever you did for one of the least of these brothers and sisters of mine, you did for me."

NOTES

1. "The Future of World Religions: Population Growth Projections, 2010–2050," *Pew Research Center*, April 2, 2015, http://www.pewforum.org/2015/04/02/middle-east-north-africa/
2. "Beyond the Arab Awakening: Policies and Investments for Poverty Reduction and Food Security," International Food Policy Research Institute (Report, Washington, DC, 2012).
3. "Egypt: Don't Cover Up Military Killing of Copt Protesters," Human Rights Watch, October 25, 2011, https://www.hrw.org/news/2011/10/25/egypt-dont-cover-military-killing-copt-protesters
4. "Who is Persecuting the Copts?" The Atlantic Council, June 7, 2016, http://www.atlanticcouncil.org/blogs/menasource/who-is-persecuting-the-copts
5. Ceren Belge and Ekrem Karakoc, "Minorities in the Middle East: Ethnicity, Religion, and Support for Authoritarianism," *Political Research Quarterly* 68, no. 2 (2015): 208–292, 285.
6. "International Religious Freedom Report for 2014," United States Department of State (DC: Bureau of Democracy, Human Rights, and Labor, 2014).
7. Belge, 283.
8. "Overview and Acknowledgements," Bureau of Democracy, Human Rights and Labor, 2015, http://www.state.gov/j/drl/rls/irf/religious-freedom/index.htm#wrapper
9. The World Factbook, "Lebanon," *Central Intelligence Agency* accessed November 28, 2016.
10. Michael Chapman, "Syria's Christian Population Drops from 1.25 Million to 500,000," Assyrian International News Agency, October 31, 2016, http://www.aina.org/news/20161031184246.htm
11. Elizabeth Berrige and David Burrowes, "*The Persecution of Christians in Iran,*" The Christians in Parliament All Party Parliamentary Group and the All Party Parliamentary Group for International Freedom of Religion or Belief (London, 2015).

12. Marwan Muasher, *The Second Arab Awakening: And the Battle for Pluralism* (New Haven: Yale University Press, 2014), 134.
13. Eliza Griswold, "Is This the End of Christianity in the Middle East?" *The New York Times Magazine*, July 22, 2015.
14. "And Then There Were None," *The Economist*, January 2, 2016.

CHAPTER 10

The "Responsibility to Protect" and the Dangers of Military Intervention in Fragile States

Anthony C. Zinni

When we see people somewhere in the world who are in danger of persecution because of their ethnicity or religious beliefs, we feel a compassionate and honor-bound need to come to their rescue. We want to protect them and ensure their sustainable security and well being. For the United States, as the most powerful nation in the world and one founded on a set of noble values and principles, it seems to be an imbedded moral obligation to act. It is not, however, a simple decision to send in the Marines. We have incurred great costs in casualties and resources and a very mixed record of successes and failures when it comes to interventions despite the well-intentioned motivations behind the commitment of our military to prevent unacceptable humanitarian atrocities.

The end of the Cold War in 1989–1990 marked the beginning of the third reordering of the world in the twentieth century. The relief and euphoria that resulted from greatly diminishing the possibility of a nuclear war led to heady talk of a new world order and a peace dividend. What happened instead was the creation of a world described by Pentagon strat-

A. C. Zinni (✉)
The Middle East Institute, Honorary Chairman, Washington, DC, USA

© The Author(s) 2018
K. C. Ellis (ed.), *Secular Nationalism and Citizenship in Muslim Countries*, Minorities in West Asia and North Africa,
https://doi.org/10.1007/978-3-319-71204-8_10

egists today as "volatile, complex, uncertain, and ambiguous." As the post-Cold War era began, leaders such as Colin Powell and Casper Weinberger provided warnings and guidelines for the use of the military in this new environment. Their criteria advised defining the national security interests involved, the setting of clear objectives, a thorough assessment of the risks and costs, setting an exit strategy, analyzing the potential consequences of our actions, determining the continuing support of the American people, and gaining broad international support for our actions.

The Clinton Doctrine, articulated by the President in 1999, stated, "We cannot, indeed, we should not, do everything or be everywhere. But where our values and our interests are at stake, and where we can make a difference, we must be prepared to do so." In the decade of the 1990s, we took on many non-traditional commitments and militarily intervened in an unprecedented number of conflicts. It seemed more of these interventions were values based as opposed to interests based; and, as some had disastrous consequences, our appetite for these missions waned. Since September 11, 2001, however, we have been knee-deep in conflicts generated by the attacks on that date. This has led to an even greater diminution in our desire to take on further military interventions. As a result, when we now see conditions in war zones and failed and fragile states that threaten entire ethnic, religious, or tribal groups, there is little likelihood of our putting "boots on the ground" to stop the catastrophic bleeding and suffering.

I have had several direct experiences with the plight of Christians in the Middle East. I was commander of the United States Central Command. That role involved being responsible for all military functions and operations in the Middle East region, and it kept me aware of the status of Christians there. As the Bush Administration's envoy to the Middle East Peace Process engaged with the Israeli and Palestinian leadership, I would often meet with the leaders of the 16 Christian denominations in the region to make sure their voices were heard, even arranging a meeting for them with then Secretary of State Colin Powell. They felt left out of the peace process and had issues regarding the status of holy sites and their peoples' welfare. Recently, as part of a delegation from the Middle East Institute examining U.S.-Egyptian relationships, I had discussions with the Coptic Pope and Muslim religious leaders in Cairo regarding anti-Christian events in Egypt during the reign of the Muslim Brotherhood.

These and other experiences made me well aware of the fragile status of Christians in the region. Their position can range from full acceptance to tolerance to uneasy co-existence to outright genocide by extremists. There clearly has been an ongoing diaspora from the Middle East that has caused Christians' numbers to dwindle in many parts of the region. The recent efforts by extremist groups like ISIS to totally eliminate Christian groups such as the Yazidis have raised alarms about a new round of genocide in Syria and Iraq. This has led to a demand in many quarters to use military force to protect the groups at risk and prevent potential religious cleansing and genocide. For many reasons, however, U.S. policy makers have been reluctant to commit military forces to this mission. Past experiences with military interventions have made them wary of such commitments.

In 2008 I participated in a study on preventing genocide sponsored by the United States Holocaust Memorial Museum, the American Academy of Diplomacy, and the United States Institute of Peace. Our task force was co-chaired by former Secretary of State Madeline Albright and former Secretary of Defense William Cohen. Our task force made five basic recommendations. The first dealt with early warning and assessing risks that would trigger actions by U.S. policy makers. The second recommendation offered non-military, early-prevention measures that could be taken for before problems reached crisis status. The third discussed preventive diplomacy in order to halt and reverse escalation. The fourth addressed military options. Our fifth recommendation involved international actions such as strengthening norms and institutions. Implementing the recommendations that required developing intelligence procedures, diplomatic actions, and international cooperation seemed reasonably achievable. The use of the military, however, was definitely a last resort decision for our leadership in the view of the task force members; the study group felt maximum effort should be exerted through non-military measures in the early stages of a growing crisis.

I was a participant in another study the year before that was organized by the Center for Strategic and International Studies (CSIS). Our commission's task was to examine the elements of national power and how they were used in dealing with global crises. Our commission's membership included retired diplomats, educators, senior military, jurists, and business leaders. Ironically, this study's conclusion determined that the use of "hard power," the military option, was far more apt to be chosen over "soft power" options such as diplomacy, economic measures, humanitarian assistance, or informational efforts. We tended to do little in the way of preventive approaches and launched the military when crisis conditions developed. Even at that point, little was done to generate what has become known as a "whole of government" effort, and the military had little complementary support or partnership. The commission concluded that we lacked a balanced use of hard and soft power. We referred to this balanced combination as "smart power."

As mentioned earlier, after the end of the Cold War there was a growing use of the military in missions dubbed Military Operations Other Than War (MOOTW), Low Intensity Conflict (LIC), Stability and Security Operations, (SASO), Irregular Warfare (IW), Small Wars, and a plethora of other terms coined to cover the sudden spate of such non-traditional military missions in places like Kurdistan, Somalia, and the Balkans. U.S. decision makers and policy makers discovered (or relearned from Vietnam days) that it was easy to get in but hard to get out; that short-term positive effects cannot be sustained without major commitments of resources; that the United Stated owned the problem once we were in; that the military alone could not provide long-term stability; that the other components of government (economic, diplomatic, informational, development) did not have the capacity in their departments and agencies needed to fully stabilize the situations; and that the international community had little stomach or in some cases wherewithal to participate and share the burden. Another lesson was brought home to me when Secretary of State Albright asked me how we retain public support for limited operations with limited objectives using limited resources. I immediately understood her question. Americans understand existential threats that require the full commitment of our military toward total victory; but these vague, draining missions were difficult to support. We cannot accept "good enough" solutions that do not provide perfect end states in governance, economic, human rights, and other conditions. Yet, the sticker shock in the expenditure of resources and casualties necessary to achieve perfect endings is equally unacceptable.

There has also been a growing realization that we rarely succeed in these missions. Our hubris in developing the doctrine and strategies to rebuild societies and bring them into the twenty-first century has run smack into the realities of cultural differences, expectations, costs, and complexities. I have been involved in many of these kinds of operations and have seen first-hand the effects of military intervention, both positive and negative.

There is no doubt that the military brings a significant and unique set of capabilities to meet emergency needs during a humanitarian crisis, man-made or natural. It can rapidly deploy large supplies of food, shelter, potable water, medical care, engineering capability, transportation, communications, intelligence, contracting, and security. We saved 500,000 Kurds in 1992 after Saddam Hussein's forces brutally attacked them and sent them bleeding into the rugged hills of southeastern Turkey. There 10,000 of the most vulnerable of them—the elderly, children, and the ailing or wounded—died before we stabilized them and brought them home. We were left no choice but to protect them from Saddam's wrath, so we maintained a secure zone for 13 years following their rescue. The mission started with 13 contributing nations, but in the end only the United States and the United Kingdom maintained a military protection force.

In Somalia, we deployed 28,000 coalition forces to save hundreds of thousand people in desperate need of food, water, and shelter denied to them by warlord militias and rogue gangs who attacked the convoys of supplies non-governmental and international relief organizations were attempting to provide. The mission was originally seen as a short-term (weeks-long) jump-start limited to provide security until United Nations' forces could assume a more powerful presence. The U.S. forces remained there for three years and found themselves involved in fighting the warlord militias and providing basic sustenance. This was a case of classic "mission creep" that can easily befall intervention forces. Secretary of State Colin Powell's famous "Pottery Barn" analogy applies: "You break it, you own it."

In the aftermath of removing the regimes in Iraq and Afghanistan, we embarked on programs of nation building, proudly flaunting our "new" concepts of counter-insurgency. It was, in fact, a rehash of our Vietnam "hearts and minds" doctrine and suffered the same fate. As usual, the military was stuck with the missions as other government agencies offered minor contributions to the effort. Consequently, the military was involved in the areas of governance, economic development, the provision of aid, and many other components necessary to totally rebuild a society. Meanwhile, U.S. popular support for these missions waned and the continuous repeated deployments severely weakened military readiness and adversely impacted the quality of life of military personnel.

Military resources tend to be expensive compared to locally or internationally contracted materiel. It may be necessary in the short-term emergency phases of a mission to use them, but continuing to provide them draws on military resources needed for potential combat missions. Depleting stocks or failing to get appropriations to cover these expenditures can harm readiness. Some effort has been made recently to preposition humanitarian stocks, which helps; however, this does not alleviate the incurred burdens for things such as fuel, maintenance, and personnel costs.

The use of the military can create problems with aid organizations operating in the same area. They do not desire to be seen as cooperating with a military force because of the political implications and unacceptability of armed forces to the locals. At times they feel the military overwhelms their efforts and credit and attention goes toward the military participants instead of the aid workers. Often there is a fear in their ranks that the military will take charge and begin directing their activities. In fairness, both the aid community and the military have worked to find acceptable ways to cooperate and to better understand each other's roles. This is not, however, an easy marriage.

One result of outside intervention is the inevitable empowerment of certain elements of society and the disempowerment of others. We saw this in Somalia when certain clans lost power and others gained power resulting from our intervention. In Iraq, the dominant Sunni, a minority, lost power to the Shi'a. Although such shifts in power may not be intended, they can present long-term problems. In Somalia, it led to attacks on U.S. and UN forces that caused the mission to fail. In Iraq, it led to Iranian influence, the development of Sunni extremist groups, and the division of the country.

When we fail, "syndromes," such as the Vietnam Syndrome and Somalia Syndrome, result. These make our political decision makers very reluctant to commit forces. President Clinton held back from committing the military in the Rwanda–Burundi ethnic slaughter. He regretted not acting but was wary of intervention after the Somalia experience.

Much talk of creating "humanitarian zones" has been going on recently as streams of refugees pour out of the Middle East and elsewhere. Nations have grown increasingly resistant to taking in more of these traumatized people due to issues of local security, economics, or identity. Proposals of "no-fly zones" and sanctuaries have been advocated. While commanding the U.S. Central Command, I had responsibility for no-fly and no-drive zones. While in Somalia we had responsibility for humanitarian zones. In effect, these were designed to be safe areas for threatened and traumatized populations. An unintended result of establishing these zones is that we become responsible for *everything* that occurs within them, often for an indeterminate time period. Those we are protecting may commit unacceptable acts. A limited protection, such as no-fly, does not prevent ground attacks on the vulnerable. The administration and governance of these zones can fall to us. These and many other considerations need to be fully thought out before we leap to a decision to create sanctuaries.

The military has cautiously embraced the expanded humanitarian, security, and peacekeeping missions that have increased dramatically in the past two and a half decades. They accept and acknowledge that they have a critical role to play in these missions. They have, however, paid a dear price for these interventions, primarily because the policies and strategies implemented were not thoroughly developed by the political leadership that launched missions that solely depended on the military to resolve the problem. The lessons we should have learned in the operations we have conducted since 1989–1990 have not been effectively captured and codified into the policy and strategy planning necessary to ensure success next time. We have for example, plenty of robust and dynamic war plans that are updated, exercised, and adjusted on a continuous basis. Yet there are no counterpart plans prepared to deal with the non-military and post-conflict aspects of an intervention. Herein lies the problem.

The Arab Spring, the Shia/Sunni Divide, and Their Impact on Regional and Geopolitical Tensions

The Answer to the Vulnerability of Arab Christians and Other Minorities Is Citizenship Rights Under the Rule of Law

Rami G. Khouri

The year 2016 has been very difficult for many people and countries across the Middle East. Whether we seek to understand the condition of Christians or other vulnerable minorities, it is useful in retrospect to appreciate the wider context of the region's changing conditions in recent years and decades, especially in view of the "Sunni–Shiite Divide." This is a narrow and somewhat exaggerated framework within which to assess minority realities and threats, but nevertheless it is the dominant lens through which the world views the conditions of countries and people who are often caught in violent and disruptive situations.

Most of us in the Middle East during the past half-century had rarely if ever actually talked about Sunnis and Shiites in the context of the current warfare and confrontation—until 2003. Before that year, when the Anglo-American invasion destroyed the Iraqi state and produced conditions that were ideal for those who promoted sectarian strife, we were of course always aware of some contentious issues between Sunnis and Shiites, especially theological differences and occasional instances of discrimination

R. G. Khouri (✉)
American University of Beirut, Beirut, Lebanon

© The Author(s) 2018
K. C. Ellis (ed.), *Secular Nationalism and Citizenship in Muslim Countries*, Minorities in West Asia and North Africa,
https://doi.org/10.1007/978-3-319-71204-8_11

where Shiites were a minority, or were a majority ruled by a Sunni minority, as in Iraq and Bahrain. In Iraq, in particular, the brutal Baathist regime of Saddam Hussein carried out grievous crimes, not only against Shiites and Kurds, but also against all other Iraqis who challenged the ruling power elite. Soon after the Anglo-American war in 2003 eliminated the Iraqi state structure, we started to witness organized sectarian attacks and provocations, ethnic cleansing, decapitations, millions of sectarian refugees, and other such developments that we still witness today in some places. Much of this was initiated by small groups of Sunni terrorists associated with Al-Qaeda who entered the ungoverned regions of Iraq with the aim of fomenting anti-Shiite attacks and laying the foundations for an "Islamic State"—which ultimately emerged years later in the form of the Islamic State in Iraq and Syria (ISIS) and its self-declared caliphate.

Such dramatic episodes are only the tip of the iceberg of people across the Middle East, affirming their narrow sectarian and ethno-national identities (e.g., Kurds, Alawites, Amazig-Berbers, Yazidis, Druze, Christians, among others) because this was the most logical, natural, and effective way for them to enjoy the rights, services, and protections that were not always available to them through their modern states. This wider context of why sectarianism has expanded so quickly and forcefully in recent decades is part of a larger tale of the fate of modern states among the ancient societies and identities of the Arab world. Within this development that mainly spans the past three or four decades, the condition of Christians as one of the largest and oldest minorities in the region is best understood through the underlying dynamics of social, political, economic, environmental, and military stresses that impact all the people of the region. Christians and other minorities tend to suffer like everyone else in the face of wars, prolonged drought, foreign invasions, or stagnant and even collapsing economies. But they also suffer in distinct ways because of their status as minorities that are easily scapegoated, their presumed links with Western or other foreign powers, their history in some cases of being favored by colonial powers or current ruling powers, or the animosity they earn because others resent what they perceive as their higher educational status, better economic conditions, or easier access to foreign emigration opportunities.

In the most difficult conditions (such as wars and occupations in Iraq, Syria, Palestine, and Lebanon, in particular) the above factors tend to cause Christians to emigrate at a higher rate than their Muslim compatriots, which adds to the already existing lower birth rate among Christians, reducing their relative share in society. Some countries where Christians used to account for around 10 percent of the total population now see that figure down to perhaps 4 or 5 percent at best—and it continues to decline in relative terms. Consequently, many people around the region and the world see Arab Christians as a threatened minority; and in some countries or regions within countries they may disappear altogether because they see no future for themselves in their ancestral land. This is due to many reasons, including recent economic stresses, political tensions, security fears, occasional explicit acts of violence against Christians, and perceptions of discrimination in a few countries. Understanding this situation in its totality requires us to look beyond Muslim–Christian relations, and rather to appreciate the much wider, deeper, and older forces that make life difficult for *all* people in many Arab countries.

Today's regrettable sectarian tensions between Sunnis and Shiites represent only the most recent serious threat that impacts the lives of millions of people, both majorities and minorities. It also highlights sectarian identity as an element of both internal stresses within states and regional conflicts among states and non-state actors. These dynamics generate dilemmas, dangers, and options that shape the lives of all Arabs, including Christians and other minorities. Beyond demeaning people across the entire Middle East, regardless of their identity or status, sectarianism now also ravages the wider world in the form of terrorism, the repercussions of fractured states, increased militancy, refugee flows, and other dynamics.

We can best grasp why this has happened by noting that Christians, minorities, and all citizens in the Arab world have experienced a series of trends in recent decades that have shaken the three consecutive orders that had defined the Arab world and the Middle East broadly for perhaps the past 500 years. The Ottoman order shaped much of the region for some 400 years, during which individual communities existed in a range of conditions and configurations, such as *dhimmi* communities, ethno-national groups, tribal groups, commercial elites, some favored minorities, and others. This gave way to the colonial period, which varied in form, intensity, and duration in different countries, and dominated Arab societies for periods ranging from a few decades to nearly two centuries. By the 1930s–1940s, decolonization had spawned mandates and nominally independent and sovereign modern states, with borders, central governments, armies, passports, and a single national identity—e.g., Jordan, Lebanon, Syria, Libya, Kuwait, etc.—that was a novelty for most Arabs or as well as non-Arabs (Kurds, Druze, Amazig-Berbers, Circassians) in Arab-majority states.

The state order that started to come into being immediately after World War I has lasted for the past century, though the borders of some Arab states keep changing, as we have seen in Sudan, Yemen, Palestine, Iraq, Syria, and Kuwait under Iraq's brief conquest. These physical borders can be erratic and fluid in places, and they are particularly politically fluid in the eyes of many of their own people, whose allegiance to a "state" identity is often less intense than their ethnic, tribal, religious, or other transnational identity.

More importantly for the condition of Christians and minorities across the Arab region, within this past tumultuous century the most fundamental concepts that define states and the lives of their citizens have never been either defined or validated by those citizens. These include core critical ideas such as statehood, nationhood, sovereignty, religiosity and secularism, communal and national identity, citizenship, governance, and the dignity of the individual that should emanate from good governance—the critical element that allows people to achieve their basic rights and have their fundamental human needs met, such as housing, schooling, health care, clean water, decent income, the rule of law, security, and stability. We as Arab citizens have never really had the opportunity, or been asked, to define what we understand to be the critical elements that create security in our lives, at the individual, family, community, or national levels. All of these elements ultimately conflate into perhaps the most important yet elusive concept that shapes the lives of individuals, communities, and states in our region, and that also has never been meaningfully defined by citizens—the concept of legitimacy. This includes the legitimacy of the state, of citizen rights, of governance and the exercise of power, and of the regional order.

This very broad menu of fundamental, even existential, concepts remains peculiarly undefined in the Arab region as a whole, which is why every single one of these critical concepts is in flux right now. Our region is so turbulent, and suffers such violence and uncertainty, because the basic building blocks of stable, satisfying states have never been put in place; and those building blocks of modern statehood that were put in place in the past century proved to be poorly anchored in the soil of society and people's identities and allegiances.

The decades of the 1970s and 1980s were a pivotal turning point in this history. In those years the old Arab nationalist order was systematically discredited by its defeat in the 1967 war with Israel, the lack of good governance, and states' inability to meet the needs of their growing populations. As usually has been the case, the exception comprised a small minority—5 to 10 percent of the Arab population—that included most citizens of oil-producing states or very wealthy people in non-oil-producing countries who monopolized power and wealth. One reason for this is that in the 1970s and 1980s our region witnessed the negative impact on families of a continuing problem: the imbalance between high population growth rates and fluctuating economic growth rates, leading to poverty, unemployment and underemployment, greater economic disparities, and heightened vulnerability and resentment among tens of millions of Arabs who could not keep up with the rising costs of their families' everyday vital needs. It is important to recall that in the past tumultuous century from 1915 to 2015, the total population of the Arab world increased from around 40 million to 400 million—among the fastest continuing population growth spurts in the world, and surely one of the reasons for the demographic, economic, social, environmental, and political stresses our region suffers today.

This pivotal turning point in the 1970s–1980s included some shifts in the broadly defining developmental and political patterns of the region, which impacted individuals and families, whether these were in minorities, majorities, or somewhere in between. I say "somewhere in between" because individuals in the Arab world, as in other countries, often have multiple and fluid identities, and they can gravitate between minority and majority status if they wish by shifting their self-identification. So an individual can be a Palestinian; a Jordanian; a Christian; a Lebanese; a Maronite; a Druze; a member of a small clan or a large tribe; an Arab; a Kurd; a Circassian; any of several types of Muslims, such as a Shiite, Sunni, Salafi, Sufi, jihadi, etc.; a progressive democrat; a narrow state nationalist; or some other self-asserted identity. Individuals identify themselves with the identity that they deem to be the most logistically useful and emotionally meaningful to them at any given moment. We have seen this fluidity expressed in public opinion polls across the region over the past 40 years: individuals who are asked about their most important identity routinely change their answers over time, saying, for example, that they are Jordanian, Syrian, or Kuwaiti, or Muslim or Christian, or Druze or Kurd or Arab, or a member of a specific tribe or tribal confederation that crosses state boundaries, or any other identity that is meaningful to them at the moment they are asked this question. Individuals usually lay claim to the identity that they feel will help them achieve the well-being and the rights of citizenship that they have not achieved through their status as citizens in a modern state. Perhaps this is because they have never been given the opportunity to define either citizenship or statehood. Citizens also regularly fluctuated among their identities in large part as a response to conditions around them, whether in their immediate neighborhood and state, or in the wider region and the world. These evolving conditions and identities that defined people's lives in the past century in fact reflect a legacy of national frailty and instability, but one that was camouflaged by several factors: many decades of authoritarian rule, the negative regional impacts of the Arab–Israeli conflict, the dulling impact of oil income, and the stultifying result of the Cold War's external constraints on internal developments. That complex legacy also ultimately resulted in the situation we suffer today in the region, including sectarian tensions and the increased vulnerability of minorities.

The developmental state was replaced by the consumer state. The ruling families and their crony capitalist friends and partners—the people around Zein Alabidine Ben Ali, Husni Mubarak, Ali Abdullah Saleh, Saddam Hussein, Hafez and Bashar Assad, Omar Hassan Al Bashir, and many other rulers whose names often are better known than the names of their countries—replaced the possibility of developing a social contract that defined how power was exercised. The concept of security replaced the concept of nationalism. The idea of the citizen was replaced by the idea of a consumer—as we've witnessed in the cases of some Arab societies that turned the opening of a McDonalds hamburger outlet into an official state event, and the inauguration of a children's entertainment fair like Legoland into a major national and developmental achievement—or wealthy countries that have sought global validation by hosting (and paying for) established international sports events like tennis or golf tournaments or car races. The critical decades of the 1970s and 1980s cemented the shift from Arab nationalist developmental states that had been improving the lives of most citizens to family-run, security-anchored, crony-capitalist-supported consumer states that spawned pauperization, marginalization, and chronic vulnerability among tens of millions of citizens.

Subsequently, in the two decades from the early 1990s to 2010, the Arab world experienced another major shift which impacted heavily the status of citizens, the nature of statehood, and the relationships between the two. From the end of the Cold War in 1990 until around 2010, the region experienced slow degradations in the fundamental quality of life of a large number of its people. It is very hard to absolutely quantify these trends, but they are clear from indicators such as poverty, socio-economic disparities, quality of education, labor force participation, productivity, labor informality, and many others that define both the ability of individuals to participate meaningfully in their society and to live a decent life, and the ability of society to provide their citizens the opportunities to do just that. In this period the Cold War powers pulled back from parts of the region for various reasons, population/economic growth imbalances persisted and worsened, and many key quality-of-life dimensions declined, such as education, income, opportunity, access to water and reasonably priced food, and family security, among others. Governments had provided most of these basic needs in the previous decades, but after 1990 they were gradually less able to do so. This was partly because they ran out of money, and partly because they did not have the technical ability or political legitimacy and credibility to be able to continue to promote broad social development. So it was no surprise, in retrospect, to see the eruption of the Arab uprisings in December 2010 and January 2011, which spread in various forms to a dozen Arab states, six of which suffered serious political and military disruption.

The mass discontent and even existential fears of citizens who were finding it increasingly difficult to meet the basic needs of their families but also were politically powerless erupted onto the surface of society during the uprisings of 2010–2011. The uprisings happened partly because people were unhappy, poor, marginalized, or inadequately served by their governments and societies; however, they mainly happened because tens of millions of people started to feel that alongside these pressures and disadvantages they were forever condemned to stay in that condition of marginalization, poverty, vulnerability, helplessness, and daily pain. Their helplessness was heightened by their hopelessness; they feared they were never going to be able to get out of their dreadful situation, and that they and their children were condemned to lifetimes of poverty and marginalization.

The equally frightening reality today is that most of the trends that sparked the uprisings—poverty, lack of opportunity, helplessness, suffering, and perpetual marginalization that tens of millions of families felt—have worsened in the past six years. Demography once again plays a major role here, for in the past six years the population of the Arab world has increased by 52 million people, from around 348 million to 400 million. Fifty-two million people have been born since 2010, when the Arab world could not meet the basic needs of its people. How will we possibly find the ability now to feed, house, educate, employ, and provide health care for another 52 million Arabs, or the six or seven million new people being born in the Arab world every year?[1]

These immense challenges that define the wider context of the Arab region are not being addressed seriously. Daily life for hundreds of millions of Arabs remains difficult, year after year, and in some cases it worsens dramatically due to wars and state collapse. All of us—whether Christians or Muslims or any other identity—will suffer from the consequences of our states' and governments' not meeting the challenges of development, dignity, and security that still are major issues for what may be a majority of Arabs. Ten key trends in particular shape the current conditions and trajectories in the Arab region, and these need to be appreciated as the main factors that make life more and more difficult for all citizens, and especially for minorities, who are easily scapegoated and discriminated against, enjoy less access to public assets, or choose to emigrate more quickly than others in society.

The first is the state fragmentation that impacts many countries, including some states that have collapsed and others that survive but are fragile at the edges. Most Arab borders are relatively porous, as states find it difficult to control flows of people or goods, whether refugees, armed militias, smugglers of arms and narcotics, or desperate people looking for any job that will give them a few dollars a day. This fragmentation has been building up for decades, and it is the result of citizens not being offered full rights, and therefore not developing full allegiance to their states and governments.

The second, related trend is the continuous contraction of the reach, impact, and even the legitimacy of some central governments. This also started in the 1970s, when the Muslim Brotherhood suddenly enhanced its following as a big regional movement anchored in local grievances. Why? Because Arab central governments were not able to keep meeting the basic needs of citizens in health, education and income, or to give voice to people in terms of their representation politically, culturally, economically, and nationally. The contraction of the central government from physical regions (especially poor and rural areas) and from big segments of some sectors (fresh water delivery, communications, education, and health care) allowed others to step in and deliver the things that citizens saw as their essential rights. Religious, tribal, and ethnic organizations were the first to step in and fill the vacuums left by receding governments. This contributed to growing sectarianism in many instances. It also created situations of shared sovereignty among the government and others in society who provided basic citizen services. The contraction of government activities that serve citizens has combined recently with a renewal of authoritarian tendencies—heavily, directly, explicitly, and eagerly supported by foreign countries, including the United States and some Western European nations, Russia, Iran, China, Turkey, as well as powers within the Arab world.

Third is the use of political violence by all states and organizations across the region. All major political actors—governments, opposition groups, foreign parties, regional powers, global powers, non-government groups, terror groups—now actively use military force and political violence and wage war in one way or another anywhere they wish to do so in the Middle East.

Fourth, sectarian polarization continues to ravage many of our societies, though it is relatively new to our region in its current violent and exclusionary form. Occasional incidents in past centuries saw sectarian fighting among a few groups here and there in Arab lands, but sectarian violence on the scale we see today has not been part of our history. Iran and Saudi Arabia are widely depicted as the two poles of today's Sunni–Shiite sectarian rivalry, and they certainly are active in challenging each other. But this alone cannot explain the sudden scourge of sectarian warfare. One element of the explanation for heightened Sunni–Shiite tensions is that the widespread lack of vital citizenship exercised through the rule of law in societies governed by legitimate ruling authorities and states in recent decades has forced people to find legitimacy, services, protection, expression, and opportunity anywhere they can. They often and most easily find these in their tribal, religious, or sectarian identities; ethno-national groups; regional affiliations; and even their local gangs or football hooligans' group. Survival, well-being, and dignity push people to belong to groups they identify with, which are often sectarian groups. These are not purely ideological reactions, but rather biological reactions. People needing to get food to feed six kids at home, while nobody at home works other than perhaps a son who dropped out of school at age 12 and washes dishes in a restaurant to bring home the equivalent of a few dollars a day, such people who need to find food and basic needs for their families will do anything to achieve that end, including illegal or violent actions such as joining extremist or militant groups. The major sectarian polarization and violence that plague the Middle East today need to be understood in a much more nuanced and accurate way than simply as the consequence of Saudi–Iranian tensions.

The fifth trend is overt, explicit, and continuing political and military intervention in Arab states by regional powers, especially Israel, Turkey, Iran, and Saudi Arabia, but also others. Such powers have long meddled in their neighbors' affairs, but they have never done it so openly, explicitly, militarily, simultaneously, and continuously. As global powers reduce or reconfigure their engagements in the Middle East, regional powers step in to fill that vacuum, which has enhanced regional rivalries as elements in the turbulence and violence in the region.

The sixth trend is the continuing rise of terrorism, especially by ISIS and Al-Qaeda, within the ongoing global war on terror that George W. Bush launched in 2001. The United States has been actively engaged in direct or indirect military actions across South Asia and the Middle East for the past 35 years or so, ever since in the early 1980s it helped Afghan and Arab groups fight the Soviets who had invaded and occupied Afghanistan. These military actions over decades have included some legitimate ones—like driving Iraq out of Kuwait, or attacking Al-Qaeda and the Taliban after the 9/11. Yet over the past 35 years of military engagements in our region most of the United States' strategic aims have not been met effectively, and new problems have emerged as a consequence of non-stop U.S. militarism. The United States has prevented Al-Qaeda and other would-be attackers from carrying out a major terror operation on the U.S. mainland since 9/11, but other goals have not been met. The Taliban are resurgent, Al-Qaeda has expanded globally, ISIS is operating in numerous countries, Egypt has a serious internal security problem, Iraq and Syria are fragile, the Iran–Syria–Hezbollah axis remains strong, Turkey is forging close links with Russia, and terror threats and attacks continue to plague many countries. The trend of continuing terrorism breeds further authoritarian responses by Arab governments that are supported by foreign powers; this in turn leads to new tensions and security threats, as new generations of hopeless young men and women become radicalized.

The seventh trend is a broad reconfiguration of the role of the big powers in the region—mainly the United States, Russia, and Europe—highlighted recently by Russia's dramatic military involvement in Syria and its enhanced diplomatic engagements with other countries, especially Turkey and Iran. The Russians, Iranians, and Turks are redefining how they engage politically and militarily in the region. The Israelis would like to do this also but they cannot because they have not resolved their conflict with the Palestinians, and they remain widely disliked by the Arab public, while some Arab governments seek to join Israel in confronting Iran. Saudi Arabia is significantly expanding its power and role in the region in a much more dynamic and even aggressive way, including its clumsy actions in Yemen and Syria; but it is learning every day as it continues to increase its political, military, and other interventions in the region.

The eighth trend is the continuing expansion of huge refugee flows across the region and further afield, as millions of people flee from Syria, Iraq, Yemen, and other lands to seek refuge, in the region mostly, but also abroad. The long-term consequences of these flows remain to be seen, including their international impact.

The ninth factor of note in the evolving conditions across the Middle East is the continuation of the Arab–Israeli conflict, which remains the oldest and most destabilizing and radicalizing force in the Middle East. The Arab–Israeli conflict between Zionism and Arabism has been going on for over a century, since the birth of Zionism in Europe, and has had huge impacts across the region in different ways, often leading to the reduced legitimacy of Arab leaders and governments in the eyes of their own people.

The tenth and most troubling issue to note is that all of these trends are continuing, while fundamental, daily-life conditions for a vast number of ordinary citizens continue to become more difficult. I would estimate that over half the 400 million people of the Arab world struggle to make ends meet and care for their families. In the case of many young Arabs, their lack of jobs or adequate income means they are not even able to marry and start families. Some surveys suggest that over 60 percent of new entrants to the labor market in Egypt go into the informal sector, because they are unqualified to do anything other than sweep floors or wash dishes and car windows. The informal sector on average may account for as much as 40 percent of Arab labor markets. The informal sector offers low pay, no job security, and no social protections like health insurance, maximum working hours, and retirement plans. It guarantees life-long misery and vulnerability, which inevitably spill over into political and social tensions, or even violence in some cases. Another danger sign: About 45 percent of students in mid-primary and mid-secondary school classes around the Arab world are not learning to read, write, or do basic math, according to standardized international test results. They will drop out of school and join the informal market, or try to emigrate, illegally in most cases.[2] Some 25 million young Arabs who should be in school are not in school, for various reasons, including wars, social and logistical issues, and the poor quality of education they witness in their midst whereby so many students learning nothing in class. Around 75 million Arab students are in school, even though many of them are not learning anything.³ So we suffer a massive structural problem inside the Arab world in terms of capturing and nurturing the enormous human potential in our region that has been driven into the ground or pushed abroad by the problem of authoritarian government and mismanagement over so many decades.

All of these problems, including inadequate water, education, electricity, and jobs, impact every Arab citizen, whether Christian, Muslim, or any ethnicity or religion. People will naturally turn back to their religion, or their tribal and ethnic identity, to find protection if the state leaves them living in conditions defined by these ten trends, as has been the case for many Arabs in the past half-century. The answer to vulnerable minorities in the Arab world, whether dwindling Christian communities in peril or any other group of people, is genuine citizenship, based on a clear understanding of the need for citizens to define and validate their own government systems, state borders, power structures, and national values. Tunisia is the first Arab state to embark on this road, and hopefully Tunisia will prove to be the Poland of the Arab world, in that Poland broke through the harsh Soviet controls in the early 1980s and ten years later the entire Soviet system collapsed in tatters. Perhaps something similar will happen in the Arab world, if the Tunisian democratic transition succeeds and sparks others in the region.

Notes

1. See: The World Bank, "Arab World." This is total population and growth rate data from World Bank; most UN data puts the total at 400 million; in any case it is always an estimate due to lack of recent censuses. http://data.worldbank.org/region/arab-world
2. Lisbet Steer, Hafez Ghanen, Maysa Jalbout, with Adam Parker & Katie Smith, "Arab Youth: Missing Educational Foundations for a Productive Life?" Center for Universal Education, Brooking Institution, February 2014. https://www.brookings.edu/wp-content/uploads/2014/02/arabworld_learningbarometer_en.pdf
3. "Regional Overview for Arab States," *UNESCO*, March 11, 2015. "Despite the growing interest in quality issues, the accumulated evidence points to the prevalence of weak pupil performance, widespread learning disparities, high repetition and low survival and completion rates in several countries in the region. Disparities in learning outcomes, while narrowing between girls

and boys in many contexts, remain significant in others, to the disadvantage of poor, rural, urban slum, indigenous and minority pupils." The data on children in school is from these UNESCO sources. http://en.unesco.org/ gem-report/sites/gem-   report/files/regional_overview_AS_en.pdf   and http://en.unesco.org/gem-report/sites/gem-report/files/157267E.pdf

The Impact of the Shia-Sunni Political Struggle and Future Strategies for Christians and Other Vulnerable Communities in the Middle East

Brian Katulis

Christians and other vulnerable communities are caught up in the broader regional struggles for power and influence currently taking place in the Middle East. Christians are but one community that has been rendered defenseless and exposed by the internal and regional Shia–Sunni sectarian struggles in Iraq and Syria.

Along with the challenge of Muslim sectarianism, the rise and fall of political Islamist forces in countries such as Egypt have placed Christians and other groups in the crossfire of a dangerous battle. Geographically, the Middle East is at the epicenter of a broader "arc of crisis" that has a signifi-cant impact on security beyond the region, as demonstrated by the recent refugee crisis in Europe. Strategically, the region has long served as a vital land and sea transit route between Europe, Asia, and Africa, and its stabil-ity is an interest of several global powers, including the United States.

B. Katulis (✉)
Center for American Progress, Washington, DC, USA

© The Author(s) 2018   195
K. C. Ellis (ed.), *Secular Nationalism and Citizenship in Muslim Countries*, Minorities in West Asia and North Africa,
https://doi.org/10.1007/978-3-319-71204-8_12

The continued presence of Christians and other vulnerable religious minority groups in the region requires a shift in policy planning on the part of the United States, Europe, and Russia toward working with regional partners to develop a positive agenda that supports religious freedom, equality, and basic rights for all its people, regardless of their religious or sectarian background.

This chapter provides a strategic assessment of the security and political dynamics reshaping the Middle East today. It then describes how these overarching security dynamics impact Christian communities across the Middle East, highlighting the diversity of circumstances facing the region's Christians. Next, it analyzes the impact of U.S. foreign policy on these dynamics during the past few years. Finally, it concludes with some preliminary analysis on the impact of President Donald Trump and his administration on these dynamics.

A STRATEGIC ASSESSMENT OF SECURITY AND POLITICAL DYNAMICS IN TODAY'S MIDDLE EAST

An intense competition for power between and within states dominates the Middle East today. This competition for power has fragmented societies on the nation-state level and shattered the regional order between those states as countries like Saudi Arabia and Iran jockey for influence and status across the Middle East. More than anything else, this competition for power is governed by the desire of both states and non-state actors to control states and determine the shape of the international order in the region. As a consequence of this desire for control, sectarian battle lines have been drawn and hardened through the Middle East.

Though this regional competition for power took root long before the 2011 Arab Spring, those revolts opened up new arenas for geopolitical struggle that only intensified the existing contest for power. This competition is multipolar; it does not fit into categories that are often used as a framework for analysis. The contest for power is frequently conceptualized as a sectarian struggle between Sunni and Shia Muslim blocs, led, respectively, by Saudi Arabia and Iran. Although this divide remains important, it is incomplete and serves to obscure other, equally important aspects of the post-2011 competition for power and influence among Sunni-majority countries in the Middle East and North Africa. The fall of authoritarian regimes in Tunisia, Egypt, and Libya and the civil wars in Syria and Yemen have created new arenas for both emerging and established regional powers to vie for influence.

Today, the struggle for influence in the region takes place in multiple areas: in politics, the media, and economy. The battle is not simply about security as traditionally defined, although this is a key component, particularly in Syria's civil war and the continued threats posed by terrorist groups in Yemen, Egypt, Libya, and Iraq. Even though cross-border conflicts between states have become increasingly rare in recent decades, countries continue to shape and alter the internal security dynamics of other countries through direct military aid and support for non-state terrorist networks.

But the new feature of the past decade has been the expansion of the competition between states in these new arenas of politics, media, and economics. In general, wealthier and more politically stable states have advanced their own national interests by offering financial support to governments and political actors in less wealthy countries gripped by deep domestic political polarization. Media outlets and support for media campaigns are an important force multiplier in this struggle. Indeed, the Middle East is embroiled in a fierce contest of ideas at the intersection of religion, politics, and violence—a struggle that manifests differently in different places but affects the entire region.

In part, this struggle is driven by a crisis of political legitimacy (defined here as having the "internal support for the system of government, expressed voluntarily by the people"[1]) decades in the making. Social contracts have eroded. The lack of open and vibrant debate about the future keeps societal discourse stuck in the past and present. The specific problems of terrorism and political legitimacy are linked to the broader challenge of the lack of political alternatives to the extremist ideologies espoused by groups such as the Islamic State. A lack of basic freedoms in many countries across the region has created an intellectual and political vacuum filled by extremism, sectarianism, and xenophobic nationalism.

Moreover, the Middle East as a whole lacks a comprehensive regional security architecture to govern and moderate geopolitical competition. The security structures that do exist are only modestly integrated, with regional states often cooperating more closely with the United States than with their immediate neighbors. This zero-sum environment encourages regional states to use whatever means at their disposal—including stoking sectarianism—to secure their own power and influence.

Both Iran and Saudi Arabia have historically supported proxy elements and other countries to advance their own geopolitical interests in the region and around the world, but the region's multiple civil wars have given them and their regional partners an unprecedented opportunity to pursue geopolitical advantage.[2] However, these external interventions have only exacerbated existing conflicts and prolonged humanitarian suffering by sharpening their sectarian[3] and geopolitical edges.

IMPACT OF REGIONAL DYNAMICS ON CHRISTIANS IN THE MIDDLE EAST

The impact this regional competition has on the Middle East's Christian population varies from country to country. Today's overall Christian community in the Middle East is estimated to range from 7.5 million to 15 million individuals, with the largest numbers living in Egypt, Syria, and Lebanon.[4] These estimates vary considerably because of the massive waves of forced migration over the past decade and the sharp growth in the number of Christians from the Middle East living in exile since the start of the new millennium. Today, Christians represent less than 5 percent of the region's overall population.[5]

The Arab Spring uprisings that began in 2011 have created new pressures on Christians, other religious groups, and nonbelievers. More than four years after the start of the uprisings, the status of Christians varies considerably across the region. In Egypt and Lebanon, there is a stronger sense of protection and security for Christians than in war zones like Syria and Iraq. But the overall regional picture looks grim, and the reactions from the United States, Europe, and other key powers to this new wave of destruction have been marginal.

Some of this deterioration in the overall status of the Middle East's Christians is the direct result of unforced errors: the 2003 Iraq War and its aftermath, for example, had devastating consequences for the Christian community there. But most of what is happening to Christians in the Middle East is the result of wider regional trends related to struggles for power and the use of religion as a tool to build influence with constituencies that have ultimately divided societies, as noted earlier.

In this context, individuals from all walks of life have become vulnerable, as respect for basic freedoms has deteriorated in specific countries. Christian communities are particularly exposed and defenseless in key countries.

Shia--Sunni sectarian struggles in Iraq and Syria have been especially brutal for Christian communities, while the challenges posed by the rise and fall of political Islamist forces in countries such as Egypt have placed Christians and other groups in the crosshairs of a dangerous political battle.

It is therefore important to analyze separate countries according to the specific challenges in each. For example, Egypt's Christians, the largest numerical group of Christians in the region, generally backed the 2013 removal of the Muslim Brotherhood from office, yet they retain some reservations about the country's current path.[6] Lebanon—which has largest Christian community as a percentage of overall population, although precise estimates are not reliable since the last official census was conducted in 1932[7]—experiences internal divisions among Christian communities that view themselves as more empowered than others in the region. Palestinian Christians living under occupation in the West Bank and Gaza face the same strains and limits as Muslim Palestinians of all walks of life. In Iraq and Syria, extreme violence and a general breakdown of order have devastated Christian communities.

Moreover, the rise of violent extremist ideologies has negatively affected Christians. Extremist movements, including the recent rise of the Islamic State, have led to new threats against Christian communities. These movements, which follow an ultra-orthodox and violent interpretation of Islam, are shredding already fragile social fabrics in some key Middle Eastern countries. Countries that have sharp sectarian and ethnic divisions appear to be most susceptible to these groups. Other Islamist groups, including the Muslim Brotherhood, often engage in sectarian discourse that scapegoats Christians and accuses them of collusion with the military and other authorities.

The Situation in Iraq: Estimates vary, but most experts conclude that the vast majority of Iraq's 1.5 million Christians have fled their homes since the United States-led invasion in 2003.[8] Many have gone overseas, and others have flocked to the Kurdish regions of northern Iraq. The rise of ISIS in 2014 has been especially devastating for the Iraqi Christian community. The ISIS seizure of Mosul and surrounding parts of the nearby Nineveh Plains devastated Christian communities that had roots in those areas reaching back more than 1500 years.[9] Christians were faced with stark options from ISIS: pay a *jizya* tax or religious levy imposed in previous eras of Islamic rule, convert, or die.[10] Most Christians fled, while ISIS terrorists have destroyed churches and other landmarks of Christian heritage.

The Situation in Syria: Representing about 10 percent of Syria's population of 22 million, the Christian community is the second largest in Middle East in terms of numbers.[11] As in Iraq, Christians in Syria have faced death, pressure to convert, or requirements to pay a special tax for non-Muslims from a variety of terrorist groups, including ISIS. Moreover, Syria's Christians are divided over where their support lies: some Christians remain aligned with the government of President Bashar al-Assad, while others have joined the anti-Assad opposition. Others have joined the millions of Syrians displaced by the civil war, requiring the same humanitarian assistance that their fellow Syrians need.

The Situation in Egypt: Egypt's Christians comprise the largest Christian community in a single country in the broader Middle East, with an estimated 6–9 million Christians.[12] They have endured waves of complicated political transitions since 2011, and increased insecurity has taken its toll on the community. The head of the Coptic Church supported Muslim Brotherhood President Mohammad Morsi's removal and has backed his successor, President Abdel Fatah al-Sisi.[13] A significant segment of Egypt's Christian population seems to have supported this move as well, but some Egyptian Christians have expressed worries that this positioning with an authoritarian government could leave them exposed to a potential backlash in the long run. Moreover, Egypt's legal code still includes restrictions on basic religious freedom, and Egypt's institutional weaknesses, including shortcomings in the police and justice sectors, have left Egyptians of all religious backgrounds vulnerable.

The Situation in Lebanon: Although numerically smaller than Egypt's Christian community, the Christian community in Lebanon remains more politically powerful than its counterparts in other countries for a number of reasons. Christians represent a larger share of the population of Lebanon compared with other countries in the region. They have been in leadership positions in government, politics, and business life for decades; the longstanding involvement of Christians in Lebanon's social and cultural life are vital to the country's heritage. However, the two main political leaders in the Christian community—Lebanese Forces head Samir Geagea and Free Patriotic Movement leader Michel Aoun—remain bitterly divided over Iran, Hezbollah, and Syria's civil war.

The Situation in Israel and the Palestinian Territories: In the West Bank, the Christian presence has dropped substantially in recent decades, including in vital places such as Bethlehem, the birthplace of Jesus. This declining presence is related to the broader factors that affect all Palestinians, including the lack of resolution to the Israeli–Palestinian conflict, the restrictions on movement and access put in place by the Israeli occupation, and the lack of economic opportunities to produce jobs. The status of Christians living in Jerusalem is better than those living in the West Bank, but the lack of resolution to the overall conflict has created greater incentives for Christians to migrate to other countries. Between 150,000 and 200,000 Christians live in Israel proper and retain deep concerns about full equality and citizenship.[14]

The Situation in Jordan: Jordan has a small native population of Christians numbering a few hundred thousand, but successive waves of refugees from Palestine, Iraq, and Syria have included large numbers of Christians. In the past decade, Jordan has become one of the few safe havens for Christians fleeing conflict and repression in other parts of the region. Though it faces the same questions on equal citizenship that plague the region as a whole, the Hashemite monarchy in Jordan has set a tone of tolerance and inclusivity toward the country's Christians.

IMPACT OF U.S. POLICY ON CHRISTIANS IN THE MIDDLE EAST

For eight years, the Obama administration's Middle East policy largely ignored and, in some cases, unintentionally abetted these destructive regional dynamics. Thanks to the war in Iraq, the Obama administration inherited a Middle East already deeply in the throes of sectarianism. The war empowered sectarian actors of all stripes, from Sunni al Qaeda terrorists to Iranian-backed Shia militias. Moreover, by toppling Saddam Hussein's regime and replacing it with a government more susceptible to Iranian influence, the war shifted the regional balance of power toward Tehran.

From the start, the Obama administration failed to push back against sectarianism in any real way. Indeed, it framed American engagement with the region in largely sectarian terms, such as President Obama's June 2009 Cairo speech calling for "a new beginning between the United States and Muslims around the world,"[15] the creation of a State Department special representative to Muslim communities, and other efforts to reach out to an undifferentiated "Muslim world," without any mention of universal values like pluralism and religious freedom. It remains unclear what these efforts achieved, aside from signaling an implicit if unintended acceptance of communal boundaries policed by autocratic governments, Islamist groups, and others across the region.

More concretely, the Obama administration's early Iraq policy helped contribute to regional fragmentation and the rise of the Islamic State in ways that remain largely unacknowledged. In particular, the administration's decision to cast its lot with Prime Minister Nuri al-Maliki after his political coalition's narrow loss in the 2010 Iraqi parliamentary elections enabled Maliki's increasingly dictatorial and sectarian behavior over the next four years. This behavior, in turn, helped create the conditions that enabled the Islamic State's June 2014 blitzkrieg. The Obama administration then forced Maliki out of power as a condition of American military assistance against the Islamic State, but the damage to Iraq and the region had been done.

The Arab Spring of 2011 in Tunisia, Egypt, and elsewhere in the region caught the administration flat-footed. Though publicly sympathetic to aspirations for greater freedom and more representative government in the region, domestic political and budgetary constraints prevented the Obama administration from backing its rhetoric with real resources. However, the administration's call for longtime Egyptian dictator Hosni Mubarak's departure from power alienated it from many of America's other long-standing regional partners, Saudi Arabia in particular.

Perceiving the United States as having hung Mubarak out to dry, these partners and the Obama administration drifted even further apart during the Muslim Brotherhood's brief time in power in Egypt. The administration's actual policy toward Egypt under the Brotherhood was muddled and allowed various actors in Egypt and the region to believe the worst about American intentions. The Obama administration's Egypt policy from 2011 onward convinced Saudi Arabia, the United Arab Emirates, and other long-standing American regional partners that they had to be more assertive in pursuit of their own regional interests.

This new assertiveness, however, has only contributed to the Middle East's social and political fragmentation. Viewing itself as losing ground to Iran in the regional competition for geopolitical power, Saudi Arabia—often in conjunction with the UAE and other Saudi regional partners—has stepped up its interventions across the region. In Syria, for instance, Saudi Arabia and other Gulf counties, most notably Qatar, have provided arms and other assistance to largely Sunni Islamist militant groups fighting the Assad regime. This aid has kept the armed opposition to Assad alive, but it has also fragmented it into competing factions unable to either defeat the regime or force it to the negotiating table. Making matters worse, this fragmentation has allowed Salafi-jihadi militants like Jabhat

Fateh el-Sham (al Qaeda's Syrian branch) and Ahrar al-Sham to take root in Syria, a development that portends increased fragmentation of Syrian society as a whole. For its part, the Obama administration's Syria policy unintentionally abetted the fragmentation of Syria by failing to effectively coordinate assistance to the armed opposition.

Similarly, the Obama administration made the United States an accessory to the fragmentation of Libya and Yemen. The merits of the initial intervention against the Qaddafi regime in Libya can be debated, but the international neglect of post-Qaddafi political rebuilding allowed Gulf states like the UAE and Qatar to treat the country as an arena in which to advance their own regional geopolitical agendas. Only at the end of the Obama administration did a more active Libya policy allow the United States to rein in its regional partners and attempt to forge a unified Libyan government.

In Yemen, the United States provided material support to the Saudi-led coalition's military campaign. Intended to roll back gains made by Iranian-backed Houthi rebels, the Saudi-led campaign has wrought widespread devastation on Yemeni society, with no end in sight. While the Obama administration attempted to broker a power-sharing agreement to end the conflict, those efforts did not prove successful. Meanwhile, Saudi Arabia's military campaign undercuts its stated broader strategic goal of reinforcing the region's state system.

In part, the Obama administration's own rhetoric only fueled Saudi Arabia's newfound assertiveness. President Obama himself publicly expressed irritation with "free riders" like America's Gulf partners, and his statement that Riyadh must learn to "share" the region with Tehran— especially after the 2015 nuclear agreement with Iran— only increased these partners' suspicions about American intentions toward them and the region as a whole.[16] Moreover, record arms sales to the Gulf States, stemming in large part from the U.S.-Iran nuclear accord, failed to provide reassurance to Saudi Arabia and other Gulf partners.

While the Obama administration failed to halt the region's fragmentation, its Middle East policy operated under multiple domestic constraints. Entering office amid an economic crash unprecedented since the Great Depression, the new administration faced a public that had soured on the war in Iraq and intervention the Middle East generally. After the 2010 Congressional elections, moreover, the administration confronted a Congress unwilling to appropriate additional funds to support transitions away from dictatorship in Egypt, Tunisia, and Libya, or even to authorize the use of force against the Islamic State. Any administration would have found it difficult to arrest the Middle East's fragmentation under these domestic political conditions.

Equally important, President Obama's correct instinct to encourage America's regional partners to take greater responsibility for their own security ran up against the region's own intense competition for power. As tragically demonstrated by Saudi Arabia's brutal military campaign in Yemen, regional partners may act in ways that worsen the Middle East's political and social fragmentation. Believing themselves to be in a zero-sum competition with Iran, American partners like Saudi Arabia have behaved in ways that undermine their stated strategic goal of reinforcing the regional state system.

The Trump Administration's Nascent Middle East Policy

President Trump's emerging Middle East policy seems likely to exacerbate the region's political and social fragmentation. His wholehearted and unqualified embrace of authoritarian governments in Saudi Arabia and Egypt—combined with statements from Secretary of State Rex Tillerson that human rights will no longer be an American priority and intimations that the United States will provide greater material support to the Saudi-led campaign in Yemen—appears likely to enable and license the destructive domestic and international behavior of those governments.[17] In short, Trump has become the "enabler-in-chief"[18] of Riyadh's evident if unwitting quest to fracture the Middle East. The perverse incentives created by Trump's regional approach can be seen in the deep schism between Saudi Arabia and Qatar, both critical American security partners in the Gulf.[19]

If Trump's Middle East policy helps accelerate the political and social fragmentation of societies across the region, the negative trends confronted by the Middle East's Christians and its other religious minorities will only grow worse as well. Many of the Trump administration's other early moves, ranging from its draconian immigration policies to its public rhetoric, have the potential to make the predicament of the Middle East's Christians even more dire than it was when Trump took office.

For one, the anti-Muslim rhetoric of Trump and many members of his foreign policy team (especially when paired with overt promises from high-level officials like Vice President Mike Pence to prioritize the "suffering of Christians in the Middle East"[20]) may have grave consequences for Christians and other religious minorities in the region. While the Obama administration exercised extreme caution when voicing concerns about religious freedom and pluralism out of fear that extremists would use such statements in their propaganda, the Trump administration's anti-Muslim rhetoric and specific emphasis on the fate of the Middle East's Christians could serve to reinforce existing extremist propaganda that regional religious minorities are nothing more than agents of a hostile foreign power determined to undermine Islam and promote Christianity. The Trump administration appears to see the United States as a sectarian actor in its own right in the Middle East.

Worse, the Trump administration's immigration and refugee policies actively undermine its professed concern for the fate of the Middle East's Christians. In one of his first moves as president, Trump slashed the number of refugees the United States would admit in 2017 from 110,000 to just 50,000. By mid-July 2017, this refugee quota had already been met.[21] As former Obama administration human rights official Tom Malinowski notes, this reduction in refugee admission slots effectively reduces the number of Middle East Christians who will be able to resettle in the United States as refugees.[22] Facing the threat of discrimination and even death in their home region, the Middle East's Christians will find the doors of the United States closed by the Trump administration.

Other aspects of President Trump's immigration policies have already had a detrimental impact. His administration's determination to deport all unauthorized immigrants living in the United States could have a disastrous effect on the many Middle Eastern Christians illegally residing in the United States.[23] In June 2017, for instance, Trump's Immigration and Customs Enforcement office arrested more than a hundred Iraqis (many of them members of the Chaldean Catholic Church) living in Michigan and scheduled them for deportation.[24] Although a federal judge halted the planned deportations in mid-July thanks to a lawsuit by the American Civil Liberties Union,[25] the case vividly demonstrates where the Trump administration's policy priorities truly lie.

Finally, the illiberal and exclusionary rhetoric and behavior embraced by President Trump both on the campaign trail and in office make it difficult for the United States to present a compelling ideological alternative to sectarianism. Trump's affinity for authoritarian strongmen ranging from Vladimir Putin to King Salman and his clear disdain for core American values like freedom of expression and pluralism will hamstring any efforts to promote these values abroad. Combined with his policy instincts and anti-Muslim rhetoric, Trump's illiberal worldview will make the lives of the Middle East's Christians and other religious minorities even more difficult in this perilous time.

NOTES

1. CAP National Security and International Policy Team, "State Legitimacy, Fragile States, and U.S. National Security" (Washington: Center for American Progress, 2016), available at https://www.americanprogress. org/issues/security/report/2016/09/12/143789/state-legitimacy-fragile-states-and-u-s-national-security/. See also Francis Fukuyama, *Political Order and Political Decay: From the Industrial Revolution to the Globalization of Democracy* (New York: Farrar, Straus and Giroux, 2014), 41.
2. Katulis and Juul, "U.S. Middle East Policy at a Time of Regional Fragmentation and Competition."
3. Stathis N. Kalyvas, "Ethnic Defections in Civil War," *Comparative Political Studies,* vol. 41, no. 8, August 2008, 1043–1068, available at http://stathis. research.yale.edu/documents/Ethnicdefection.pdf; Emile Hokayem, "'Assad or We Burn the Country': Misreading Sectarianism and the Regime in Syria," *War on the Rocks,* August 24, 2016, available at http://warontherocks. com/2016/08/assad-or-we-burn-the-country-misreading-sectarianism-and-the-regime-in-syria/
4. Phillip Conner and Conrad Hackett, "Middle East's Christian population in flux as Pope Francis visits Holy Land," Pew Research Center, May 19, 2014, available at http://www.pewresearch.org/fact-tank/2014/05/19/ middle-easts-christian-population-in-ux-as-pope-francis-visits-holy-land; Nina Shea, "The Middle East's Embattled Christians," National Review, December 23, 2009, available at http://www.nationalreview.com/article/228851/middle-easts-embattled-christians-nina-shea
5. Conner and Hackett, "Middle East's Christian population in flux as Pope Francis visits Holy Land"; PBS Newshour, "Facing Uncertainty, Middle East Christians Are Increasingly Emigrating," September 17, 2012, available at http://www.pbs.org/newshour/bb/religion-july-dec12-christians_09-17/
6. Multiple CAP interviews, Egypt, October 2014.
7. Central Intelligence Agency, "The World Factbook: Lebanon," June 20, 2014, available at https://www.cia.gov/library/publications/the-world-factbook/geos/le.html
8. Tim Arango, "In Iraq, Traditions of Christmas Found Only in Memory," *New York Times,* December 24, 2014, available at http://www.nytimes. com/2014/12/25/world/middleeast/iraq-christians-ousted-by-isis-celebrate-christmas.html?_r=0; Greg Botelho, "Amid killings and kidnappings, can Christianity survive in the Middle East?", CNN, February 27,

2015, available at http://www.cnn.com/2015/02/27/middleeast/christianity-middle-east/

9. Holly Williams, "Iraqi Christians: 'We need somewhere safe to live,'" CBS News, August 12, 2014, available at http://www.cbsnews.com/news/iraqi-christians-we-need-somewhere-safe-to-live/

10. Daniel Burke, "ISIS to Christians in Mosul: convert, pay, or die," CNN Belief Blog, July 21, 2014, available at http://religion.blogs.cnn.com/2014/07/21/facing-fines-conversion-or-death-christians-flee-mosul/

11. BBC News, "Syria's beleaguered Christians," February 25, 2015, available at http://www.bbc.com/news/world-middle-east-22270455

12. Conrad Hackett and Brian J. Grimm, "Global Christianity: A Report on the Size and Distribution of the World's Christian Population" (Washington: Pew Research Center, 2011), available at http://www.pew-forum.org/files/2011/12/Christianity-fullreport-web.pdf; Central Intelligence Agency, "The World Factbook: Egypt," June 22, 2014, available at https://www.cia.gov/library/publications/the-world-factbook/geos/eg.html

13. Johannes Makar, "The Egyptian Pope's Risky Partisanship," Carnegie Endowment for Inter-national Peace, February 26, 2015, available at http://carnegieendowment.org/sada/index.cfm?fa=show&article=59195&solr_hilite=

14. Jonathan Lis, "Israel recognizes Aramean minority in Israel as separate nationality," Haaretz, September 17, 2014, available at http://www.haaretz.com/news/national/1.616299; Adalah, "Palestinian NGOs in Israel reject the 'Sectarian Representation Law': 'We hold on to our Arab Palestinian Identity,'" February 27, 2014, available at http://www.adalah.org/en/content/view/8250

15. https://www.whitehouse.gov/the-press-office/remarks-president-cairo-university-6-04-09; http://www.state.gov/r/pa/ei/biog/230768.htm

16. http://www.theatlantic.com/magazine/archive/2016/04/the-obama-doctrine/471525/

17. Anne Applebaum, "Trump's bizarre and un-American visit to Saudi Arabia," *Washington Post,* May 21, 2017, available at https://www.washingtonpost.com/news/global-opinions/wp/2017/05/21/trumps-bizarre-and-un-american-visit-to-saudi-arabia/; Jennifer Rubin, "Trump's un-American speech in Saudi Arabia," *Washington Post,* May 21, 2017, available at https://www.washingtonpost.com/blogs/right-turn/wp/2017/05/21/trumps-un-american-speech-in-saudi-arabia/; Karen DeYoung and Missy Ryan, "Trump administration weighs deeper involvement in Yemen war," *Washington Post,* March 26, 2017, available at https://www.washingtonpost.com/world/national-security/trump-administration-weighs-deeper-involvement-in-yemen-war/2017/03/26/

b81eecd8-0e49-11e7-9d5a-a83e627dc120_story.html; Conor Finnegan, "Tillerson: Pushing human rights abroad 'creates obstacles' to US interests," *ABC News,* May 3, 2017, available at http://abcnews.go.com/Politics/tillerson-pushing-human-rights-abroad-creates-obstacles/story?id=47190743

18. Dan Benaim, "The Problem Isn't Just Who Trump Has Offended—It's Who He Hasn't," *Foreign Policy,* July 11, 2017, available at http://foreignpolicy.com/2017/07/11/the-problem-isnt-who-trump-has-offended-its-who-he-hasnt/

19. CAP Middle East Team, "A Guide for Those Perplexed About the Qatar Crisis," June 21, 2017, available at https://cdn.americanprogress.org/content/uploads/2017/06/22065035/3QatarCrisis-brief.pdf

20. Julie Zauzmer, "Pence: America will prioritize protecting Christians abroad," *Washington Post,* May 11, 2017, available at https://www.washingtonpost.com/news/acts-of-faith/wp/2017/05/11/pence-america-will-prioritize-protecting-christians-abroad/

21. Jaweed Kaleem, "U.S. hits cap of 50,000 refugee admissions," *Los Angeles Times,* July 12, 2017, available at http://www.latimes.com/politics/washington/la-na-essential-washington-updates-u-s-hits-50-000-cap-on-refugee-1499890506-htmlstory.html

22. Tom Malinowski, "Donald Trump's Phony Compassion for Christians," *New York Times,* February 5, 2017, available at https://www.nytimes.com/2017/02/05/opinion/donald-trumps-phony-compassion-for-christians.html

23. Tom Gjelten, "After Fleeing Persecution, U.S. Christian Refugees Now Face Deportation," *National Public Radio,* July 8, 2017, available at http://www.npr.org/2017/07/08/535959270/after-fleeing-persecution-u-s-christian-refugees-now-face-deportation

24. Lauren del Valle and Sonia Moghe, "Iraqi Christians in Michigan Fear Deportation," *CNN.com,* June 16, 2017, available at http://www.cnn.com/2017/06/16/us/aclu-files-against-ice-for-iraqi-nationals/index.html

25. Ben Solis, "Judge finds he can halt deportation of endangered Iraqi immigrants," *MLive.com,* July 11, 2017, available at http://www.mlive.com/news/detroit/index.ssf/2017/07/judge_finds_he_can_halt_deport.html

Epilogue

Kail C. Ellis

SHIA–SUNNI RIVALRY AND THE SHIITE CRESCENT

In an interview on December 9, 2004, King Abdullah II of Jordan was asked if he feared the Shia majority might win the Iraqi parliamentary elections that were scheduled to be held in January 2005. The king replied that the worst-case scenario would be if an Iranian-influenced government came to power. "Some red lines would have to be drawn," he said, "because what you are doing is creating an issue in Iraq that goes beyond the borders of Iraq that would affect the stability of the Gulf countries, Saudi Arabia and the rest of the Arab peninsula."[1] The king's statement reiterated his comments in an interview with the *Washington Post* the previous day. In that interview, he expressed his apprehension over the emergence of a new "Shiite crescent" stretching from Iran into Iraq, Syria, and Lebanon that would alter the traditional balance of power between the two main Islamic sects and pose new challenges to U.S. interests and allies. "Even Saudi Arabia is not immune from this. It would be a major problem. And then that would propel the possibility of a Shiite–Sunni conflict even more, as you're taking it out of the borders of Iraq."[2]

The term "Shite Crescent," coined by King Abdullah, has found widespread resonance among policy analysts, political leaders, academics, and

K. C. Ellis (✉)
Arab & Islamic Studies, Villanova University, Villanova, PA, USA

© The Author(s) 2018   209
K. C. Ellis (ed.), *Secular Nationalism and Citizenship in
Muslim Countries*, Minorities in West Asia and North Africa,
https://doi.org/10.1007/978-3-319-71204-8_13

others who have used it as a shorthand to explain the current chaos and conflicts in the Middle East. Many commentators, however, have pointed out that the king did not intend to use the term in a sectarian sense. Rather, he was cautioning against political alignments and violent bloodshed that could arise from a sectarian religious divide. Nevertheless, using a term that evokes sectarianism and conjures up a primordial blood feud whose long duration makes it seem unresolvable, as shorthand to explain or dismiss important policy research and the socio-economic and political underpinning of society, is dangerous as it has the potential to obfuscate attempts to make sound policy in a complex region.

It is undeniable that an ongoing conflict exists between Shiites and Sunnis in the Middle East. To understand its dynamics, it is important to determine whether that conflict is ideological, that is, part of the Iranian–Arab rivalry, or an inter-Arab conflict over power sharing. According to Keyhan Barzegar, it is an inter-Arab conflict: "Given Iran's political dynamics and the existing cultural-societal and historical distinctions between the Persian and Arab masses, the realization of an ideology-dominated Shiite crescent, is rather difficult, if not impossible."[3] This argument stresses that national identity rather than religion or ideology is a force of unity and solidarity in the region and that Iraqi, Lebanese, and Syrian Shiites are first Arabs and only then Shiites, and Iranian Shiites are first and foremost Persians. This cultural distinction and unique identity, according to Barzegar, arose mostly from the absence of interaction among the people as well as the misinformed policy of the Sunni governing elites and outside powers which define Iran as the region's major threat.[4]

Instead of being ideological or religious, Barzegar argues that Iran's attempts to create a coalition of Shiite-friendly governments are more defensive and pragmatic than expansionistic. For the last two to three centuries, Persia was encircled by unfriendly foreign powers such as the Ottoman Empire, Russia, and Britain, and more recently, the Baathist regime of Iraq and the Taliban. Given that this was the source of great tension, war, and instability, it is credible that Iran's aims are primarily oriented at building a secure environment on its borders and creating economic opportunities for strategic purposes.[5]

Finally, while for the foreseeable future, the two primary powers, Saudi Arabia and Iran, will continue to project their geopolitical influence by using their interpretations of Islam as instruments of foreign policy, it will be important for policy-makers and world leaders to realize that the danger lies in politicizing sectarian identities and seeking to diffuse them.

Internal problems will also need to be addressed as the danger of sectarianism will only intensify if, as is the case in certain Sunni countries in the Arab world, the treatment of Shia communities who have been historically treated as threats to the regimes, and not as citizens with national identity, natural rights, and responsibilities is not addressed.[6]

SECTARIANIZATION

In their study, *Sectarianization: Mapping the New Politics of the Middle East*, Nader Hashemi and Danny Postel challenge the assumption that the current instability in the Middle East is an outcome of the seventh-century Sunni and Shia split in Islam. While sectarian conflict between Muslim groups has intensified dramatically in recent years, the authors seek to understand this hostility by developing the thesis of "sectarianization," rather than through the lens of "sectarianism" that clouds the complex realities of the region's politics. The authors argue that "the current instability is more accurately seen as rooted in a series of developmental crises stemming from the collapse of state authority."[7]

AUTHORITARIAN REGIMES AND ECONOMIC DEVELOPMENT

The central focus of the sectarianization thesis is political authoritarianism, a form of political rule that has long dominated the politics of the Middle East. "Authoritarian regimes in the Middle East have deliberately manipulated sectarian identities in various ways as a strategy to deflect demands for political change and perpetuate their power," the authors maintain. "This anti-democratic political context is essential for understanding sectarian conflict in Muslim societies today, especially in those societies that contain a mix of Sunni and Shi`a populations."[8]

Hashemi and Postel's sectarianization thesis, in particular their analysis of the failure of authoritarian regimes to create a unifying national narrative, establish modern egalitarian policies, and mobilize national resources to overcome backwardness and advance their economies, is reflected in the chapters of this volume. In his chapter, *The Vulnerability of Arab Christians and Other Minorities Is Citizenship Rights Under the Rule of Law*, Rami Khouri contends that Christians, as well as members of all religious and ethnic communities in the Middle East, have been harmed by regimes that concentrated their efforts on securing power and manipulating their base by appeals to Arab nationalism and/or to Islam. These attempts to impose unity have always left parts of the population without the rights of the dominant community.[9]

Furthermore, Khouri notes, in neglecting economic development, authoritarian regimes have ensured that the resulting poverty and inequality of citizenship will accelerate the downward spiral to subsequent generations. Without jobs or adequate income, the future generation will not be able to marry and start families, as over 60 percent of new entrants to the labor market in Egypt, for example, go into the informal sector, which accounts for 40 percent of Arab labor markets. This generation is unqualified to do anything other than sweep floors or wash dishes and car windows. It goes without saying that the informal sector offers low pay, no job security, and no social protections like health insurance, maximum working hours, and retirement plans. It guarantees life-long misery and vulnerability, which inevitably spill over into political and social tensions, or even violence in some cases.[10]

Persecution Versus "Christian Agency"

Although socio-economic stagnation, emigration, political instability, and the seemingly unending wars and conflicts in the Middle East overwhelmingly account for the declining numbers of Christians relative to the Muslim population, the persecution of Christians in the region cannot be discounted as a factor. Nevertheless, to concentrate on persecution in isolation of the socio-economic and political factors would be a great disservice to Christians. Scholars such as Paul Rowe have emphasized that to view Christians solely as "victims of persecution or mere relics of a fading past runs the risk of once again robbing Christians of agency as powerful actors in their own societies."[11] Bernard Heyberger, a scholar of Eastern Christianity, acknowledges that while "news abounds regarding violence and injustices committed against Christians in various countries and about their ever-shrinking numbers due to emigration, this approach depicts Christians only as victims and prevents us from understanding their actual situation in their home countries or in their diaspora."[12] To change the dystopian view and emphasis on persecution, scholars such as L.C. Robson cite recent scholarship that has sought to position Christians and Jewish communities as integral parts of the larger societies to which they belong— culturally, politically, and demographically.[13] This approach is taken by Sidney Griffith, Bernard Sabella, Anthony O'Mahony, Tarek Mitri and Sami El-Yousef in this volume.

"Minorities" Versus "Presence"

In addition to changing the depiction of Christians as "victims" is the equally problematic reference to them as "minorities." Arab Christians do not consider themselves minorities; rather, they regard themselves as members of a pluralist society, albeit one in which they have suffered discrimination. Andrea Zaki Stephanous, president of the Protestant Community of Egypt, and General Director of the Coptic Evangelical Organization for Social Services, remarks, "One is aware that Christians will not accept that they are members of a minority." He continues, "Copts argue that they are not a minority, and Maronites consider themselves as founders of Greater Lebanon and the ruling group." Thus, the term "minority," when used in this context, refers to groups that differ from the majority in one variable, or more. "In the case of Copts, they differ only in religion."[14]

As the term "minority" is not accepted by Arab Christians, an alternative approach is to refer to them in terms of "presence," as advocated by Cardinal Leonardo Sandri in his greeting to the Villanova conference on Christians in the Middle East, and reiterated by the al-Azhar statement, "Freedom, Citizenship, Diversity and Integration," of April 13, 2017, which declared that Christians are not "minorities; only citizens." The al-Azhar declaration carried with it the essential corollary of equal citizenship, a view emphasized in this volume by Elie Chalala and Fateh Azzam, who recognize the importance and indispensability of human rights and the equality of citizens, codified in positive law, as antidotes to sectarianism.

Several years after the Arab uprisings of 2011, the status of Christians varies considerably across the region. In Lebanon, there is a stronger sense of protection (since Christians constitute about 35–40 percent of the population), than in conflict zones such as Syria and Iraq. In Egypt, however, there has been an increase in attacks on Copts in recent years that has caused alarm in the West and friction with the Vatican. In 2011, Egypt recalled its ambassador to the Vatican, Lamia Aly Mekhamar, when Pope Benedict XVI criticized the government for not doing enough to protect Coptic Christians after the bombing of churches and clashes between Muslims and Copts. The ambassador rejected the criticism and reiterated that Copts are integral to Egypt, have all the protections of any other Egyptian citizens, and that the bombings were terrorists' attacks directed against all Egyptians.[15]

Diplomatic relations with the Vatican were restored in 2016, paving the way for Pope Francis's historic visit of April 2017. Since 2013, however, Egypt has seen a renewed wave of attacks against Christians when the military, led by Abdel Fattah al-Sisi, overthrew President Mohamed Morsi, the country's elected president. Sensitive to the criticism that his government was not doing enough to protect Christians, al-Sisi assured the Pope that "Egypt is on the front lines of the confrontation against terrorism, which our nation is bearing with steadfastness and sacrifice. [We are] determined to defeat it and end it and to hold on to our unity and not let it divide us."[16]

While Egypt has not experienced the horrific violence that has engulfed Syria and Iraq, its Christian community continues to feel the full force of Islamist militants, with recent bomb attacks on several churches. The 2017 Palm Sunday bombings of Coptic churches in Egypt killed scores of worshipers and targeted the Coptic patriarch. The patriarch survived, but the violations of the rights of Copts to practice their religion have continued through more church bombings and the targeting of pilgrims traveling to monastery shrines. These incidents have shattered any sense of protection and confidence in the Egyptian government's willingness and ability to safeguard the Christian community.

Related to the attacks on Christian churches is job discrimination and the effects of the blasphemy law that Egyptian Copts complain they experience. Copts claim they are denied top jobs in many fields, including academia and the security forces,[17] while another major concern is the anti-blasphemy law that has been used over the past years to target Christians, Muslims, and non-believers for 'contempt of religion.'[18] The most prominent complaint by Copts, however, is the lack of religious freedom. The building and renovation of churches is limited by law as all churches must be licensed for building or renovation. In practice, licensing is subject to strict regulations and to the whims and prejudices of local officials with long delays for approval. To circumvent these obstacles, Egyptian Christians have resorted to building illegal churches, which in turn have been a major trigger for sectarian violence in some rural areas.[19]

SAFE ZONES FOR REFUGEES AND THE DUTY TO PROTECT

Another major concern for regional stability is the internal refugee crisis in Syria (estimated 7.6 million), as well as the massive influx of four million refugees to Turkey, Lebanon, Jordan, and Europe that has created a massive refugee crisis unseen since World War II.[20] Statements by the U.S. administration and government leaders in Turkey, Lebanon, Saudi Arabia, Qatar, and Jordan have indicated an interest in creating so-called safe zones for the displaced in Syria. The impact of these refugees on Lebanon's long-term stability motivated U.S. Congressman Darin LaHood to introduce H.Res.252 in April 2017, expressing the view of the House of Representatives on the challenges posed to Lebanon's stability of the estimated 1.2 million Syrian refugees and support for the establishment of safe zones in Syria.[21] Proponents of this plan argue safe zones would allow civilians fleeing conflict to be safe from attacks and receive humanitarian assistance, while limiting the need for cross-border displacements and facilitating refugee returns. Safe zones would provide relief and ease the tremendous burden on host countries such as Lebanon, Jordan and Turkey. The concept appeared to be favored by U.S. President Donald Trump, who has said he wants to establish safe zones for refugees in Syria to discourage them from fleeing to other countries.[22]

Although the president has not provided details about the proposed zones, except to say he would try to persuade Persian Gulf states to pay for them, current reports indicate that he is expected to order the Pentagon and the State Department to develop a plan for safe zones, a move that could require significantly more U.S. military involvement in Syria. The Pentagon has warned that policing these zones would be difficult in a war-torn country filled with armed groups.[23]

The implications for religious and ethnic communities of safe zones are discussed in this volume by Alon Ben-Meir and Anthony Zinni. Their discussion of the plight of refugees reiterates Pope Francis's concerns in his letter to Christians in the Middle East of December 21, 2014, where he stated, "The tragic situation faced by our Christian brothers and sisters in Iraq, as well as by the Yazidi and members of other religious and ethnic communities, demands that all religious leaders clearly speak out to condemn these crimes unanimously and unambiguously, and to denounce the practice of invoking religion in order to justify them."[24] Nevertheless, according to General Zinni, the implications of the "duty to protect" need to be carefully assessed, and must include carefully defined national security interests before undertaking any such initiatives.

The dilemma of how to protect refugees is thoroughly addressed in a recent study by Alex J. Bellamy, in *Responsibility to Protect: The Global Effort to End Mass Atrocities*. Bellamy's position, like Ben-Meir's, is that there is also a "duty to prevent" conflict: "If the institutional and political capacity necessary to maximize the effectiveness of these [preventive] measures is developed, then the frequency with which governments are forced to choose between standing aside and going to war for humanitarian purposes will be reduced."[25] Importantly, Bellamy cautions against using human rights per se as rationale for intervention. He reminds us that human rights was used to justify the 2003 U.S. invasion of Iraq, a rationale that was subsequently discredited by Human Rights Watch.[26] The optimal course of action is prevention, and the heeding of warning signs before military intervention is even contemplated—"As is now known only too well, the carnage of Bosnia, the genocide in Rwanda and the reign of terror in Darfur were all predicted before the event ... A more accurate analysis of the warning signs might identify earlier opportunities for constructive third-party engagement."[27]

Aside from the feasibility of establishing safe zones is the issue of their effectiveness. The UN and other aid officials have raised concerns about placing displaced people in so-called safe zones in Syria. The term is a misnomer, they claim, as such zones would actually place refugees in *unsafe* conditions, limiting their ability to flee to other countries. These critics contend that governments should carefully examine the implications of such a policy before establishing any safe zone or safe area, whether by the parties to the conflict or the UN Security Council.[28] The UN High Commissioner for Refugees, Filippo Grandi, is also opposed to establishing safe zones, stating, "With the fragmentation, the number of actors, the presence of terrorist groups, it's not the right place to think of that solution."[29]

CONCLUSION

As noted in the introduction, several scholars hold the position that the region's current instability is more accurately rooted in a series of developmental crises stemming from the collapse of state authority than to sectarian conflict. Religious identities are more prominent today in Middle East politics and, according to the authors cited, political elites have often manipulated sectarian identities as a strategy for deflecting demands for political change and perpetuating their power. It is not ideology or loyalty to a particular religious sect that drives the politics of the region but rather, as described by Hashemi and Postel, "the toxic brew of authoritarianism, kleptocracy, developmental stagnation, and state repression."[30]

The sobering conclusion of these analyses is that daily life for hundreds of millions of Arabs, whether Christian, Muslim, or members of other groups, will remain difficult in the foreseeable future. In some cases, life will worsen due to continuous wars, unresolved conflicts, and state collapse that already have been catastrophic for the Middle East.

It may be difficult for some observers to appreciate that at the heart of instability in the region are the fundamental issues of economic stagnation, lack of education, authoritarianism, and state repression, rather than the easy explanation of religious rivalry or persecution, per se. As the authors cited have emphasized, only an appreciation of the region's history and development will serve to illuminate an understanding of the Middle East. Bernard Heyberger, Ussama Makdisi, L.C. Robson, and Paul S. Rowe, as well as the contributors to this volume have pointed out that sectarianism was a nineteenth century construct that was part of the process of creating nationalist identities that more recently has developed into a dualist view of the world as East vs. West, or Christianity vs. Islam. The study of Christians in Islamic countries serves to undermine dualist versions of the world or the so-called "Clash of Civilizations" by offering a more fluid and more complex analysis that serves to counter culturally based bifurcations.

Moreover, as noted by Cardinal Sandri, Christianity is indigenous to the region. Therefore, Christian faith cannot be separated from any consideration of the Middle East, as it is part of the region's fabric. In his words: "Faith generates culture; therefore, it should be stressed that the Christian presence in the Middle East has contributed decisively to the history of these peoples and nations, both in the past as in the present, through literary figures, philosophers, artists and thinkers, also in the social and political fields."[31]

An important example of the Christian contribution to Arab culture is the role of Christians in promoting the Arabic language and in the growth of the periodical press. As described by Albert Hourani, the careful study of the Arabic language, undertaken by Christians in the eighteenth century for practical reasons, led to a passionate love of the language and its literature. Prior to this time, the government in Cairo and Constantinople had published the only important newspapers, and these contained only official news. While a few papers were published in French, Greek, and Armenian, virtually none were published in Arabic until the 1860s. With the increase in the number of printing presses, Arabic writers, and the reading public, as well as the comparative liberalism of the Turkish and Egyptian regimes of the time, the creation of private newspapers and periodicals was made possible. According to Hourani, "For the next

30 years these were to be mainly in the hands of Lebanese Christians, whether they were published in Beirut, Cairo, or Constantinople; for a whole generation the reading public of the Arab countries lay open to the ideas of the new writers and thinkers of Lebanon."[32]

By their love of the Arabic language and their embrace of the historical and philological Western sciences, Arab Christians rediscovered and constructed the history and sources of their heritage and that of the Islamic Middle East, thereby contributing to the making of modern identities, especially Arab identities of the entire Middle East.[33] This contribution must not only be studied and understood but also celebrated.

NOTES

1. "Chris Matthews interview with King Abdullah II of Jordan," *Hardball with Chris Matthews*, MSNBC, December 9, 2004, http://www.nbcnews.com/id/6679774/ns/msnbc-hardball_with_chris_matthews/t/king-abdullah-ii-jordan/#.
2. Robin Wright and Peter Baker, "Iraq, Jordan See Threat to Election From Iran: Leaders Warn Against Forming Religious State," *Washington Post*, December 9, 2004, p. A01, http://www.washingtonpost.com/wp-dyn/articles/A43980-2004Dec7.html
3. Keyhan Barzegar, "Iran and the Shiite Crescent: Myths and Realities," *The Brown Journal of World Affairs*, Vol. XV, No. 1, Fall/Winter 2008. https://www.brown.edu/initiatives/journal-world-affairs/151/iran-and-shiite-crescent-myths-and-realities
4. Barzegar, ibid.
5. Barzegar, ibid.
6. Fadi A. Haddadin, "The 'Shia Crescent' and Middle East Geopolitics," January 31, 2017, *Foreign Policy Association*, https://foreignpolicyblogs.com/2017/01/31/shia-crescent-middle-east-geopolitics/
7. Nader Hashemi and Danny Postel, "Introduction: The Sectarianization Thesis" in Nader Hashemi and Danny Postel (eds.), *Sectarianization: Mapping the New Politics of the Middle East* (Oxford, New York, Oxford University Press: 2017), p. 19.
8. Ibid, p. 5.
9. Rami Khouri, *The Vulnerability of Arab Christians and Other Minorities Is Citizenship Rights Under T\the Rule of Law*.
10. Ibid.
11. Paul S. Rowe, "The Middle Eastern Christian as Agent," *International Journal of Middle East Studies*, vol. 42, No. 3 (August 2010), pp. 472–474.

12. Bernard Heyberger, "Eastern Christians, Islam and the West: A Connected History," *International Journal of Middle East Studies*, vol. 42, no. 3 (August 2010), pp. 475–478. http://www.jstor.org/stable/40784825

13. Robson advocates support of recent scholarship that seeks to change the idea that Arab Christians constituted segregated and victimized communities in the 19th and 20th centuries. L.C. Robson, "Recent Perspectives on Christians in the Modern Arab World," *History Compass, 9/4,* 2011, pp. 312–325.

14. Andrea Zaki Stephanous, *Political Islam, Citizenship, and Minorities: The Future of Arab Christians in the Islamic Middle East* (Lanham, MD, University Press of America: 2010), p. 11.

15. Egyptian Ambassador to Vatican: "We don't share the view Christians are persecuted in Middle East." Published on Jan 12, 2011. https://www.you tube.com/watch?v=Tp3s55s9aSM. Egypt has recalled their ambassador to the Vatican for consultation in light of the Pope's remarks on the need for the Egyptian government to do more to protect its Christian minority. Egyptian Ambassador to Vatican "We don't share view Christians are persecuted in Middle East," ROME REPORTS in English, 4,052 views.

16. Philip Pullella and Mahmoud Mourad, "Pope Francis denounces barbarity during Egypt visit, preaches tolerance,"
    Reuters, #WORLD NEWS APRIL 28, 2017. http://www.reuters.com/article/us-pope-egypt-idUSKBN17U0U4

17. Pope Francis arrives in Egypt on historic visit: Catholic pontiff's two-day visit is aimed at fostering peace between the Muslim and Christian-minority community, April 29, 2017. http://www.aljazeera.com/news/2017/04/pope-francis-arrives-egypt-historic-day-visit-170428113013811.html

18. Marina Barsoum, "Egypt's anti-blasphemy law: Defence of religion or tool for persecution?" *ahramonline*, Sunday 15 May 2016. "On June 12, 2016, the Egyptian government clearly stated its opposition to scrapping a part of Article 98 of the Egyptian Penal Code which significantly penalizes "defamation" of "religions" with a 6-month to 5-year prison sentence. The legal ambiguity of "defamation", coupled with a track record of using this Article against Copts and liberals, has, according to its detractors, rendered it unfit to stand with a constitution that, at least in theory, guarantees freedom of expression." http://english.ahram.org.eg/News Content/1/151/216896/Egypt/Features/Egypts-antiblasphemy-law-Defence-of-religion-or-to.aspx

19. Declan Walsh, "A Hidden Church in Cairo Pins Its Hopes on Good Will from the Pope's Visit," *New York Times*, April 28, 2017. https://www.nytimes.com/2017/04/28/world/middleeast/cairo-pope-churches.html?emc=eta1. See also, "Egypt: New Church Law Discriminates against Christians," *Human Rights Watch*, September 15, 2016. "On August 30,

2016, Egypt's parliament passed a new law that allows governors to deny church-building permits with no stated way to appeal, requires that churches be built "commensurate with" the number of Christians in the area, and contains security provisions that risk subjecting decisions on whether to allow church construction to the whims of violent mobs. For decades, Egypt's courts interpreted an 1856 Ottoman decree as giving the president sole power to permit church construction. In 1934, the Interior Ministry set out restrictive rules for church construction. More recently, several Egyptian governments discussed issuing a "unified" law for houses of worship for all religions but never did. https://www.hrw.org/news/2016/09/15/egypt-new-church-law-discriminates-against-christians

20. More than four million Syrians have now fled war and persecution and become refugees in neighboring countries, making the Syrian conflict the UN Refugee Agency's worst crisis for almost a quarter of a century. UNHR, July 9, 2015. http://www.unrefugees.org/2015/07/total-number-of-syrian-refugees-exceeds-four-million-for-first-time/?gclid=Cj0KCQjw--DLBRCNARIsAFIwR24Iy8MGymjGN_P69SmfUgJ00OZLH8XEqmAuEt2x1N9gWc_HDWeD55IaAidKEALw_wcB&gclsrc=aw.ds

21. Rep. Darin LaHood, H.Res.252—Expressing the sense of the House of Representatives on the challenges posed to long-term stability in Lebanon by the conflict in Syria and supporting the establishment of safe zones in Syria. https://www.congress.gov/bill/115th-congress/house-resolution/252

22. Julia Edwards Ainsley and Matt Spetalnick, "Trump says he will order 'safe zones' for Syria," Reuters, http://www.reuters.com/article/us-usa-trump-syria-safezones-idUSKBN1592O8

23. *Radio Free Europe, Radio Liberty,* "UN Refugee Chief Doubtful About Trump Plan for 'Safe Zones' in Syria," February 04, 2017, https://www.rferl.org/a/un-refugee-chief-grandi-doubtful-trump-safe-zone-plan-syrian-refugees/28278661.html

24. Pope Francis, *Letter to the Christians in the Middle East*, December 21, 2014. https://w2.vatican.va/content/francesco/en/letters/2014/documents/papa-francesco_20141221_lettera-cristiani-medio-oriente.html

25. Alex J. Bellamy, *Responsibility to Protect: The Global Effort to End Mass Atrocities* (Cambridge, UK, Polity Press: 2009), pp. 3–4.

26. "War in Iraq: Not a Humanitarian Intervention," *Human Rights Watch*, January 25, 2004 7:00PM EST https://www.hrw.org/news/2004/01/25/war-iraq-not-humanitarian-intervention

27. Alex J. Bellamy, op. cit. p. 53.

28. "Q & A: Safe Zones and the Armed Conflict in Syria," *Human Rights Watch*, March 16, 2017 https://www.hrw.org/news/2017/03/16/q-safe-zones-and-armed-conflict-syria#_Have_there_been

29. *Radio Free Europe, Radio Liberty*, "UN Refugee Chief Doubtful About Trump Plan for 'Safe Zones' in Syria," February 04, 2017, https://www.rferl.org/a/un-refugee-chief-grandi-doubtful-trump-safe-zone-plan-syrian-refugees/28278661.html

30. Nader Hashemi and Danny Postel (eds.), op. cit. p. 21.

31. Letter of Greeting to participants in the Villanova Conference on Christians in the Middle East, December 6, 2016.

32. Albert Hourani, *Arabic Thought in the Liberal Age: 1798–1939* (Cambridge University Press, Cambridge: 1983), p. 95.

33. Heyberger, op. cit.

INDEX[1]

A

The absence of national security for individual, family and community as a cause of poverty, unemployment and underemployment, 184

Ahl al kitab, 4, 47, 155

Ahl al-dhimmah, 2, 4

Aid organizations suffers from military intervention, 176

Al Bustani, Butros, 91–93, 103

Al *Nahda* Literary awakening, 13

Al Quds first newspaper in Palestine (1908) established by a Greek orthodox Palestinian family, 94

Al Tasamoh (forbearance) *wal Tasahol* (and open-mindedness or leniency), 103

Alawite communities, 68, 145

Ali, Muhammad initiative (1769-1849), 94, 97

Alliance of the Christian church and the authoritarian regime, 144

Arab Christian survival, the role of the Arab Muslim elite to maintain sectarian diversity in the Middle East, 140

Arab Christians and the cultural renaissance in the Arab Islamic world, 13, 89–104

Arab nationalism was rejected in favor of Arab/Islamic unity, 151

Arab Spring 2011, vii, 10, 12, 13, 16, 18, 70, 156, 202

Arab *Umma*, 111

Arabic awakening, 92

Arabic sources of Christian heritage, 11

Authoritarian regime, ix, 9, 10, 14, 107, 115, 140, 196, 211, 212

B

Baghdad in Abbasid time (1258), 11, 43

Blasphemy laws, 9, 160, 161, 214

---

[1] Note: Page numbers followed by "n" refers to notes.

© The Author(s) 2018
K. C. Ellis (ed.), *Secular Nationalism and Citizenship in Muslim Countries*, Minorities in West Asia and North Africa,
https://doi.org/10.1007/978-3-319-71204-8